Alyn
Love
Mam & Dad

HISTORY OF THE HAMLET OF GELLIDEG

F. J. PEDLER.

HISTORY OF THE HAMLET OF GELLIDEG

BY

F. J. PEDLER

MERTHYR TYDFIL:
JOSEPH WILLIAMS & SONS (MERTHYR), LTD., GLEBELAND STREET

—

MCMXXX.

Cardiff Academic Press
St Fagans Road, Fairwater, Cardiff CF5 3AE

British Library Cataloguing in Publication Data

A catalogue record for this book is available from the British Library.

ISBN 1 899025 12 X

First published 1930
Joseph Williams & Sons (Merthyr) Ltd.

Front cover illustration: Heolgerrig Brewery

Printed & Bound in Great Britain by
Antony Rowe Ltd.

This edition
published in Great Britain by
Cardiff Academic Press
St Fagans Road, Fairwater, Cardiff CF5 3AE
1998

Cardiff Academic Press Ltd.

INTRODUCTION.

A SHORT time ago I began a series of articles in the *Merthyr Express*, describing certain tramps I took around the Merthyr Parish boundaries. At first I had no conception that the descriptions would run to such length; but as one thing led to another, and the plan of the district had to be followed most carefully, the work became rather voluminous. The more I delved into the history of famous spots or of outstanding personalities, the more interesting did the work become.

Having been approached by several readers, who had read the articles and were desirous of seeing the work preserved in a more convenient form, I turned over the question in my mind whether it would be wise to print the articles in book form. Was the subject matter of sufficient historic interest to warrant its publication? How many people would care to read such a book? These were some of the questions that crossed my mind.

To have dealt with the whole of the boundaries of the Merthyr Parish on the same lines as I have adopted for the Hamlet of Gellideg would have meant many years of extra labour and research, therefore I have confined myself entirely to my native hamlet. I claim to have a specially intimate knowledge of it, because I was born in it, brought up in it, worked most of my lifetime in it, and for nearly a quarter of a century was a public representative of it.

Historians like Charles Wilkins and T. E. Clarke have compiled valuable histories of Merthyr Tydfil, and I have been much indebted to them for their work, more especially to the former. But the "History of Merthyr Tydfil," valuable as it is, is very bare in parts, and I have tried to fill in as much as possible concerning the history of the hamlet. In this work I have tried to describe things and places which I thought to be of interest. Something has also been written about several of the original old characters of the district, many of whom have left quaint anecdotes of their habits and customs in the old days. The growth of the various religious causes, as well as the development of education, have also been attempted.

Personally, I feel that the present generation ought to be better versed in the history and geography of the locality in which they live. To-day the children in our schools know far more of the details concerning the murder of Thomas à Becket in Canterbury Cathedral than they do of those old Puritans who assembled at Blaencanaid. They learn about water-power being used to work the mills of Yorkshire, but do not know the various uses to which water was put locally in connection with the iron and steel trades. They can tell you the height of Mount Everest, but never seem to have heard of Twyn y Ddisgwylfa or Penylan. Perhaps the blame lies with lack of sufficiently interesting reading material; and I trust that this volume, and the proposed new Reader to be produced by the local branch of the N.U.T., will do much to fill the gap.

People who live in a district of this type are more fortunate than townspeople, insofar as they can trace certain landmarks much more easily. They ought to know the chief historical sites, the roads, paths, brooks, farms, old and new methods of land cultivation, the source of the domestic water supply, and place-names and their meanings. Then there are places of worship, mills and factories, methods of mining, and the manufacture of iron and steel.

The district under observation is the ancient Hamlet of Gellideg, one of the five parochial districts of Merthyr Tydfil. Its area is about eight square miles, and of this area coal and iron-ore are found in abundance for six-and-a-half square miles underneath the surface. The hamlet lies between the River Taff and the western boundary of the Parish, along the mountain top, being bounded on the north by Cwm Ffrwd and on the south by Nant y Graig. There is no doubt that most of the district was well wooded before the Ironworks took their toll for smelting purposes. The land was formerly well cultivated, judging from the number of important farms; but the land nearest the scene of industry was quickly covered as the works developed.

When the iron industry began flourishing about the middle of the 18th century, people began flocking to this district owing to the scarcity of labour-power. The native population had been formerly dependent on the land and its produce. Now Bacon introduced families from Gloucestershire and Worcestershire to work for him. Houses were built and the population grew rapidly. It was a case of migration of labour-power from the rural to the industrial district. In 1801—the year of the first census—out of a population of half-a-million in Wales, Merthyr had 7,705, the number of houses being 1,404. Cardiff's population was then 1,870, and Newport's 1,423. In 1841 Merthyr had as many people as Cardiff, Newport and Swansea put together. But as a result of the building of the T.V.R., a remarkable change came about, for it was the coal export trade that regulated the growth of Cardiff. In 1881 the population of Cardiff was 82,000, that of Merthyr was 48,000, The collieries and the ironworks continued to develop, Merthyr becoming the greatest iron manufacturing town in the country.

I wish to tender my warmest thanks to all those who have been so kind and ready to assist me with any information that they had at their disposal. I have endeavoured to make the work as interesting and instructive as I could, and hope the reader will derive some amount of pleasure in perusing it. Some are inclined to say, "But what is the use of these long-forgotten things—these ruins, and these old levels and mine-pits?" To them I can only say, "It is through the Past that you can better understand the Present."

F. J. PEDLER.

Heolgerrig,
April, 1930.

INDEX TO CONTENTS.

History of the Hamlet of Gellideg.

CHAPTER I.

MERTHYR PARISH CHURCH TO PONTYCAPEL—CWM FFRWD TO THE MILLSTONE—THE FINGER POST—BRYN Y GWYDDEL—CARN Y FRWYDR—CARN TYLE HIR.

ABOUT the middle of the 18th century, when the village of Merthyr Tydfil was very small and of little importance (the iron and coal industries not having commenced as yet), there were in the vicinity of the Old Church a few small thatched dwelling-houses. It was here that the whole business of the village and parish was carried on, and markets were held weekly in the street. Twice a year, fairs were held also in the same place. One of these fairs was known as " Gwyl y Pasg Bychan," and young and old enjoyed themselves by taking part in all sorts of amusements. It was the prevailing custom at " Y Pasg Bychan " to form a procession, which was headed by the parish clerk or other officials, to march over the parish boundary. This was known as "beating the bounds," and is in vogue even at the present day in some English parishes. Therefore a start was made from the fair. The official would be followed by a large number of the younger generation, and we can imagine their whistling, singing, and merry shouts of laughter. Off went the noisy motley crowd to the nearest part of the northern boundary of the parish, which was Cefn Coed y Cymmer, at the junction of the Taf Fawr and Taf Fechan, then proceeding alongside the former river, to the junction of the Ffrwd at Pontycapel. There a little ceremony was performed. One of the youngsters was grabbed, and a few strokes with the hand or the birch were administered with the customary admonition: " You will remember this part of the boundary of the parish."

Then Nant Ffrwd, which was a county as well as a parish boundary, was followed. Entering Cwm Ffrwd, there came into view one of the most romantic ravines in the parish. The scenery on both sides is varied and very beautiful. Gnarled oak mingles with smooth silvery birch and stately ash. Festoons of ivy adorn the gloomy recesses, under the overhanging wall of rock, like curtains at the entrances to magic caves. There are three waterfalls, over which the silvery waters tumble into the dark pools below, and the trees which overhang the ravine in parts almost obscure the sky.

The first brook that enters the Ffrwd is the Scwrfa, on the left, about a hundred yards above the bridge. The brook falls over a cliff which is semi-circular in shape and about six feet in diameter. It drops from twelve to fifteen feet, and, owing to the continual running of water, the sides of the rock are as smooth as glass. There is another small cataract, about a hundred yards above in the Scwrfa, which is worth seeing. It can be reached by following the Scwrfa footpath, after crossing the stile on Pontycapel Road. The name of this brook owes its origin to the custom that prevailed during the 18th century of prospecting for iron ore. On the mountain side above Clwydyfagwyr, and near the source of this brook, there is an old embankment of a pond, known locally as Pound Scwrfa. Occasionally, this embankment was opened, and the water would flow with great force through the bed of the brook, washing loose earth and exposing the layers and nodules of iron-ore in its course, which would be collected after the flood. This system was known as "scouring,"—hence the name Scwrfa, which was a common term in the early iron districts.

Following the Ffrwd for about three hundred yards, we enter a great gorge with steep cliffs on each side. Then immediately we reach Pwllyn Pren Fall, from sixteen to eighteen feet high, and a little higher there is another fall known as Pwll Annie Fall, which is about twelve feet high. The place between the two falls is very slippery and dangerous, although one can, with care, manage to reach the top of the Pwllyn Pren Fall. There is something very interesting to a geologist in the neighbourhood of those falls which I am tempted to describe. The water that percolates the rocks on the northern side of the brook, or Nant Ffrwd, is fully saturated with carbonate of lime in solution. One can see small fern, moss, and withered wood, encrusted with stalagmite, and presenting a very pretty sight. Below the fall, the rock has been caved by the action of water, and affords good shelter. On some of the ledges where water has been continually dropping, small hollows have been formed, saucer-shaped, inside which are small pebbles which have helped to carve out the hollow. Here and there in the brook may be seen large lumps of calcareous tufa, which is similar to large quantities that can be seen in the Taf Fechan, below Vaynor Church.

Being anxious to see Cwm Ffrwd in its winter garb, accompanied by two friends I visited it on a January day, after two weeks of severe frost. We were astonished at the magnificence and splendour of the spectacle. We often speak of decorating our homes at Christmastime, but let us pay a visit to Cwm Ffrwd during frosty weather, to see Nature's decoration. The sight is unforgettable. Although the trees, ferns and plants have lost their

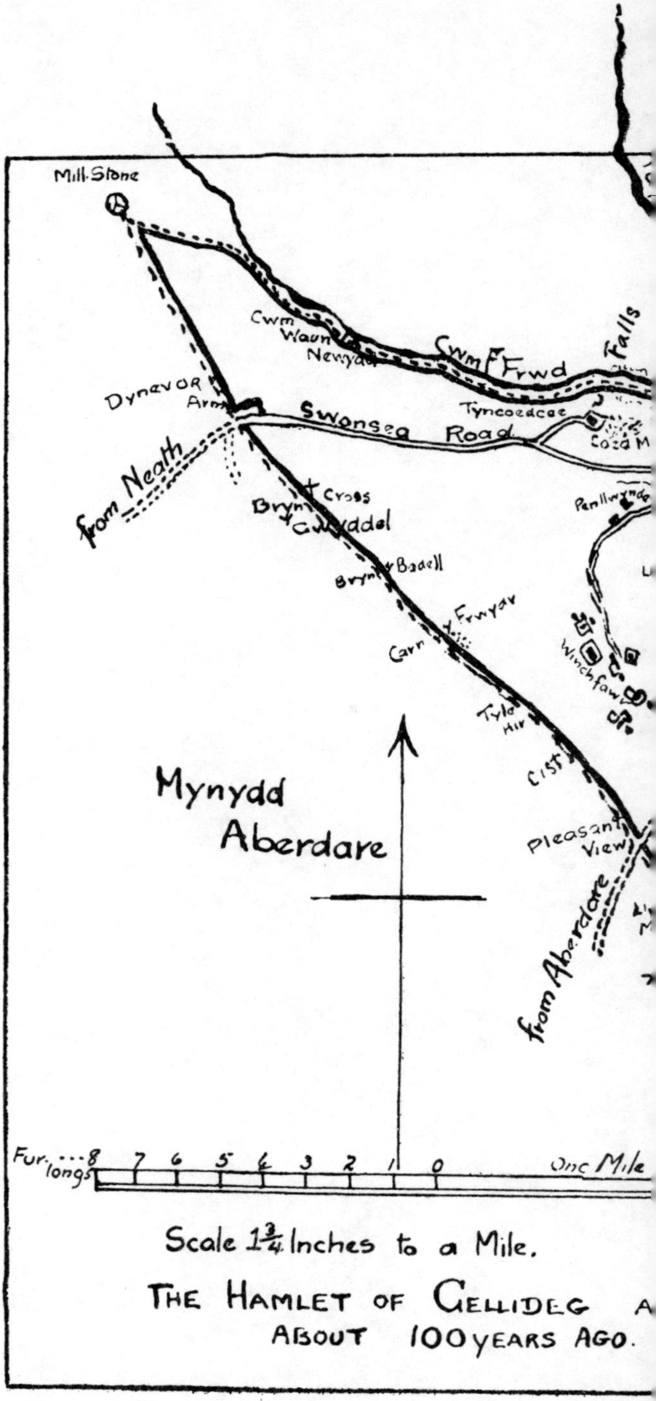

THE HAMLET OF GELLIDEG A
ABOUT 100 YEARS AGO.

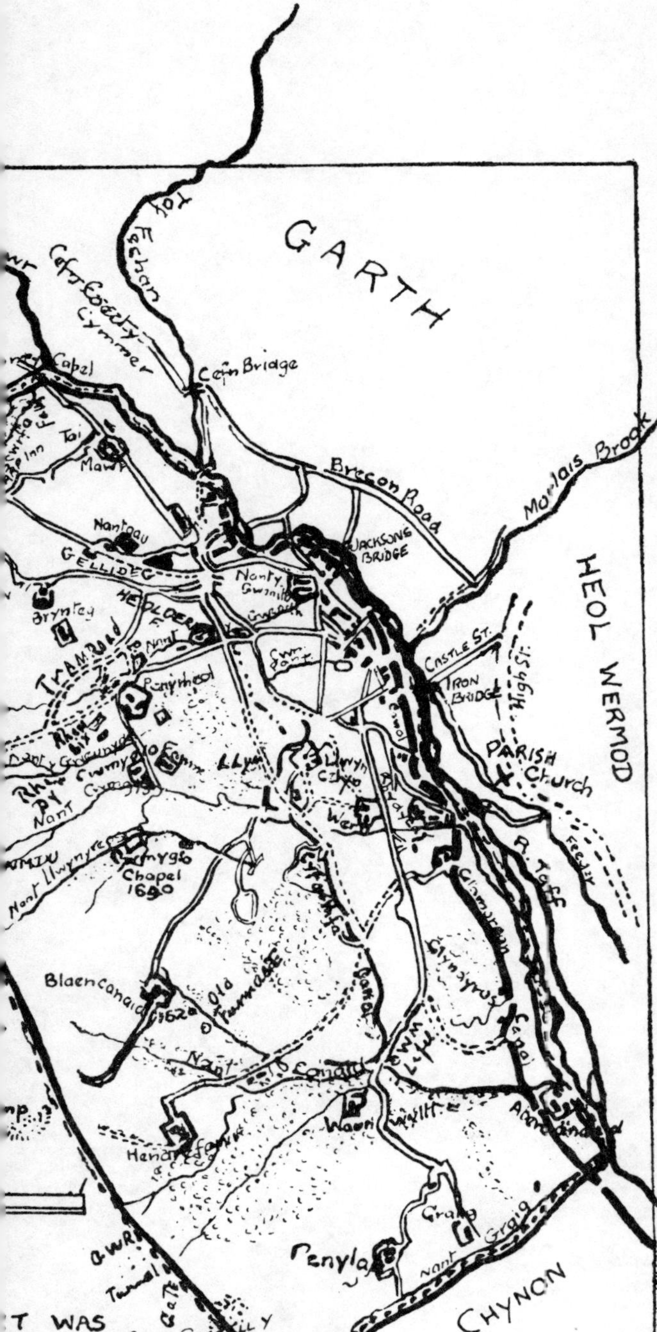
GARTH
Cefn Bridge
Brecon Road
Morlais Brook
JACKSONS BRIDGE
HEOL WERMOD
CASTLE ST.
IRON BRIDGE
High St.
PARISH Church
R. Taff
GELLIDEG
Nantgau
Brynteg
TRAMROAD
Penyrheol
Chapel 1650
Blaencanaid
Old Furnace
Canal
Hendrefawr
Penylan
Graig
Nant Graig
GWR
Tunnel
CARN CASTELL Y MEIBION
T WAS
TAF A CHYNON
FJP 1930

fragrance and been stripped of their foliage, the old gorge is fully compensated by Nature clothing it with a wonderful winter garb. Thousands of icicles can be seen overhanging the cliffs on either side, some of them four or five yards in length. In one place we saw a long string of ivy leaves, hanging from the fern and moss-covered cliff, about ten yards in length and at a considerable height, and the dark green leaves tipped with tiny icicles. It gave a chandelier-like effect, upon a magic background in the Frost King's icy palace. In the narrow gorge near Pwll Pren waterfall, we saw a tree which had fallen right across, resting on the cliffs on either side, about a dozen yards above the water. The moss-covered stalactite and stalagmite on the northern side looked beautiful in their ice-covered aspect. The lover of Nature in all its moods would be amply compensated were he to pay a visit to Cwm Ffrwd in winter.

Now I shall continue my journey along the boundary up the Ffrwd, passing Coed Meurig Farm on the left and Ffrwd Isaf on the right. The next farm we pass is Ty'n-y-Coedcae, until recently the residence of Mr. Lewis Jenkins. The family has occupied the farm for very many years. Next we come to the furthermost farm on the boundary—Cwm Waun-newydd. This is now in ruins, and the land has been linked up with that of Ty'n-y-Coedcae. At some distance above Cwm Waun-newydd there is a fence which continues along the boundary of the parish over the mountain, passes a mill-stone, and in a direct line meets Cwm Nanthir, where Nant-y-Deryn joins Nanthir above the Aberdare waterworks in Cwm Ynysmintan. After reaching the mill-stone, we have come to a most interesting point on the boundary of the parish. Here three parishes meet, viz., Merthyr Tydfil, Aberdare, and Penderyn. In addition, the counties of Glamorgan and Brecon meet here.

I should like to know by whom the stone was placed at this spot. It is a large stone composed of mill-stone grit, four feet in diameter and nine inches thick at the edge. It is embedded deep in the fence, and, lying flat, the upper surface can be seen without difficulty. Now the curious thing about the stone is this: In the centre there is an iron plate with three divisions. The sector facing Aberdare Parish has the letter "A" in it; the one facing Penderyn, the letter "P," and the one facing Merthyr the letter "M." If the centre of the stone could be seen, we should be able to say whether it was the upper or the lower mill-stone. We can be sure that, at such an important spot, the official in charge of the tour round the parish boundaries would again seize one of the unfortunate boys and administer the customary punishment with decided emphasis on: "Remember you well, my boy, this mark of the parish boundary."

Turning southwards from this stone, we proceed towards the Swansea Road, following a straight line of fence or raised boundary bank to the Finger Post. This passes through a bog. On the Merthyr side is a high hill known as Twyn Du. Next we come to a dry flat area with numerous heaps of stones, within a circle of about a hundred yards diameter and of varous sizes. The fence passes through one of these on the western side, and the stones have been used for making a part of the fence. All the other heaps are on the Merthyr side. For what purpose they were placed there is a matter of speculation. We do know that centuries ago the mountain tops were inhabited by Britons and other Celtic races. Therefore it may be that the heaps are remnants of hut circles, which typified the mode of dwelling adopted on dry mountain tops by the primitive tribes.

Now we reach the boundary stone near the Dynevor Arms on the Swansea Road. In those early days there was no public house at this spot. According to one of the rate books, the Finger Post was rated in 1842, at a gross value of £16 10s., with a rateable value of £15 5s. The owner and tenant then was Jenkin Jenkins. To-day anyone desirous of visiting this neighbourhood can easily get there by bus, and many places of interest can be visited.

Next we come to the source of Nant y Gwyddel, which runs to the Aberdare side. Then the Dyllas, Llwydcoed and Aberdare Road, which joins the Swansea Road opposite the Dynevor Arms, is reached. After crossing the road, we pass, on the Merthyr side, a field, and on the Aberdare side, an old inn. At one time this inn was known as "The Giant's Grave," but later it was named Fairfield House, and is now a dwelling-house.

Following the boundary in this space, we pass through some patches, where the furthest northern outcrop of iron ore on the boundary is to be found. The patches extend over the boundary on either side. Now we climb the hill of Bryn y Gwyddel, on the summit of which may be seen some boundary stones. Again the mark of the limits of the parish would be impressed upon one of the lads.

Next we come to a very strange mark, in the form of a large mound cross about twenty-three yards in length and lying a little to the south of the summit of Bryn y Gwyddel, which is 1,260 feet high. On the Ordnance Map, at a point a little south of this, there is marked Bedd y Gwyddel (The Irishman's Grave). What can we glean from these foreign place-names—Bryn y Gwyddel and Bedd y Gwyddel? Let us go back to the fifth century, to the time when Brychan Brycheiniog wielded great power as ruler and Prince of Brycheiniog. He was the son of an Irish king, Anlach by name, who, according to tradition, brought Christianity into

South Wales to the Welsh people. Brychan had a very large family, many of whom lived in the neighbourhood of Merthyr, which was quite near to the Lordship of Garth Mathrin or Brycheiniog, and which was governed by a Regulus — a title which Brychan bore. One of Brychan's daughters, named Tanglwys, lived at a place afterwards named Hafod Tanglwys—now called Aberfan. Gwladys was another daughter, from whom the name Capel Gwladys was derived. Then there was a son, Rhun, giving rise to the name Pontyrhun, at Troedyrhiw. Another son, Sanos, give rise to Kilsanws. But the name we are most familiar with is that of Tydfil, the martyr. These are only a few of the place-names bestowed in honour of Brychan's children.

On one occasion, Brychan paid a visit to the residence of his daughter at Hafod Tanglwys. He was then very old, and a large family gathering had assembled. It was the time when South Wales was very much troubled by the invasions of the Irish Picts, and the family, no doubt, had felt the effects of these very acutely, and had met for consolation. Having learnt of this gathering, the invaders rushed down the mountain side in great numbers, and, swarming into the residence, slew the aged Brychan and a number of his family, while those that were able to escape fled towards the hills. It is said that Tydfil was slain on the spot where St. Tydfil's Church is built at Merthyr Tydfil, and also that many of the churches built after this cruel massacre were dedicated to the children of Brychan. We might assume, therefore, that many of the crosses which can be seen throughout South Wales, in mound form or carved in stone, owe their origin to this early Christian family. (May I suggest that the crosses are undoubtedly Christian.) I have seen the cross mentioned by Mr. Meredith in his article to the "Merthyr Express." This was found on Mynydd Merthyr above Mountain Ash, and is now in the National Museum of Wales. It is cut or carved in a very rude primitive manner, out of a sandstone of the Pennant rock, which is to be found locally. At the Cyfarthfa Castle Museum there is another stone with a similar cross. This is a red sandstone, and the outlines of the cross are better carved. It was presented to the Museum and came from Vedw Hir Farm, Llwydcoed.

There is also a tradition that in the 11th century, after the days of Iestyn ap Gwrgant and Rhys ap Tewdwr, a great battle took place between the Normans and a large body of Irishmen, and that the Irish leader, who was a giant amongst his men, was slain and buried on the hill now known as Bryn y Gwyddel.

Now we pass through Pant Bryn Mân and up Bryn Padell, passing Ffynnon Bryn Padell. Here, by the aid of ditching in former years, the water of the spring is made to run into both the Aberdare and Merthyr parishes. At the top of this hill was once a " carn," known as Carn Gwenllian Dociar ; and though now there is nothing resembling a " carn " to be seen, there is a story connected with it. In the neighbourhood of Aberdare there lived an old lady named Gwenllian, who, when a child, was taken up the mountain by her father for a walk. The times were then full of unrest. Many years later she married a man named Dociar, and she related to him the story of her visit to the mountain top when a child. She remembered seeing her father placing something in a heap of stones and carefully covering it up. Both decided to visit the place again : and upon reaching the spot, they found a large heap of stones, or " carn." They began searching at the spot where she thought her father had concealed something—and something was found, but what it was no one got to know. The "carn" then became known as Carn Gwenllian Dociar. Concealing valuable things was customary in the olden days.

Next we come to Pinnau Duon Patches, where the thin beds or iron ore, which are above the 4ft. coal seam, are to be found. The iron ore is known as the upper Pinnau Duon (or Black Pins). The 4ft. seam and the pins were all worked in the open from the Llwydcoed side by Fothergill to meet Cyfarthfa on the other side.

A very important part of the boundary next comes into view. This is Carn y Frwydr. It is a " carn " of considerable size, built near the rampart of a hard sandstone rock, 1,430 feet above sea level. There has been some excavation, but there are no records of any results. The rock upon which the " carn " is built is known as the Cockshutt Rock, which is a firestone, and which was used in building Cyfarthfa Castle. This rock varies in thickness, and serves as a division between two classes of coal seams in the district. All the seams of coal below, from the Gorllwyn Seam downwards, are of steam coal qualities ; from the Abergorky Seam upwards there are the semi-bituminous or binding coal seams.

There seems to be more than a passing word to be said for Carn y Frwydr. At present, the " carn " is very scattered. When visiting this place, which is easily accessible from Winchfawr, one is greatly impressed, when standing on the " carn," by the undulating state of the surrounding surface. For about 250 yards, looking south-eastwards, there can be seen two or three rows of depressions, mostly circular. I have personally reckoned over one hundred of these, and am of opinion that they have been made for a definite purpose, the earth being thrown out and banked up between the pot-holes. On the north and west sides is the rampart, which originally must have been much larger than it is at present, the banks and ditches having been reduced in course of time. There is no record whether this place was fortified at one period, but everything points to its having been used for defensive purposes. There is a tradition that some of the struggles of Iestyn ap Gwrgant and Rhys ap Tewdwr took place in the neighbourhood. Besides, there is a possibility that the place was occupied before the 11th century by a community of the old Britons, who inhabited the mountain tops. Were this the case, and the circular pot-holes proved to be pit dwellings, there must have been a very large community at this place. All such places were protected by some sort of enclosure, either in the form of earthworks or palisades. Before leaving this important part of the boundary, the person in charge of the procession would take hold of another of the youngsters, and administer a few strokes with the admonition : " You will remember this mark on the parish boundary."

We now pass through Pant Waun Wair and the source of Nant y Derlwyn, which runs down past the Dyllas Colliery and Level, Hen Ffwrnais y Garn, and the old collieries of Ysguborwen. Then we continue towards Carn Tyle Hir, between two conglomerate stones of large size. On one of these is the bench mark, the usual crow's foot. A little higher we reach Carn Tyle Hir, the highest place on the boundary in this locality, 1,505 feet above sea level. The view from here on a fine clear day is magnificent. Here the width of the mountain ridge is over half-a-mile. Right through the " carn " there is a fissure in the rocks, caused by subsidence, and visitors to this spot must be careful, lest they let anything drop into it. There are also other dangerous places in the vicinity, for which huntsmen especially should be on their guard when hunting. The " carn " is not a large one, and on each side there are two pot-holes, all four holes being similar to those around Carn y Frwydr, and having been made for some special purpose in olden times. A visitor to this spot would be well repaid were he or she to proceed a little westwards over the top, to the ramparts overlooking Ysguborwen, this part being known as Carn Buarth Maen, and its highest point as Twyn y Ddisgwylfa. A wide vista of typical Welsh mountain scenery unfolds itself. The descent at first is a little steep, but then it sweeps away gently towards the Aberdare valley, taking in its course dark patches of woodland, white-washed farmhouses, and large tracts of fern whose darker green contrasts with the tawny stretches of coarse grassland. Then on the opposite side of the valley the mountain rises again—more sharply this time, it seems—into veritable ramparts, stern and forbidding. But we must return to the boundary. The mountain top here is quite dry, there being no bogs.

CHAPTER II.

CISTFAEN—PLEASANT VIEW—TWYN MELYN—GWERSYLL Y WERFA (WERFA CAMP)—CARN LAS—G.W.R. TUNNEL—MOUNTAIN ASH ROAD—CARN CASTELL Y MEIBION—PENYLAN MOUNTAIN AND FARM—GRAIG FARM—GRAIG BROOK—GETHIN RAILWAY—GRAIGOLA PIT (OR PWLL Y WITW)—ABERCANAID RIVER BRIDGE—GLAMORGANSHIRE CANAL.

BETWEEN Carn Tyle Hir and the boundary stone at the roadside near Pleasant View, there can be seen a " cistfaen," the burial place of some primitive Briton. The old " cist " is from five to six feet in length, about two feet in width, with the usual long slabs on either side. It has been explored at some distant date, but I am unaware of any record of its contents. Before descending to the road, a large circular pot-hole can be seen, and quite near there is a flat stone with the bench mark—the crow's foot—upon it. This mark had been covered over, but owing to the mountain surface being burnt, it came into sight again. In olden days these marks indicated the path along the mountain tops, which early surveyors adopted as lines of demarcation, although, as we can readily see from the Ordnance Map, they do not always coincide with the boundary line.

Now we pass, on our left, Pleasant View, built in 1858 by Mr. Lewis Pugh. From the stone at the roadside, which is 1,365 feet above sea level, we pass on to Twyn Melyn, on the Ordnance Map marked Llwyn Melyn. Opposite the Pleasant View, which is 1,400 feet above sea level, are the remains of bonfires, and also one of those peculiar large pot-holes. On the left of the boundary line is the old path known as Cefn y Ffordd, and further east is Carn Buarth Maen, just above Cwmdu Old Farm. The old "carn" has long since disappeared.

Next we pass through Pant Rhiw Feurig, where on our left are to be seen the remains of three " carns " and some small quarries. Here the Pennant rock, which crops out in thin layers, has been quarried for use at the Cyfarthfa Ironworks. The stone was dressed on the spot into small slabs five inches square and one-and-a-half inches thick, and then conveyed in carts to the Cwmdu tramway, where the trams were loaded and then taken to Cyfarthfa Yard. Thomas and Samuel Rees, of the Court, Merthyr, and Werfa—noted men in their day—travelled often through Pant Rhiw Feurig on their way from Merthyr to Llwyn y Werfa.

Now we must climb Rhiw Feurig Hill in order to reach Gwersyll y Werfa, where the boundary has recently been fenced with wire by the owner. Here we reach another point of much historical interest. At the top of the rise, about 80 yards west of the fence, are the remains of an old camp on a stretch of flat ground. It is an earth-work of primitive construction and semi-circular in shape. The distance between both ends of the crescent is roughly 60 yards, and the trench is about five feet deep at the present time. Recent excavations have revealed that the original depth of the trench was three or four feet more, and that it had been cut through rock foundation. At the surface the trench is, on an average, about three yards wide. The excavated earth was thrown on the inside. There are also inside the camp the remains of two " carns," which have been formerly investigated, but with what result we know not. As the mountain top here is narrow and flat, and the spot a very prominent one, there is no doubt that the builders of the camp recognized its strategic possibilities, for on the northern, eastern and western sides the hill is very steep. The southern side is open and flat. There are various names given to this position : Twyn Gwersyllfa, Gwersyllfa'r Werfa, and Twyn y Cyffion. Earth-works of this description are very primitive. It is possible that they are pre-Roman, and may be 3,000 or 3,500 years old. Nothing definite has been found to prove the date of its construction or occupation. Quite near the camp there are indications that even this elevated position might have been cultivated many centuries ago. Right above the old Werfa Farm—the ancient residence of the Rees family, of the Court and Werfa—there may be seen what appear to be furrows over the mountain top. It is said that furrows may be discernible on mountain tops for 1,000 or even 1,500 years after cultivation has ceased. According to the place-names and judging from its position, it seems very likely that it was a camp of special military importance.

Continuing along the boundary, we reach a large " carn " known as Carn Las. This also has been opened, but again the result of the search is unknown. It is about 200 yards from the camp. Down below, on our left, lies the old Hendre Fawr Farm, and in the distance, to the rear, Blaencanaid Farm can be seen. We now follow a fence and wall for about half-a-mile from Carn Las over flat ground. A solitary larch tree breaks the monotony of the surroundings, on the right of the wall. Some years ago an attempt was made at reafforestation here ; but, out of a large plantation, there are only a few trees left. The young trees failed to thrive. Another half-mile brings us to a stone stile in the wall. At this point the G.W.R. tunnel pierces the mountain, and its direction can be traced by observing the telegraph posts, which pass over the mountain. The height above sea level is 1,345 feet here. As the Merthyr end of the tunnel is only 630 feet above sea level, we can easily estimate that the tunnel is at a depth of 715 feet from the mountain top.

The next important place we come to is Carn Castell y Meibion, and on our right is the gate through which the road leads to Cwmpennar and Mountain Ash. Three mountain paths converge upon this spot: the road from Abercanaid and Waunwyllt, following the direction of the railway tunnel; the Cefn y Ffordd over the top from Pleasant View; and the other way from Hendre Fawr and Blaencanaid—they all meet at the gate.

Before ascending Penylan Mountain, let us proceed along the Mountain Ash road for about 600 yards. Inside a mountain wall on our right there is another large "carn," which has been opened and the "cist" exposed. The grave has been formed with large flat stones at each side to a depth of three feet, and close by is the large flat slab which was used as the cover. There is also a large mound of earth and small stones near by, which does not seem to have been opened. The mountain here is known as Tyle Robert, and overlooks Cwmbach, Aberdare. There is a fine view of the Cynon and Cwmaman valleys.

But we must return to the boundary line, which runs through Carn Castell y Meibion. This is a large "carn" over which the boundary wall has been built. There are two walls built at right angles to one another; one follows the boundary almost to the summit of Penylan, while the other leads downwards to Waunwyllt. The "carn" may be seen at the apex of these walls. Now why was this place called Castell y Meibion? The surrounding district was probably inhabited by the old Britons when Gwersyll y Werfa and Tyle Robert were sites of great importance. Such an important point on the boundary, where so many roads converge, must surely be impressed on the young mind, so again a youngster was seized, placed across the knee, and went through the usual ritual: "My boy, you will surely remember this mark of the parish boundary"!

After a brief halt, the march is continued to the summit of Penylan, which is 1,620 feet above sea level. This mountain is known as Mynydd Merthyr, but, at this particular spot, as Mynydd y Ddisgwylfa. Many people go into transports of rapture over the scenery of Snowdonia, the Lake District, or the Alps; but have they ever experienced the thrill which pervades one when the summit of Penylan is reached? What a panorama unfolds itself! Some months ago I paid a visit to the spot with a Sunday School class on a glorious Saturday afternoon in August. We could all see the Bristol Channel quite easily.

The boundary now turns southwards. As it is my intention to deal with the hamlet of Gellideg, in which we will find much to interest us, we will now leave the boundary and confine ourselves to that ancient parochial district. It is strange how ignorant we are, on the whole, of the history and geography of our local surroundings. Here there are many interesting spots within easy reach. We pass them often, but give not a thought to their history. Many local historians have touched the fringe of many an interesting spot or object in the neighbourhood, but the accounts have been very bare. The area comprised in my subject will be confined to the interior of the ancient division or district known as the Gellideg Hamlet.

The parish of Merthyr Tydfil was anciently divided into five parochial districts or hamlets, these being—Gellideg, Tâf a Chynon (west of the river Taff) ; Garth, Heolwermod, and Fforest (east of the river Taff). I have been unable to find the necessary information as to when this division into hamlets took place, although they are mentioned in the old Parish Register as far back as 1704. The question naturally arises: When did Merthyr Tydfil become a parish? Again: How and when was the County of Glamorgan thus named? The first survey and division of Wales that we know of was made during the Roman occupation in 207 A.D. The town of Caerwent (the Isca Silurum of this period) was, from an inscription that has been found, the administrative centre of the canton of the Silures. This division was made on the cantonal system, which was the general method adopted in the civil areas.

The second division of Wales was made in 877 A.D. by Rhodri Fawr, King of Wales. He divided the country into three parts: Gwynedd, or North Wales; Powys, or Mid Wales; and Deheubarth, or South Wales. Morgannwg, or Glamorgan, was then a separate and independent district governed by its own lord or prince, but it covered a much greater area than it does at present. It is said that in 945 Wales was divided by Hywel Dda into counties similar to those made by Alfred the Great in England. The next division took place after the Norman Conquest, by Sir Robert Fitzhammon in 1090. Glamorgan was then divided into lordships and given to the twelve knights who had assisted him in the conquest of Iestyn ap Gwrgant's lordship, viz., Glamorgan. But it was a long time before tranquillity was restored. There were several rebellions against Norman rule, the chief being those of Ivor Bach, Llewelyn Bren, Prince Llewelyn (the last), and Owain Glyndwr. During the rule of Llewelyn, the last native Prince of Wales, a survey was made of the whole of Wales, by his command, in 1282—some time before he was slain near Builth.

The Lordship of Senghenydd was one of those given to one of the knights. In Llewelyn's survey, part of this Lordship was divided into six parishes according to population, these being—Eglwys Elian, Llanfabon, Gellygaer, Merthyr Tydfil, Aberdare, and Llanwyno; but there is no definite information as to when the whole of Glamorgan was divided into parishes. The sub-division of the parishes into parochial districts took place later, but it is not known at what particular time. In that valuable little leaflet compiled by Major F. T. James entitled "Notes from the Old Parish Register from 1703 to 1763," published in 1925, there are many references to the hamlets: Garth in 1704, Fforest in 1705, Gellideg in 1718, Tâf a Chynon in 1704, and Heolwermod in 1712. Therefore it is reasonable to assume that the division was made previous to 1700.

The Reform Act of 1832 gave power to Merthyr, Aberdare, and a part of Vaynor, to be constituted into a Parliamentary Borough, entitled to send one representative to the House of Commons. Mr. J. J. Guest was returned unopposed to the following Parliament in 1835. For the new Parliamentary Borough a map was specially prepared by Robert Dawson, a lieutenant in the Royal Artillery, on a scale of two inches to the mile, showing the boundary within the parish, as well as that of Cefn Coed in the Parish of Vaynor. This map was prepared from the ordnance survey map, and as no date appears upon it, it is quite likely that it was prepared from the ordnance survey map of 1824, which was the date ot the last survey previous to 1832. It indicates the parliamentary boundary (in pink), as well as the hamlet boundaries.

The Hamlet of Gellideg is bounded on the south by Nant-y-Graig, on the east by the river Taff, on the north by Cwm Ffrwd, and on the west by the parish boundary, at a point in which we digressed for a space of time. We will now take up our itinerary again.

Descending Penylan Mountain, we follow a brook called Nant-y-Graig, and on our left pass Penylan Farm. This was the birthplace in 1815 of the eminent sculptor, Joseph Edwards. He was the son of John Edwards (Shon Penylan), a stone-cutter, and became one of the leading sculptors of his time. Examples of his work, in the form of carved tomb-stones and mural tablets, can be seen at local cemeteries and places of worship. At Ynysgau Chapel there is a memorial tablet to Edward Harri; but the most imposing and beautiful example of his work is the family tomb of the late William Harris (senior) at Cefn Cemetery. The vault is surmounted by an exquisitely carved figure of an angel. William Harris was High Constable of Merthyr in 1863.

Next we come to Graig Farm, where once lived a family of note, the Morgan family, who owned and resided on the estate for a long period, and played an important part in the old town of Merthyr and in the district of Plymouth. Since the beginning of the last century, a considerable number of coal mining operations have been carried on in the Graig Estate. Now we come to the old Gethin and Castle Pit Railway, which has been acquired by the G.W.R. Nearby is Abercanaid Railway Station, and also some houses known as Graig Cottages. All these are within the hamlet. A little lower down is the old disused Graig Pit, known as " Pwll y Witw." This pit was worked under the direction of Mrs. Lucy Thomas of Waunwyllt, and is an important landmark in the economic history of the South Wales coal trade. The name " Lucy " is still preserved in a more recent colliery undertaking, but how many people associate it with this female pioneer of the coal industry ? If the Graig Road is followed downwards, the canal is crossed near the old Graig Methodist Chapel. There are some houses here, too, on both sides of the canal, known as Graig Houses (Tai'r Graig), as well as the site of " Yr Hen Dai," " Tai'r Gerddi," on the lower side, near the old pit, traces of which have become almost obliterated.

The Graig Brook continues its course under the Glamorganshire Canal, passes Llwyn-yr-Eos House, and enters the Taff near Abercanaid Bridge. About a hundred yards above this bridge, another brook pours its waters into the river. This is the Canaid Brook, and the confluence of brook and river gave rise to the name Abercanaid. "Aber " signifies the joining of two streams of different names, or again, the joining of a lesser with a greater body of water.

It would be appropriate at this stage to give an account of the Glamorganshire Canal, which runs right through the area I am describing, and which has played such an important part in the early industrial development of the district. The making of the canal was the second venture to improve the transport facilities in a rapidly growing industrial district. The first venture was the road made by the iron-master Anthony Bacon. part of the cost coming from public subscriptions ; and the second was the canal, which was constructed by the leading iron-masters of that time. The company was formed of about seventy-five proprietors, the chief of whom were Richard Crawshay, Thomas Guest, John Hall, Richard Hill, and the three brothers Homphray. The Bill asking for the necessary powers for construction was presented to Parliament on May 18, 1784, but was not actually passed until January 21, 1790. The canal was to be made from Cardiff to Merthyr. The Company was empowered by the Act of Parliament to raise £60,000, with further instalments of £30,000 and £10,000, making a grand total of £100,000. Powers were conceded to levy rates of transport for certain articles not exceeding fivepence per ton per mile, and for certain specified articles a rate not exceeding twopence per ton per mile.

The canal was commenced in August, 1790, and was partially opened as far as Navigation (now Abercynon) in 1794. In June, 1798, the whole length from Merthyr to Cardiff—where a little extension work to the sea had been carried out—was completed, and the canal was opened for navigation. In the Cyfarthfa Museum there is an engraving of this canal on a copper plate, and I have reason to believe that it was made before the work was commenced. It shows the proposed canal, the river Taff, and a considerable part of the Merthyr—Cardiff Road. It also shows a branch canal from the main canal to Dowlais, which begins a little above Parliament Lock, then proceeds almost in a straight line across the Taff, and on to Dowlais Works along the south side of the Morlais Brook and Penydarren Works. Here is a table of references inscribed on the plate and dated 1790 :—

REFERENCES.	LENGTHS. M.F.C.				FALLS. FT.	INS.
From A at Dowlais to B near Merthyr Bridge	1	5	6	...	411	0
From C at Cyfarthfa to B as above	0	3	5	...	8	0
From B near Merthyr Bridge to D at crossing of the river below Quakers' Yard	8	5	0	...	279	0
From D at crossing of the River Taff to E at New Bridge	3	1	7	...	78	6
From E at New Bridge to F at Melin Griffith Works	7	6	4	...	130	6
From F at Melin Griffith to G at the bank below Cardiff (at high tide)	5	0	2	...	51	9
To Low Water	0	0	0	...	20	8

A description of a journey along the canal in one of the coal or iron barges of that period would be most interesting, and it is surprising that no writer has left us an account of canal life in those busy days.

After some years of transport on the canal, it was found that the system of distribution was too slow to keep up with the pace of industrial development. The coal and iron magnates turned their attention to a faster and more efficient means of transport. Isambard Brunel, one of the greatest civil engineers of the day, was consulted and asked to report upon the possibility of a railroad between Merthyr and Cardiff. His report was issued in February, 1835. In it Brunel states that Mrs. Lucy Thomas, of Waunwyllt Collieries, was the only supplier of coal from the Merthyr Valley to Cardiff, the quantity supplied annually by her being 30,000 tons.

CHAPTER III.

GLYNDYRUS — UNDERTAKINGS OF ROBERT AND LUCY THOMAS — THOMAS MERTHYR—OLD CYFARTHFA TRANSPORT ROAD—OLD CWM LEVEL—CYFARTHFA CANAL—CWM PIT AS A BALANCE PIT — CANAID BROOK—G.W.R. TUNNEL—WAUNWYLLT—MELIN GANAID—THE OLD FURNACE—BLAENCANAID—HENDRE FAWR.

THE Canaid Brook, as we have seen, enters the River Taff a little distance above Abercanaid Bridge. Following the brook, we see not far away the Old Pit on the left, quite near the canal. Here the 7-ft. seam of coal was worked very successfully by the Plymouth Company. The pit engine was of an unusual type for a colliery, being a vertical marine engine, and suitable, considering the very limited space on the bank of the canal. I have heard some of the workmen engaged there say that a " face " of from 300 to 400 yards of 7-ft. coal was worked very successfully on the " long wall " system. On the right of the road was the old ventilating shaft, the fan of which was worked by an electric plant producing its own power.

Next we come to Upper Abercanaid Old Dock. There seem to have been two " docks." The one on the lower side is a fairly large one, being over eighty yards in length and of substantial workmanship. It is entered from the canal under the tow-path bridge. On the upper side there are the ruins of another old " dock." The remains of old workings, including a shallow old pit of a primitive kind, are to be seen on this side. These are relics of the concerns of Robert and Lucy Thomas, who utilized the " docks " for the loading of coal for canal transport. Quite near is another relic of the same period—a shoot or tip over which were emptied the tramloads of coal into the boats below. To the right of the brook and above the canal is the little village of Upper Abercanaid, in which was the old residence of Mr. Thomas W. Lewis, the father of Sir William Thomas Lewis, afterwards Baron Merthyr of Senghenydd. There are also the ruins of an old chapel.

Behind this village is the old Glyndyrus pumping shaft, which in its time dealt with a tremendous volume of water from the mine and coal workings. The engine was a Cornish double pumping engine, the beam or horse-head 36 feet in length and of tremendous weight. The date on the beam was 1839 ; the depth of the pit, 150 yards ; length of stroke, 3ft. 6ins, four to five strokes per minute ; diameter of plunger or ram, 13½ ins. There were also pumps attached, with the same beam and rods, from a small pit near-by known as Tasker's Pit, worked from a depth of 50 yards.

The diameter of this plunger was 14 ins. Now the three plungers forced together a tremendous volume of water continually; the length or height of exit in one single pipe was one of the greatest in South Wales. All the pits have now been dismantled and the water allowed to flow over the top into the canal.

A little northwards along the canal and we come to Glyndyrus Farm, once the residence of Thomas and Lucy Lewis, and which was in existence as far back as 1700. There are two locks in the canal near-by, kept at one time by the local bard, William Moses (Gwilym Tew o Lan Taf). Glyndyrus and the Upper Abercanaid neighbourhood was of great importance during the early period of coal and iron-stone mining, in the time of Anthony Bacon, Rd. Hill and Rd. Crawshay. It is said that the first coal used for iron-making at Plymouth Ironworks was worked in this neighbourhood, and carried by mules and horses across the river.

Continuing up the Canaid Brook, on the right we pass Pwll Tasker, 50 yards deep, which was sunk by Mr. George Tasker, who also sank Gethin Pit. Pwll Tasker was sunk to the 9ft. seam. Near by are the Glyndyrus levels, both starting together, which for many years served as outlets for the drainage of the Cyfarthfa undertakings in this area. Tasker also made the cutting to these levels. On the right is the old disused Glyndyrus Pond, made by the Canal Company for the purpose of supplying the canal with water; and a little way above, underneath the railway line, are two levels entered by a single arch. From the arch the levels, which were known as Leflau Thomas Lewis, branched—one producing coal and the other mine. There is a stock of unused mine on the bank at the present time. The Gethin and Castle Pit railway is next crossed, with the G.W.R. Crossing to the right. Here also is the south end of the Ynysfach line which proceeds from Pen Yard, Ynysfach. Between this and the Gethin line was an old level called Leval Will Ellis, from which various seams of coal were worked to the Aberdare boundary. Coming back to the brook, we see on our left the Lucy Collieries, worked under the direction of Mr. Gomer Thomas and Company. On the right is a shallow old pit known as Pwll Patch, where the 3ft. and 4ft. seams were worked, and which served as a connection between Cwm Pit and the Glyndyrus workings. Proceeding under the G.W.R. line to a point nearly opposite the signal box, we reach the junction of the Canaid and Waunwyllt brooks, and emerge on to the Graig and Waunwyllt road. Our course up to this point has been rather tortuous and difficult to follow, but here we are on safe ground.

Opposite the signal box there is an arch over the brook, and between this and Graig Bridge, between brook and road, is the oldest level worked by the Cyfarthfa Company and known as Leval Cwm, in which the 4ft. seam was worked extensively. To locate the old level, it is necessary to look over the wire fence or view it from the bridge, as there is nothing to suggest the existence of a level to the casual passer-by. At one time there was a farmhouse near the confluence of the brooks, known as Cwm Canaid, but the old homestead has been long covered over by the Cwm Pit tips. In his " Notes of the Old Parish Register," Major F. T. James refers to the farm as Cwmglymais, which was the name it went by in 1717. He is also of opinion that the name should be Cwm Camlas, from the old Cyfarthfa Canal which passed close by; but I fail to see how this can be so, as this canal only came into existence towards the close of the 18th century, as I shall try to describe immediately. Since the old farmhouse has been covered over, the land has been known as Tir Cwm Canaid. Parts of this old canal can be seen at various places alongside the Cwm Pit Railway; there is a good stretch near the Canaid Brook and the G.W.R. Now this canal must not be confused with the Glamorganshire Canal. It is rather difficult to give the exact date of its construction, but most probably it came into being with the advent of mining operations in the Canaid Dingle between 1780 and 1790. The customary transport before that time—of wood, mine, or coal—was performed by mules or horses, loaded with panniers or baskets hanging on each flank. Carts were also used later. Thus the coal and other materials were taken from the Canaid Brook to Cyfarthfa Works. There was a fairly good road made almost in a straight line from the Works to the source of supplies. It commenced from the Swansea Road, passing the mountain-side screen, and proceeded along the tramroad which runs through the archway of the B. & M. Railway. Of course, when the road was in use there was no screen, tramway, arch, or railway. It then crossed the Penyrheolgerrig Road near the old farm, went through the site of the Coedcae Pit tip, passed the western end of Upper Colliers' Row, then by the Llyn (Llwyncelyn Lake), continued behind the Upper Wern, and then over a bridge across the Cwm, the pillars of which are still to be seen. After that it followed the course of the present Cwm Pit railway, passing in front of Lower Colliers' Row. As the quantity carried by horses and mules was very limited, and the loading and unloading took time, the business was necessarily slow. Production increased, but the transport facilities could not cope with it. Necessity became the mother of invention, and a scheme for better transport suggested itself: a canal would be the very thing to supply the necessary want.

The Cyfarthfa Canal was made some years before the bigger canal, but I am not certain who was responsible for its construction. I think it must have been made before the time of the engineer Henry Kirkhouse. One by the name of Thomas had control of the minerals and transport before Kirkhouse came on the scene. This Thomas was very likely the shrewd person mentioned by Charles Wilkins, who foresaw the possibility of making a canal from Canaid Brook to Cyfarthfa. In the Merthyr Library there can be seen an old map showing this canal: its course can be followed quite easily. In his " History of Merthyr " Wilkins states that the starting-point is Blaencanaid, which is misleading. I shall deal with it briefly, indicating the portions of it which are uncovered. The Cwm Pit tip covers the south-west end, but a short stretch can be seen on the upper side of the Graig Road near the Canaid. Passing the site of Pwll Carage on the left, and crossing Cwm Pit siding, a long stretch can be seen, with alders growing on each side. Next we reach the Parish Road and the Fan tips. The Fan Pit at this spot was used for many years as the ventilating shaft for Cwm Pit; here the old canal has been covered. At the rear of Lower Colliers' Row was the Waun Level, where the yard (or upper 2ft. 9ins.) and 4ft. seams were worked to the Aberdare boundary. Next came Colliers' Row Level, on the 6ft. seam. I am not certain whether the canal entered this old level—the position was very convenient; the waterway passed quite near and proceeded in front of Colliers' Row. Then we come to the screen, which was built over the site of Colliers' Row Pit (Pwll Bach), and in which were worked the Bute and 9ft. seams. This screen dealt with all the coals brought down from the Cwmdu Collieries, now worked by Mr. Gomer Thomas and Co., as well as the output of the two Colliers' Row Drifts, Lefal Pownd, Canal Level, and many other levels in the vicinity. Now we reach Canal Level; the canal passes quite near the entrance. From its name, it is evident that boats from the canal were taken in a little way to be loaded, as it has been ascertained that a place for loading was discovered inside. The Bute and 9ft. seams proved to be in excellent positions, and hundreds of acres of those seams have been worked there by various contractors. Following the canal again, we reach the bridge pillars which supported the bridge crossing the Cwm. It passed between the pillars, under the bridge, and wound around the dingle before crossing the Cwm Pit line. This line was not in existence at that time. I am trying to describe the course of the canal with the aid of present day landmarks. Then it went parallel with the line on the lower side opposite Upper Wern, entered Llwyncelyn Lake, and passed by Llwyncelyn Signal Box, behind which is still to be seen an old stone arch through which it passed. It is seen that a great bend was made here, probably made purposely for the convenience of Llwyncelyn and Ynysfach Works, situated a little distance below this point, which was the site of the earliest of the Cyfarthfa furnaces. From here, the waterway took its course over a flat stretch to a pond near the lower end of Upper Colliers' Row, continued in a straight line across the Heolgerrig Road, and under the B. & M.R. bridge and into the Cyfarthfa Works. The purpose of the canal was to provide cheaper, better and speedier transport than existed previously. Small iron flat-bottomed boats, or barges, were used, drawn by one or more persons according to the number of boats joined together. The old canal was in use up to the period 1835—1840, when mechanical power robbed it of its function. We can assume, therefore, that it was utilized for transport purposes for half a century. When Mrs. Mary Simons of Brynteg Farm was a young girl, she assisted her father, Mr. Howel Giles, in the task of hauling these boats along the canal.

Now we will turn our attention towards Cwm Pit, Melin Ganaid, and Blaencanaid. Not far from the spot where the canal strikes the brook at equal level, and situated between the Canaid and Waunwyllt Brooks, is Cwm Pit, sunk in 1845 to a depth of 150 yards, passing through most of the coal seams from the 20in. to the 7ft. seam. At first the old pit was worked as a balance pit, which was the earliest type of local pits, and it would not be out of place to attempt a description of the working of one of these. A plentiful supply of water was the first essential, this being secured by making a storage pond near the pit. At the pit bottom there had to be a system of drainage to lead away the surplus water. The two pit cages were fitted with tanks underneath, sufficiently large to hold a weight of two tons of water respectively, with a self-acting valve at the bottom of each. The winding-chain, fastened to the top of each cage, was a combination of three separate chains tied together by small wooden blocks, fitted through three opposing links; the whole made a triple-stranded chain, which was practically flat and pliant enough to pass over the large sheave at the top. Underneath each cage was fastened a heavy chain with large links and used as a balancing chain. The balance and winding chains were of equal weight, so the cages with an empty tram in each would equally balance. To set the cages in motion, a working balance was necessary. Now let us suppose there was a ton of mine or other material to be raised from the pit bottom. The banksman—the official in charge of the lowering or raising the cages—manipulating a water-valve, regulated the desired quantity of water necessary for his working balance. The cage at the pit bottom, the water in which had been released, would be one ton heavier than the one at the top, therefore the banksman would supply the upper cage with two tons of water, thus causing the cages to be set in motion. This operation was repeated when the empty cage reached the bottom and the load had reached the bank. When the load reached the top, the banksman locked his brake during the process of unloading or loading. Signalling was effected by tapping upon one of the iron guide-rods. It can be seen what an important part was played by water-power, and the necessity for its storage and drainage. In due course, the industrial revolution made itself felt locally by the ousting of the balance pit system by its new rival—steam-winding power. Some of the old mine-pits clung to the balance system even after steam-power became widespread. A few years before Cwm Pit was closed, a new ventilating shaft was sunk close by, and an electric plant installed for working the fan and other purposes.

Now I have two brooks to follow—the Waunwyllt Brook on the left, and the Canaid Brook on the right. Nearly opposite Cwm Pit is the G.W.R. tunnel, opened in the year 1853. The line rises gradually by a few feet towards the centre of the tunnel, and I have been told that water was conveyed by means of troughing from near the tunnel to the G.W.R. station at Merthyr, there being a natural flow. On a Saturday evening in 1874 a terrible accident occurred at the above station. The B. & M. train had just reached its destination, when a number of loaded wagons broke loose in the tunnel and careered madly towards the Merthyr Station. The stationary train was struck with such force that it was knocked clean through the station end, and half of the engine was embedded in the solid wall in front of the station. As the B. & M. train had only just arrived, many people were injured as a result of this terrific impact.

At a little distance above the tunnel is Waunwyllt Farm, the old residence of Robert and Lucy Thomas, who played such an important part in the pioneer days of the South Wales coal industry. They first worked their coal, and then brought it up to Merthyr to be sold, for domestic purposes, in a yard opposite the Corner House Inn, Penry Street. Soon they discovered that the coal from the 4ft. seam, which they were working, was of exceptional quality for steam-raising purposes, and a great business very soon sprang up. They only carried on for about six years on the Waunwyllt land, owing to some difficulty with the land-owners. By agreement, new works were opened on the Graig Estate, on a new system of payment; the stipulation was that they must pay a royalty of 9d. per ton to the owners of the estate. Previously, the custom was to pay lump sums annually for the privilege of working the minerals. The pit they sank on this estate was known as Pwll y Witw, because the widow (witw) carried on the business after the death of her husband, Robert Thomas.

Passing Waunwyllt Farm is an old road, which meets the other roads on the mountain near Carn Castell y Miebion; it passes through the target site formerly used by the Merthyr Volunteers. Many a shot was fired here by the recruits, who came up from the town to practice. I am afraid that more shots found their billets in the surrounding woods and mounds than ever found the " bull," judging from the amount of lead fragments scattered about. Next we enter a large quarry from which stone was obtained for the construction of the tunnel. The rock is of the Pennant formation, of which the rugged and craggy Penylan is made. After passing through the quarry, we come across one of the tunnel shafts, or air-pits, seen at the side of the pathway. Now we pass through a gateway in the wall, and the path gets steep and rugged on its course to the top. To the right is the Waunwyllt brook. The old farm of Hendre Fawr takes up a prominent position on the same side. It is very old, and at one time belonged to the Rees family, of The Court and Werfa. The height above sea-level at this point is 1,000 feet. Hendre Fawr is mentioned in the old Parish Register in 1714 (Major James' Notes). In many places above the farm there are signs of early cultivation, there being the marks of old, nearly obliterated furrows, even at the summit of the mountain. The name of the old homestead sounds rather ancient, like Hendre'r Gelli and Hendre'r Mynydd, in the Rhondda Valley. These are all isolated places. Nothing is recorded, and nothing indicates whether there was an old town, as the literal meaning implies. It may at one time have been a very substantial homestead, or a group of dwellings, but more than likely it was a winter residence. " Hafod " signifies a summer residence, while " Hendre " often signifies a place of residence during the winter. Another form of the word is Hen-dre-fa Fawr. If we assume that the mountain top a few hundred yards above was inhabited in very early times, in the neighbourhood of Gwersyll y Werfa and Carn Castell y Meibion, where indications point to the fact that the mountain top was cultivated, there is reason to believe that the old place was frequented occasionally, if not permanently, by certain people. The spot is well-sheltered on three sides—on the southern side by Penylan, on the western side by Twyn y Werfa, and by the Blaencanaid ridge on the northern side. Towards the east a very wide expanse of gently sloping land opens out towards Merthyr and Dowlais. These positions served a double purpose : they were strong points for military defence in case of attack by an enemy, as well as protective barriers against the winter storms for the peaceful haven amid the hills.

I shall now return to Cwm Pit, and follow the course of the Canaid Brook, which, from its junction with the other brook, is arched for about 250 yards. After crossing the Cwm Pit Incline, we reach the old Cwm Felin Drift, now disused, in which various seams were worked. The ravine here is the home of a large variety of birds : jays, in their beautiful coloured plumage, dart screeching hither and thither ; the chatter of magpies makes discord to the full-throated warbling of blackbird and thrush ; the black-cap twitters in sharp staccato notes, while finches of many kinds pour their melody into the woodland choir ; and even the queen of song has been known to visit the locality. In 1926 I had the greatest gratification when I heard her at midnight on the 1st of July. In the company of many others I visited Melin Ganaid for the express purpose of hearing the " light-winged Dryad of the trees " (as Keats describes her) " singing of summer in full throated ease." Punctually at one o'clock the first note was heard. Perfect silence reigned around—not a breeze was felt. A whisper went through the company : " Dyna'r eos," and we listened attentively. For over two hours we listened to the enchanting trilling, and when we left the spot she was still singing—

" Perhaps the self-same song that found a path
  Through the sad heart of Ruth, when sick for home,
She stood in tears amid the alien corn ;
  The same that oft-times hath
Charmed magic casements, opening on the foam
  Of perilous seas, in faery lands forlorn."

Her singing could be heard at a distance of half a mile. It was one of the happy events that good fortune brings during one's lifetime.

Just before we reach Melin Ganaid, a small brook enters the Canaid, which is known as Nant yr Hen Odyn, there being a waterfall from seven to eight feet in height at the junction. A little higher up, this stream crosses the Parish Road leading from Merthyr to Hendre Fawr and the mountain top. We now reach Melin Ganaid. It is here that the old Parish Road crosses the Canaid Brook at the upper end of the building, which was once in the possession of Thomas Rees, of The Court and Werfa. The road was mainly used for communication between these two residences. Reference is made to Melin Ganaid in the " Notes on the Parish Register " in the year 1714. On the 4th of October, 1926, I paid a visit to the place, and made inquiries of the occupants whether they knew of any relics of the old mill, such as machinery, mill-stones, or masonry ; and, if possible, to provide any information as to the working of the mill—whether the motive power was water or derived from a " gin," which was an apparatus set in motion by animal power—that of horse, ox, or mule, as is often the case in chaffing operations on farms. Nothing was learnt of the method employed, but, fortunately, on the end wall of the upper house, not far from the foundation, we found a date. The wall had been tarred on two occasions, and one of the occupants remembered hearing the mason, when repairing, saying that there was something like a date there, but no further notice was taken of it; she, however, remembered the place in the wall. Taking up this cue, we set about rubbing, scrubbing, scouring and washing in earnest, until the following date came into view: (?) I R 1726. I failed to find the G before the I R, the stone having been probably chipped. The original date must have been G.I.R. 1726 (George I Rex. 1726), as George I was the reigning monarch over Great Britain from 1714 to 1727.

Thomas Rees, of Werfa, bought the Court Estate from Thomas Lewis, of the Fan, about 1727; he also became owner of Melin Ganaid and Hendre Fawr. He was living at the Court when Howel Harris preached there, in front of the house, to whom he had given permission to do so. Thomas Rees died in 1787, leaving five sons, one of whom—Samuel—inherited The Court and Werfa, while the other four shared the remainder of the property.

After Anthony Bacon's departure from Cyfarthfa Works, Cockshutt held them alone for a while; he then left to join Thomas Rees, of the Court, in the working of the Canaid Mill, which seems to have carried on a flourishing trade at the time. All the grinding for the neighbouring farms was done at this mill, and William Williams ("Billy Blaencanaid") remembered the time when, as a young man, he drove his horse loaded with sacks of grain there very often.

Now what is the origin of the word "Canaid"? It has been a difficult question to solve, for those who have attempted it; therefore, when the doctors disagree the disciples are free. "Canaid" or "Cannaid" means luminary or luminous, something that has to do with the shedding of light; or we might interpret it as the disseminating of knowledge. If "Canaid" means "light," what "light" could have been cast in this place to give rise to the name? The sun is a luminary body: so is the moon a secondary luminary body—they cast their light far and wide. But what has cast its light in this very valley to be worthy of the name of a luminary? Could it be the glare of beacon fires, centuries ago, on the summits of Penylan, Twyn y Werfa, or Penllwyn Melyn? Or was it that cast by the Druids, the priests of the ancient Britons, when inhabiting the mountain tops in the vicinity, or by other Celtic races? Is it not possible that this light was cast and spread by those who worshipped at Blaencanaid, at the beginning of the 17th century, namely, the True Light—the Son of Man and the Son of God, who declared that He was the Light? This early place of worship spread its light far and wide beyond the Canaid valley.

Some are of opinion, since the word "cannu" means "to whiten," that the name arose, possibly, from a bleaching factory that may have been situated at some period at Melin Ganaid, where articles were whitened on the grass in the sun's rays. Another explanation is the appearance of the brook itself as it meanders downwards from its source in Pantrhiwfeurig. As it makes its way through coarse grassland, bordered by sedge, moss and rush, its crystal waters gleam in the sunshine.

To the right of the road, at the rear of Melin Ganaid, there is a stile to be crossed to enter the Blaencanaid land, and at a little distance inside is Nant yr Hen Odyn, on the right hand side. If this brook is followed for about 300 yards, a small furnace of very primitive character is reached. Wilkins, in his "History of the Iron and Steel Trades," is of the opinion that this particular furnace belonged to the earliest type used for iron smelting; further, he goes on to say that "it is one of the most interesting of those old furnaces, and may be seen nestling in a hollow under Blaencanaid." Its construction is simple to a degree, and close by is a level of the smallest kind. Now both level and furnace are almost obscured by bramble, fern, thorn-tree and ivy. In point of size, both seem to have belonged to the pigmies. The level was opened much later than the period of the furnace, by Richard Thomas, of the Lord Raglan Inn, Cefn Coed, about 1860. A short time ago, with the kind permission of the late Thomas Williams, of Blaencanaid, I cleared out the old furnace, and found it was stone-built. It was about eight feet high at the back, while the diameter in the middle was four feet six inches, diminishing towards the base to two feet. The inside wall was covered with clinker. The upper front portion had fallen in, and at the bottom there was a small aperture about 15 inches square. About 18 yards above the old furnace there is a waterfall, about eight feet high. The brook passes right through the garden at the rear of Blaencanaid Farm, and its water is utilized by the occupants for domestic purposes.

I have now reached the farthest place of note in the Canaid Valley. Here the present tenant, Mrs. Mary Williams, was born. She is of a genial character, and is never happier than when relating the historical events connected with the old farm, which has been in the possession of the family for many centuries. The farmhouse was rebuilt in 1840. There is a date—1819 J.M.—on the front of the barn wall. According to tradition, Blaencanaid was the first meeting-place of dissenters, or Nonconformists, in Wales—the date mentioned being 1620. It may have been at an earlier date. Thomas Llewelyn, of Rhigos, was the supposed founder of the Blaencanaid Society, and to him was given one of the few licences to preach and expound the Gospel to the people of Wales. The Society that met to worship at Blaencanaid was constituted a regular church in 1642. It is said that a few societies had been constituted regular churches between 1639 and 1642.

In the Blaencanaid Church, Independents, Baptists, Quakers and Unitarians worshipped together ; but trouble arose regarding the freedom of conscientious worship, and clandestine meetings had to be held, even during the night. In front of the house there is a large cone-shaped yew tree, which indicates something unusual in the old homestead. Underneath the house there is a kind of cellar, from nine to ten feet in length, seven to eight feet in width, and arched over with stone to a height of six feet. The floor is on a rock of soft shale. There were two flights of stone steps serving the entrance ; one of these is open, but the other has been walled up from the second step from the bottom. The old cellar was discovered about fifty-five years ago. It had been previously covered over, but fell in and had to be re-covered.

A visit was arranged to the farm a few years ago, and the cellar was cleared out and opened for inspection by Coun. Marsh (Vice-Chairman of the Museum Committee), Mr. Cooper (Curator of the Cyfarthfa Museum), and myself. We found everything as stated, but nothing to indicate the purpose of the place. Nobody seems to know definitely to what use it was put. There has been, and there undoubtedly will be again, much controversy as to what use this cellar was put ; but in the absence of authentic record, it is useless to make any definite statement. Some claim that mass was celebrated in it for persecuted Roman Catholics, a priest coming occasionally from Brecon for the purpose. Others claim that the Dissenters used it in secret for their devotional practices. The fact that there is an old yew tree in front of the farm does not prove that it must have been a place of worship. Yew trees were often grown around the homesteads in the olden days, to supply the bow for hunting and military purposes. The Black Archers of Llantrisant used the bow of yew very effectively at Crecy and Agincourt. But the founding of the Blaencanaid Society in 1620 is absolute fact. This was the year of the landing of the Pilgrim Fathers, who left England to seek religious liberty : and their action was only one example of what was taking place in the country. Blaencanaid became the headquarters of a "church" which comprised a district of several square miles. Here, those who sought religious liberty came from long distances on horse-back, or on foot, to worship in their own simple way far from the stern and forbidding eye of authority.

CHAPTER IV.

RHYDYCAR—WERN—CWMYGLO LEVEL AND OTHERS—PWLL ROPIN—PENCAE—PENYCOEDCAE—GELLI DDU—CWMYGLO FARM—CWMYGLO OLD CHAPEL—WAUN PENYRHEOL—LLWYN YR EOS—CWMDU COLLIERIES—CWMDU OLD PIT—CWMDU FARM—FORTY COLLIERS' LEVEL.

AS the method of exploring the hamlet is by following the brooks to their sources, we now reach the brook at Rhyd-y-car. In an old tithe map of 1850, this is named Nant Cwmyglo, but in recent ordnance maps the lower part is named Nant Rhydycar. There is reason to believe that the present course is not the original one followed from the Glamorganshire Canal to the River Taff, as the tipping of the huge Rhydycar cinder tips has altered the configuration of the ground, causing the alteration in its course. In the old plan that has come to my notice, at Cyfarthfa Museum, of the proposed canal, and dated 1790, there are shown the courses of most of the brooks before the canal was made. It shows the Rhydycar Brook running almost in a direct line to the Taff, a little way above Caedraw Bridge. Its new course is much longer ; it now meets the Taff between the Willows and the New Gasworks, nearly opposite Nantyrodyn on the other side. The Canaid also has changed its course according to the plan ; its original bed was north of the old Abercanaid Farm, since the construction of the canal its course has been diverted south of the farm. Brook and farm have long been covered over by tips.

Rhydycar has played an important part in the early coal and iron industry. There are two very old farms—Lower and Upper Rhydycar Farms. Probably there was a third farm between these and Ynysfach. The brook passes between the two farms, and on the north side are two long rows of workmen's dwellings of a very old type. It is rather difficult to state what was the original extent of these farms, because the land has been covered over by huge tips and the construction of the canal through the land. The appearance of the old homesteads, with their massive oak beams, as found in all old farmhouses, suggests that they date very far back. There is a reference to Rhydycar in the Old Parish Register (according to the "Notes" of Major F. T. James) as far back as 1715. Rowland Thomas (Idris Ddu) says in his manuscripts that a lease of Rhydycar was granted to a certain John Williams, Glamorgan, for a term of 21 years, by the Earl of Talbot and Hensol and a Richards of Cardiff, in the year 1744. William Richards, of Glyndyrus, held the land of Rhydycar for three years, but afterwards relinquished it. The said John Williams then granted a sub-lease to Llewelyn John and Morgan Jenkins for the remaining 18 years of the original lease. Idris Ddu said that a copy of this lease was in his possession. In 1763 Rhydycar came into the possession of Anthony Bacon, the iron-master, for the purpose of making a thorough investigation of the mineral wealth underlying the land. In 1765 Anthony Bacon and one Browning obtained from Earl Talbot and the said Richards a 99 year mineral lease at a rental of £100 per annum, of all the coal, ironstone, etc. This lease gave them the right of working all the minerals over a very wide area, from Nant Canaid to Nant Ffrwd, between the River Taff and the western boundary of the parish. Liberty was also granted them to build works where it was suitable. Most of the farms had surface leases, so before Bacon could destroy the surface of the land, he had of necessity to buy up the farm leases, which he did in due course. Some of the first leases taken over by him were those of Rhydycar, Bryntegail Fawr (which was between Upper Rhydycar and Ynysfach), Llwyncelyn, and Abernant y Gwenith. With these I shall deal in due course. Other farms came into his possession as the land was required for works purposes. This proved the death-knell of the farming community in the hamlet. The sturdy stock of yeomen farmers were supplanted by miners and iron-workers. What a glorious stretch of rustic beauty there must have been then from Ffrwd to Canaid : smiling cornfields, sparkling brooks, and patches of woodland reaching down the gentle slopes to the Taff. Now the ugly scars of industry, in the form of pit mounds and cinder tips, ruined buildings and subsidences, deform the whole countryside.

In the same year (1765) Bacon bought up the Plymouth mineral lease from Guest and Wilkinson at a rent of £100 per annum.

The question often asked is, How did the name Rhydycar come into existence ? "Rhyd" means a ford—a place to cross a brook or river, without the aid of a bridge (as Rhydychen—Oxford). "Car" means a vehicle. Therefore the name implies a place for a vehicle to cross a stream or river. It may be that the brook was at one time called Nant Car, and the crossing would therefore be Rhydycar. In Cwmtaf Fawr and Cwmtaf Fechan there are brooks called Nant Car.

Let us seek an explanation from another angle, and betake ourselves to the time prior to the making of the canal and the extensive tipping operations. The old Parish Road passed both the old Rhydycar farms, and by so doing crossed the brook near the site of the present rows of workmen's dwellings. This road crossed the canal a little above Upper Rhydycar, coming directly from the River Taff, joining a road that came from the direction of Llwyncelyn, and met the Rhydycar road somewhere between the canal and the river, both using the ford as a crossing place. The roads mentioned are shown in part on different plans and maps. The distance from Rhydycar Farm to the Parish Church is only about 320 yards, and from the crossing of the canal about 250 yards. I am, therefore, of opinion that where these roads crossed the river together was the ford that gave rise to the name Rhydycar. This ford must have been a little way above the site of the present Caedraw Bridge. It is quite possible that a road existed direct from lower Rhydycar to meet the others before crossing the river. People should not be misled into thinking that the present Parish Road is identical with the old road. This is far from being the case, especially with regard to the part nearest the town.

At the lower end of Upper Rhydycar there was an old mine level known as Hen Lefal Capel, and the field that was in its vicinity was known as Cae'r Capel. Now it would be interesting to know how these names came about. I have asked many, but so far have failed to get an explanation. One person suggested that it might have arisen from the old chapel at Cwmyglo, because the level was worked in that direction ; but I am inclined to think that it arose through the proximity of the level to Capel y Plwyf (the Parish Church). As the level's course was straight for a considerable distance, a person looking out from the inside could see the Parish Church without difficulty, as it was only about 330 yards away, there being no tip to obscure the view in those days. The old level was later used as a water-course, and also as an entrance into the old workings for many years.

Higher up on the left of the brook is the old Rhydycar pumping shaft, now dismantled, the water being allowed to form an outlet which forms part of the brook below. The engine was a double-acting Cornish engine, and one of the finest in South Wales. The pit was about 75 yards in depth. The diameter of the plungers was 19 inches ; length of stroke 3ft. 6ins., and it was able to make ten to twelve strokes per minute in case of need. At Glyndyrus, the length of the rods and the weight of the column of water was so great, that a great deal of care was exercised not to overwork the engine. Not far from here is the old Rhydycar Mine Pit, in which both coal and mine were worked. The lowest coal seam—the Gellideg—was worked here. There was a connection between this pit and Colliers' Row Pit (afterwards the Fan Pit, on the Gellideg seam). On the right of the brook are the huge shale tips of the Ynysfach Mine Drift, the entrance to which can be seen, as well as its old engine-house, towering high as a memorial to the old drift. It was driven in a southerly direction, connecting with the two Rhydycar Pits, Colliers' Row Fan Pit, and also Cwm Pit. Near its entrance is the site of the old Ynysfach Coke Ovens, to which I shall refer when dealing with Ynysfach Works, Llwyncelyn, and the Llyn.

Following the Ynysfach line southwards to a point near the Wern Road, we reach the site of the old coal-separating machine. In this neighbourhood the brook has been arched over for a long distance, only to reappear again at the rear of the old Wern Farm. A few scattered houses have been passed, but now we reach one of the oldest landmarks in the hamlet of Gellideg. The Wern is mentioned in the Parish Register in 1714. The old road which passed the Wern joined the road at Rhydycar and crossed the Taff at the ford. The present occupier of the newest part of the old homestead is Mr. John Jones. He has acted as bailiff of the Cyfarthfa land for many years, having been appointed to succeed his father in that capacity. The first occupiers of the farm of whom I have an account were Morgan William Williams and Mary his wife. They had five sons—William (Billy Pencae), who later lived at Pencae, just above the Wern, and afterwards kept the Travellers' Rest at Heolgerrig; David (Dafydd o'r Wern), who lived at Cwmdu Cottage, near Pleasant View, and died at Barry; Gomer (Gomer o'r Wern) lived and died at the Wern; Richard (Richard o'r Wern) worked first as an archer at Cwm Pit, and afterwards opened "patches" on the Aberdare Mountain; Lewis (Lewis o'r Wern) spent the greater part of his life at Coedcae, in the Rhondda, but died at Nelson.

The big field which is situated between Wern Farm and Llwyncelyn belonged to the Wern, and has been known as Wern Field. What is now known as Upper Wern was undoubtedly a part of the old Wern Farm, the fields of which joined those of Cwmyglo Farm. Here lived for many years the late Mr. John Williams, a former manager of Cwm Pit; he was popularly known as John Williams, Pwll Cwm. The large oak beams in these old farms are remarkable for their size, and are a subject of wonder. Not long ago I paid a visit to the old Wern, and was taken around the oldest part. I measured a beam over the fire-place which was 18 inches square and about nine feet in length. There was another one as well, which was 16 inches square. How long they had been there was a matter of speculation, but it was evident they were then in the last stage of decay. In this district there is a plentiful amount of alder trees, from which the farm derived its name, "gwernen" being an alder tree.

Coming from the farm, and crossing the B. & M. line to the Gethin line, we see on the left of the brook the drift which was opened by Mr. Henry Lewis, of Cae Mari Dwn, and taken over by Mr. Gomer Thomas and Co. when the Cyfarthfa lease expired in March, 1924. Here the 7ft. and lower 2ft. 9ins. coal seams, as well as a large layer of fire-clay, were worked. Crossing the Cwm Pit railway, we reach the site of the old Cyfarthfa canal. Following the bank between the Cwm and the canal, we can see a fine avenue of alders which stretch their branches across the canal. Then we come to the pillars of the ruined bridge, underneath which was the canal, and over which went the road. At a point a little to the left, we lose the track of the brook, as it disappears into a buried archway. A large quantity of coal was handled at this place when the canal was in use. Upper Wern is a little to our right, and a short distance further on are the Incline, Y Llyn, and Llwyncelyn.

We have now reached Cwmyglo, with huge mounds on either side of the brook. The first level we come across, on the left, is Lefal Will Shon Dafydd, worked on the 9ft. seam; then we cross the old road or path from Llwyncelyn to Blaencanaid. The late Thomas Williams, of Blaencanaid, told me that in the old days it was called "Heol Ceffyl a Phwn"—no doubt owing to the fact that only a horse laden with commodities could negotiate it, carts being out of the question. Further away, on the left, is Lefal Pen Machine, where a great amount of the yard and 4 feet coal seams were worked. After passing the tramroad, which crossed the dingle, we reach the ruins of Robling's Pit on the right, in which coal and mine were worked. It was sunk to a depth of about 100 yards, and in it were worked to the Aberdare boundary, the Bute, lower 2ft. 9ins., 7ft., and the Gellideg seams. The huge mounds (now commonly called "Tips John Williams") of this old shaft indicate that the workings must have been very extensive. The pit has been disused for many years, but it was about 1923 that the pit head-gear was dismantled and a wall built around the top of the shaft. All the old pits have been dealt with thus to ensure safety.

Down in the dingle near here was Hen Lefal Cwmyglo, one of the earliest of the Cyfarthfa coal levels. It was an extensive undertaking, employing about 25 horses, and the 9ft. seam was worked to the Aberdare boundary. At one time the coal was taken down to the canal, and near the bridge it was transferred to the small boats, which in turn conveyed it to the works. A little higher, on the left, is another old coal and mine level. The mine layers were what were known as the lower soap veins, lying between the 9ft. and 6ft. seams, but the latter was the seam mostly worked here. A considerable amount of "patch" work has been carried on in this neighbourhood.

Above this place is Penycoedcae, built previous to 1830, and known as well by the name Y Pedwar Tŷ. Next we reach a very old residence called Gelli-Ddu, built by Morgan Shon Dafydd. The dwelling was rebuilt a few years ago. Gelli-Ddu is situated at the junction of two brooks—Nant Llwynyreos and Nant Cwmyglo and Cwm Du. Now Cwmyglo means "The Coal Dingle." I don't think you could find a dingle in which there are more seams outcropping than this one. But the name Cwmyglo was used at a very early date indeed. Wilkins mentions Cwmyglo Farm as being a very flourishing one in 1600 and bearing that name. The society of religious dissenters came there from Blaencanaid about 1670. Cwmyglo Chapel, hidden in the dingle, within easy reach of the farm, was built in 1690. There is a record of Edward Harri, of Gyrnos, being born at Cwmyglo Farm in 1694; and Cwmyglo is mentioned in 1714 in the Parish Register. All these dates were many years previous to the time when coal began to be worked for industrial purposes, therefore we can gather that the old yeomen farmers must have used it on a small scale, and bestowed the name Cwmyglo upon the scene of their source of supply.

Next we reach the site of Cwmyglo Farm, now in desolate ruin, but a very historic local landmark. Its age is uncertain, but we have seen that it dates very far back. Originally it was one farm, but after the departure of Edward Harri to Gyrnos, there were two farms—Cwmyglo Uchaf and Cwmyglo Isaf. About 1670, the Nonconformists who had worshipped at Blaencanaid from the early days of the 17th century, had reason to remove their church, which had been constituted as such in 1642, to Cwmyglo Farm. This homestead was very commodious, more convenient, and the farmer a staunch member of the Blaencanaid church. Edward Harri was born at the farm four years after the building of the meeting-house or chapel, and tradition says that his father or grandfather had been minister at Blaencanaid. During the stay at Cwmyglo Farm, the membership of the church had greatly increased. It was doubtless much easier to reach Cwmyglo than Blaencanaid. Shon Dafydd, father of the builder of Gelli Ddu, is known to have lived at Cwmyglo in 1770.

Cwmyglo Brook runs through a very large meadow anciently known as Waun Penyrheol. If we follow it, we reach Cwm Du Colliery, now disused, and the old Cwm-Du Pit, which was one of the first pits sunk (about 1840) in Cyfarthfa. I have evidence that Rowland Thomas was a contractor at this pit in 1849. Coal only was worked there. Next we reach Cwm-Du Farm, from which Walter John and his wife Rachel were buried in the years 1771 and 1778 respectively. They lie in the Parish Churchyard. For many years this farm was used as a shepherd's cottage under the Cyfarthfa Company. Henry Davies was shepherd there for 35 years. Now we get into one of the mine patches, known as Patch Richard Thomas, and have reached the source of the Cwmyglo Brook near Pleasant View. To our right are Cwm Du Cottage, Tai Herbert Lloyd, Beili Glas and Cornel y Waun. Near the old tramroad, close to the brook, there was a level with a queer name. It was called the Forty Colliers Level.

Let us now return to Gelli-Ddu and follow the Llwynyreos Brook. We pass through some patches or small quarries before reaching the ruins of the historic chapel of Cwmyglo, built in 1690. It stands at the junction of another brook with the main one, in a well-sheltered hollow. One would have to approach very near to this hollow before realising that there was a building there at all, as the place is well-wooded. From what I can gather, the building—which of recent years has been considerably damaged—was of two parts. In the smaller portion can be seen, on one side, holes in the wall for the reception of the cross-beams. There could be seen, many years ago, the dividing wall and a space through which entrance was afforded from one part to the other. The walls have been reduced to such a state that a description of the building is well-nigh impossible, but I remember seeing a flight of narrow stone steps at the rear, and what I should take to be an entrance in front, facing Gelli-Ddu. Clarke, in his "History of Merthyr," describes the chapel as being built of loose stones, on the principle which is known as dry-walling. If he had made a close examination, he would not have written that, as the walls were built of stone and mortar. The mortar used (samples of which are in my possession) was of a special quality and difficult to remove from the stones. Direct evidence of such old places is lacking. Shon Llewelyn, of Cefn Coed—who was born in 1691 and died in 1776—wrote his autobiography in verse. In this we glean that he was received into membership at Cwmyglo at the age of 21 by the Rev. Roger Williams, but that prior to his being finally accepted he was placed on probation for six months. The Rev. James Davies was also joint minister with Roger Williams at this time. The sixty-year lease having terminated, the church was removed to a more convenient meeting-place; this was Ynysgau, beside the Taff, and the year in which it took place was 1749.

Near the old place of worship the 6ft. coal seam crops to the surface, while just above the surface is covered with a tremendous thickness of glacial drift, in which are embedded a variety of rocks, limestone, red sandstone, ironstone, conglomerates, grit, mixed with boulder clay. I shall deal with the Cardiff Corporation puddle field when following the course of the next brook.

About 400 yards to the left of the chapel ruins is a quarry from which were obtained the stones required to build Cyfarthfa Castle in 1825, the rock being known as the Cockshutt rock, which we previously found outcropping at Carn y Frwydr. Llwynyreos, almost completely hidden in the dingle, is next reached, the name signifying that the spot was once the haunt of the nightingale. The only colliery that remains working in this locality is now reached. It is Cwmyglo Drift, worked by Mr. Gomer Thomas and Co. The source of the brook is just beyond the mountain fence, with Cwm-Du between the two brooks. The surface here is broken and uninteresting.

CHAPTER V.

THE IRON BRIDGE—PARLIAMENT LOCK—BLONDIN—PENRY STREET—SURGERY—CWMPANT BROOK—YNYSFACH WORKS—THE ABERDARE ROAD—CWMPANT—PWLL PHIL REES—LLWYNCELYN—LIME KILNS—CYFARTHFA CHURCH—RAILWAY CROSSINGS—TAI MARK GRAI—NANT-YGWENITH BROOK.

THE old Iron Bridge was built in the year 1800. It was cast at Cyfarthfa Works according to the plans of that eminent mechanical genius, Watkin George, and constructed under his supervision. Nothing in the way of painting or tarring the ironwork has been done since its construction. There is no record of an earlier bridge at this point, but there probably was a ford. The old bridge is still used by pedestrians, but it has been closed to vehicular traffic since the building of the new iron bridge in 1879, which is a great improvement on the old one. About a hundred yards below there are two weirs, one of which turns a great quantity of river water into the Plymouth Feeder, while the the other, just below, has on top of it a line of large iron pipes three feet in diameter, leading from near the canal lock, right over the river, into the feeder on the other side.

Why was Parliament Lock so called ? I have been told that litigation took place regarding the use of river water for canal purposes, because in dry weather the Plymouth Feeder supply would be greatly reduced. Consequently a line of iron pipes was laid to carry the surplus water from the lock into the feeder, rather than allow it to pass down the canal. As the issue was decided in Parliament, the lock came to be known as Parliament Lock. There was a road, near this lock, which crossed the river over a bridge into Bridge Street. In the old plan of 1790 showing the proposed canal, river and road are shown. I have reason to believe that some kind of bridge originally existed at this place, about 275 yards below the Morlais Brook.

Bridge Street and High Street were the two main streets of Merthyr then, and joined at the gate-house (now the Court Arms). The old road from the river crossing curved around the eastern corner of Canal Square into Penry Street, passing Merthyr Tavern, which was built early in the last century. It is now occupied by William Jones, the herbalist. Formerly it was kept by a Mr. and Mrs. Morgans, afterwards of the Ship Brewery, Georgetown. Mrs. Morgans was a sister of John Williams, Felin Frâg.

In the above-mentioned plan a branch of the canal is shewn proceeding from a little distance above Parliament Lock, along the southern side of Morlais Brook, all the way to Dowlais Works. If we refer to the data of altitudes and distances of the proposed canal, we find the fall from Dowlais Works to Merthyr Bridge to be 411 feet. At that date (1790) there was no bridge above the weir, but there may have been a ford just above the site of the Iron Bridge. I do not think that a tramroad was made, because before 1791 there was not a single yard of iron rail in South Wales, although by 1811 there were 150 miles of tram rails. By 1814 Dowlais alone had 30 miles of underground tramroads. The projected branch canal to Dowlais never materialised. After a few years, the Dowlais and Penydarren Works seemed to have prospered greatly, and in 1793 Jackson's Bridge was built over the Taff, and a tramline laid by the Canal Company for their convenience. Later, when Messrs. Guest, Hill and Homphray wanted to promote a better system of transport—viz. the Taff Vale Railway—the Canal Company strongly protested, stating that they had done everything possible for the convenience of the works. They had built a bridge; made a tramway from the canal, and paid the excavator £1,100 for that work. Therefore I think this tramline was outside the original contract for the canal, and made later.

Reverting to the river, it would be interesting to know that about 60 years ago, Blondin, the famous equilibrist, paid a visit to the town, and, amidst tremendous excitement, walked over the river on his high tight rope, a little way below the present Iron Bridge, the rope being fixed from the roof of the "Duke Bach" in Bridge Street to a point on the far side of the river. Proceeding westward from the Iron Bridge along Penry Street, we see on the right what were once two very old shepherds' houses, whose foundations are much lower than the present roadway, with the brook which enters the river, near the bridge, at their rear. These belonged to the Wern Farm, which formerly extended to the Cwmpant Brook. Next we reach the Holly Bush Inn, and then, close by, the Corner House, which was a very noted public house during its occupation by William Jones and his wife Hannah. Their son, nicknamed "Will Corner House," displayed great skill as a harpist, and often played the accompaniment to many a stepper, gigger, dancer and singer. The old platform upon which Will played is still in its place. The Corner House was an important house of call for the boatmen, who slept at night in their cabins on the canal; and it naturally became a sort of headquarters for the canal folk—a place for amusement, gossip and brawling. The old road passed near the end of this house, over the arched brook, and followed the right side of the Cwmpant Brook. On the other side of Penry Street is the block of buildings, almost the whole of which is owned by Mr. Jack Collins, fruiterer, and a well-known local sportsman.

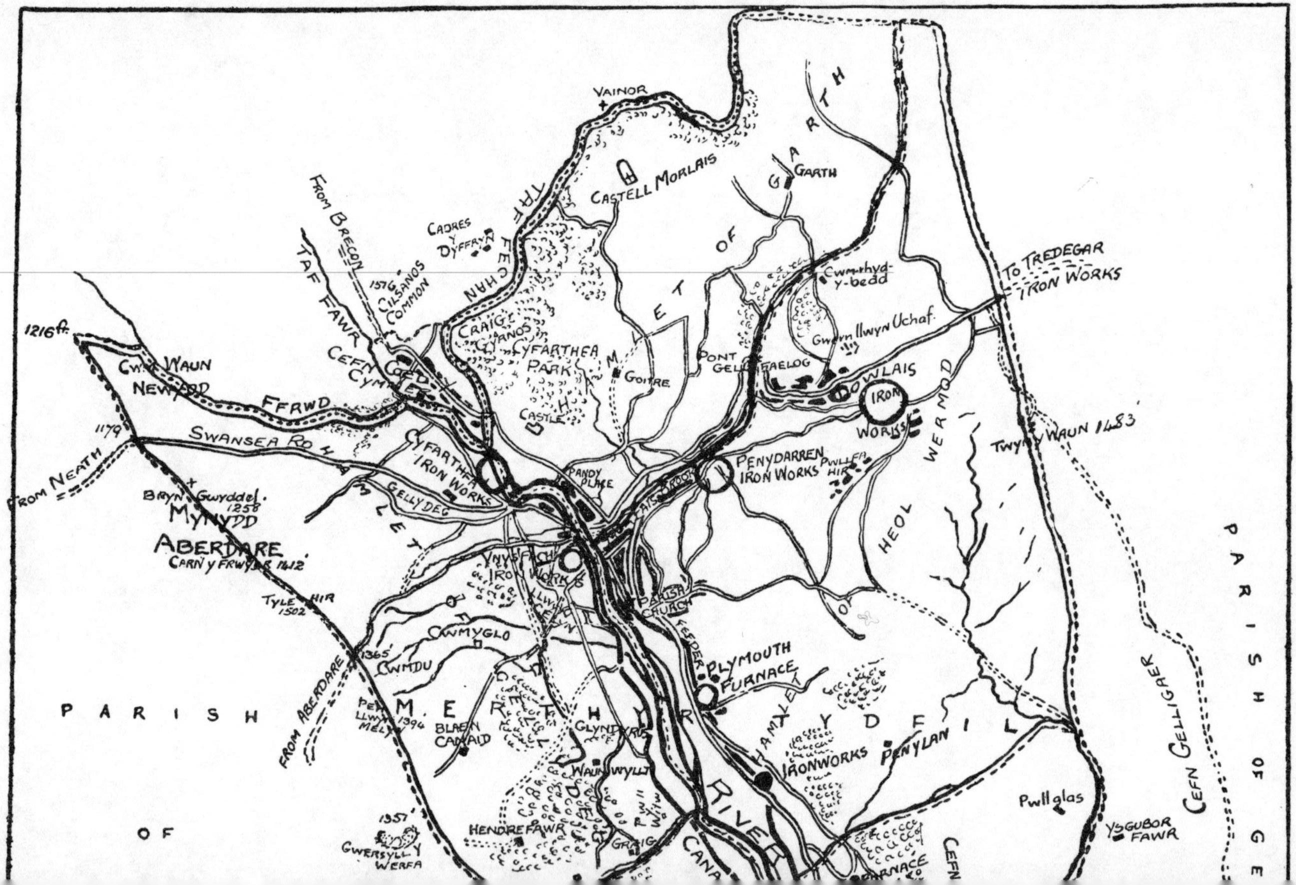

PARISH OF GE
CEFN GELLIGAER
YSGUBOR FAWR
Pwllglas
TO TREDEGAR IRON WORKS
TWYN WAUN 1483
VAINOR
CASTELL MORLAIS
GARTH
HAMLET OF GARTH
Cwm-rhyd-y-bedd
Gwern llwyn Uchaf
DOWLAIS IRON WORKS
HAMLET OF HEOL WERMOD
PENYDARREN IRON WORKS
PWLLFA HIR
PONT GELLI FAELOG
Goitre
CYFARTHFA PARK
CASTLE
TAF FECHAN
CADRES Y DYFFRYN
CILSANOS COMMON 1576
CRAIG CYFARTHFA
CEFN COED Y CYMMER
FROM BRECON
TAF FAWR
FFRWD
CWM WAUN NEWYDD
1216 ft.
1179
FROM NEATH
SWANSEA RD
CYFARTHFA IRON WORKS
GELLYDEG
HAMLET OF
PANDY PLACE
BRYN Gwyddel 1258
MYNYDD ABERDARE
CARN Y FRWYDD 1612
TYLE HIR 1502
YNYSFACH IRON WORKS
PARISH CHURCH
FEEDER
PLYMOUTH FURNACE
HAMLET
IRONWORKS
PENYLAN
MERTHYR TYDFIL
CWMYGLO
1365
CWMDU
FROM ABERDARE
PARISH
OF
PEN LLWYN MELYN 1394
BLAEN CANAID
GLYNDYRUS
WAUN WYLLT
HENDREFAWR
GRAIG
1357
GWERSYLLY WERFA
RIVER
CANAL
CEFN
FURNACE

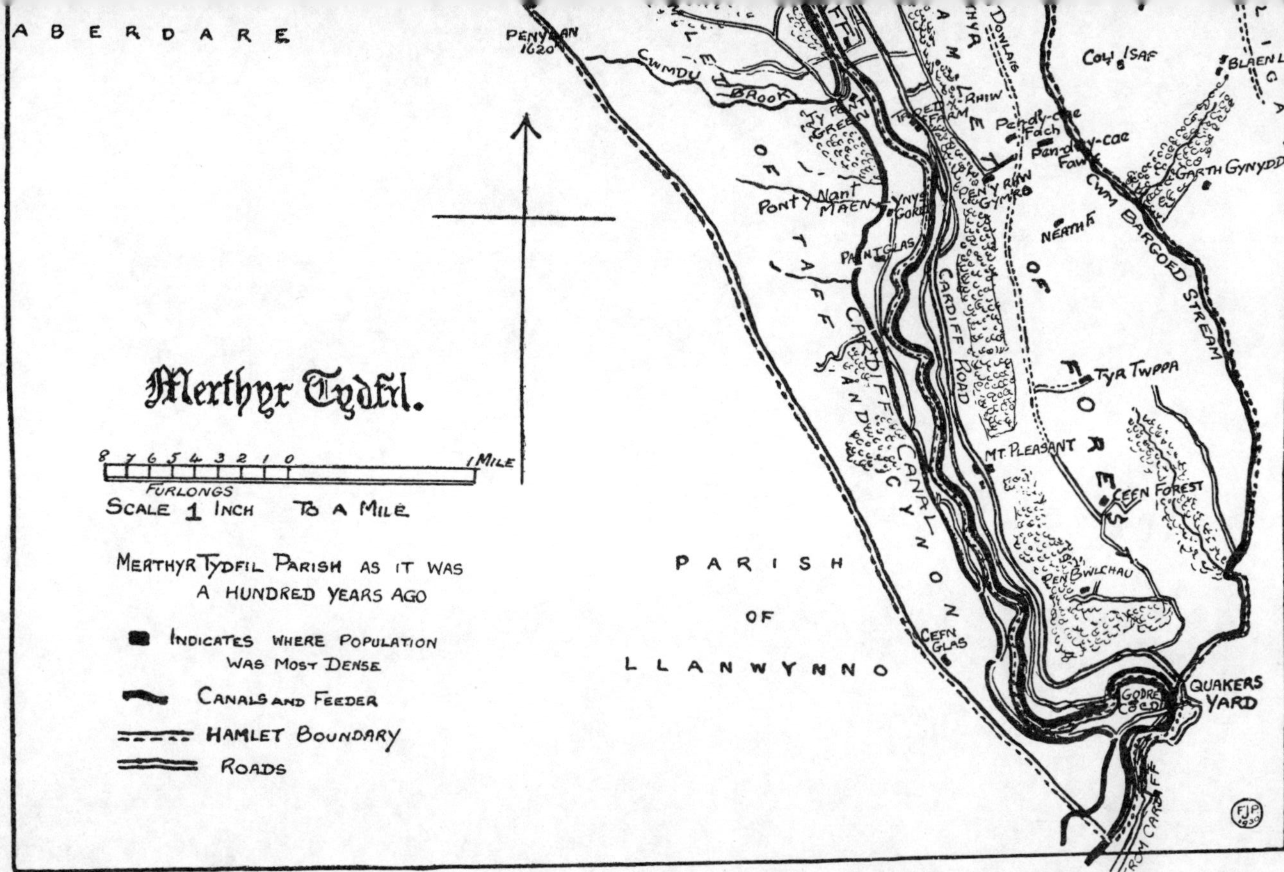
Merthyr Tydfil.
8 7 6 5 4 3 2 1 0 1 Mile
Furlongs
Scale 1 Inch To a Mile
Merthyr Tydfil Parish as it was a hundred years ago
Indicates where population was most dense
Canals and Feeder
Hamlet Boundary
Roads
ABERDARE
Penyfan 1620
Cwmdu Brook
Ty Pont Green
Pont y Nant Maen
Ynys Gored
Pantglas
Cardiff Canal
Cardiff Road
Taff and Cynon
Parish of Llanwynno
Cefn Glas
Mt. Pleasant
Pen Bwlchau
Cefn Forest
Tyr Twppa
Neath F.
Pen y Rhiw Gymro
Pendry-cae Fach
Pendry-cae Fawr
Rhiw
Dowlais
Cwm Bargoed Stream
Coly Isaf
Blaen Llwynau
Garth Gynydd
Godre Coed
Quakers Yard
From Cardiff
FJP 1930

Penry Street was named after the eminent painter, Penry Williams, one of our greatest Welsh painters. He was born, in 1802, in the house now owned and occupied by Mr. Collins, and in one of the rooms of which can still be seen the picture racks which held some of the painter's compositions. William Williams, the artist's father, was a house painter. There is an admirable portrait of him, executed by his brilliant son, at the Cyfarthfa Art Gallery, as well as numerous oil paintings, water colours, and pencil sketches. Most of his pictures depict Italian peasant life and Italian landscape, and reveal wonderful technique and admirable judgment in the use of colour. The artist spent a great deal of his lifetime in London and Rome, in the great galleries of which his work was hung side by side with that of the most eminent painters of his day. Penry Williams died in Rome. According to an old deed which came under my notice, the house where he was born was sold by his sister, Sophia Williams, spinster, and one John Davies, to Daniel Jenkins, of Abercanaid, May 17, 1850, for £60.

At the rear of Penry Williams' house, in Canal Square, lived John Williams. He came from Pentyrch early in the last century, and built the house in which he afterwards lived ; then he built a malt mill, and close by sank a well. The latter was 120 feet deep, lined with stone walling four feet in diameter, the water being used for domestic and mill purposes. This John Williams went to America, leaving the entire business to his son John, who had come with him from Pentyrch at the age of seven. A daughter of the latter informed me that her father kept the malt mill going as well as working as a blacksmith at the smithy near the Corner House for 56 years. He died about 1900 at the age of 86. He was known as " John Williams, Felin Frâg," as it was he who prepared the malt for all the local brewers, including the Evans of Six Bells. His daughter, Mrs Thomas (widow of the late Tom Thomas, miners' agent) informed me that her father was a cousin of Taliesin ap Iolo (son of Iolo Morgannwg), and also of Morgan William Williams, of the Wern She also remembered her father supplying people with water from his well at a charge of a halfpenny per week. This was before the building of the Pentwyn Waterworks in 1858, which ensured a constant and abundant supply of pure water to the town. Below the weir, and on the right bank of the river, there was another spring and spout of pure water. An old inhabitant, Mr. Len Graham (now 78 years of age), remembers people coming in dry weather as early as four o'clock in the morning to wait their turn to fill their utensils at this spring. There are other wells on the canal bank which I will deal with later on.

Next to the block of houses in Canal Square is the old coalyard of Robert and Lucy Thomas, of Waun Wyllt, and afterwards used by Mr. Ben Lewis, but now serves as a stores. Below Canal Square there were two timber-yards—one kept by a Mrs. Cole and the other by Benjamin Evans—both eventually being taken over by the father of the late John Jenkins. There was also a blacksmith's shop, where we lingered many a time to see nails being made.

After crossing the site of the lock bridge, there was to be seen on the right of the road, the overflow from the canal, where many a patient animal quenched its thirst, and had the mud of the day's toil washed away from its weary legs. On a fine summer's day, when the sun would be in the south-west, a rainbow-like effect could be observed in the thin sheet of overflowing water, if gazed at from the road. On the left-hand side of the road, there is a row of substantial houses, known as Fairfield Terrace, in the centre of which is the Miners' Arms public-house ; then there is the Cyfarthfa Surgery, formerly known as Ynysfach House. Here a fairly long list of doctors and surgeons have rendered excellent service to the workmen of Cyfarthfa and their families in the past. In this list we find the names of Drs. David Davies and his son, Edward Davies, Wills, Crocket, Webster (sen.), Rees, Burke, James, Flood, and Webster (jun.). From the Surgery the Cwmpant Brook runs on the left of Aberdare Road, underneath a row of houses.

Returning to Ynysfach Square, two rows of workmen's buildings of an early type are to be seen, known as Tai Ynysfach ; and if we pass between them, we enter Ynysfach Works, where I have reason to believe there was built a forge at a very early date. Wilkins, when comparing the rateable value of property at different periods, states : " The date selected is 1769, when the ironworks had not begun to make any perceptible influence. There was a small forge at Dowlais, another at Ynysfach, and the furnace at Cyfarthfa—these, with the one at Plymouth, being the only fore-runners in the valley." Three dates were taken for comparison : 1769, 1866, and 1905 ; and the following are two examples from the list :—

RATEABLE VALUE.

	1769			1866			1905	
	£	s.		£	s.		£	s.
Blaencanaid	8	15	...	81	10	...	45	0
Penylan	5	0	...	59	0	...	59	0

In 1801 two furnaces were built at Ynysfach, for Richard Crawshay, from plans prepared by the brilliant engineer Watkin George, by a Merthyr man—one Thomas Jones. On the north corner of the front of the cast-house are the initials of the builder, T.J. ; and on the front of each furnace is a plate bearing the date of building. The iron plate has corroded so much that the date is not now discernible, but on the key-stone of the arch in front of the cast-house, the date 1801, followed by the initials C and G, can be seen. I have often wondered what the initials meant. Watkin George had served his master well, and it is said that Richard Crawshay had offered him a share in the works, which offer he accepted. Can the letters signify Crawshay and George, or Crawshay, Gyfarthfa? The two furnaces are built in one block, with one cast-house for both. Watkin George was a captain over the first volunteers in Merthyr, and often, during inclement weather, drilled his men in this cast-house. It is said that one of the furnaces had not been out of blast for a period of 35 years.

In 1836 two more furnaces were built by Thomas Jones at Ynysfach, in addition to those he erected in 1801. They were of a more substantial nature than the first ones, being separate, whereas the others were in one block. Although their use has been discontinued for very many years, they can still be seen. During their period of activity, these furnaces were recognised as the best in the valley, and capable of a large output of iron. Until recently, the date stamp—W.C. 1836—could be seen on stones and iron plates in front of the furnaces. The Ynysfach Works were connected with the upper works by means of a tramroad, known as the Red Mine Tramroad, because the red foreign ore, brought up on the canal barges to Pontstorehouse, was afterwards taken from this point to Ynysfach Works. What does the name Ynysfach mean? "Ynys" may mean an island, or a flat meadow beside the bank of a river. There was a possibility of an island being formed as a result of flooding south of the Cwmpant Brook, hence the name, which signifies a little island. At one time, there was to be seen a great rock in this locality, the base of which lay nearly in line with the present John Street, and which continued in a southerly direction through the site of Ynysfach Works. Now may I suggest that occasionally the Cwmpant Brook overflowed its southern bank near the lower end of what is now John Street before the tip came into existence? No houses had then been built at this spot. On both sides of the brook there is a great depth of river gravel and shingle, which seems to suggest that the Taff River bed was much wider than it is at present at this part of its course.

Between Ynysfach Works and Aberdare Road, and behind Tai Ynysfach, there are two old houses, at the rear of which there was an old level known as Lefal Fwyn (Mine) Ynysfach. Here were worked the lowest workable mine veins—the "Rosser" and "Garw" groups, with a seam of coal underneath from 18 to 20 inches thick. As a rule, the miner would work the coal for a certain distance first, then the veins could be worked more easily. This level was one of the nearest to the river in this locality, and was connected with Pwll Phil Rees up above. On the right of the tramroad near Aberdare Road is the old Ynysfach Coal Yard, and I have been told that the corner house at the roadside was once occupied by the late David Morgan (Dai o'r Nant), the miners' agent. The whole of the row of houses here has been built over the Cwmpant Brook. The Colliers' Arms is on the left hand side, while on the opposite side of the brook is an old-type row of workmen's dwellings. In the bottom house lived Howel Watkins, the weigher (father of John Watkins, Aberdare Road); John was born here 72 years ago. Howel had control of the coke pits and ovens, as well as the tipping of ash between the Yard and Cwmpant Brook. Later he was appointed weigher, hence the name "Hywel Pwyswr."

Following Aberdare Road, we pass the southern end of John Street, and from here the road becomes very steep; then White Row is passed before reaching the top of the steep little hill in Bethel Street known as "Y Trip Bach." Here there used to be an old public-house named Mount Pleasant, kept by a certain Jenkin Jenkins, whose nickname, "Shinkin Coker," at once suggests his being employed at the coke ovens. Next we reach the corner house, at the top of the big hill (better known as "Y Trip Mawr"), which I think was built by the Cyfarthfa Company, and at one time occupied by Mr. Hansard, the furnace manager; now it is occupied by Mr. Richard Maliphant. A very important landmark has now been reached—"Pen y Trip Mawr." On this point five roads converge: the Heolgerrig Road (formerly Penyrheolgerrig); the Cwmpant Road from Llwyncelyn; Aberdare Road from the town; George Street from Georgetown; and Nantygwenith Lane. The latter was the main road connecting Nantygwenith and Llwyncelyn, and also Nantygwenith with the town. When Richard Crawshay died at Cyfarthfa House, June 27, 1810, aged 71, the funeral procession proceeded from his residence through Nantygwenith Lane, passing the site of Cyfarthfa Church, where there was then a field. It then turned down Aberdare Road, crossed the original Iron Bridge, and turned down Bridge Street; then through the lower part of the town it continued on its way to Llandaff Cathedral.

If we follow the Cwmpant Road southwards, at the corner on our right there used to be the Cwmpant Field, which attracted many of the old-time circuses that visited the town. A little further on is Nant Cwmpant Bridge, from which the brook has been arched over with brick and stone as far as the B. & M. Railway near Upper Colliers' Row. This was done about the time when Cyfarthfa became a steel-works, as additional tipping space was required. Now the whole field on both sides of the brook has been covered by huge towering heaps of slag aud cinder from the works. Boys thought it a great feat to pass through the above-mentioned tunnel, as inside it was totally dark and there were many small pools to negotiate. Years ago, large ash trees grew beside the brook, above the bridge. At the top of the field, on the left of the brook, was a large sand quarry which furnished the works with sand. It is strange how this came to be deposited here, unless we can ascribe its presence as being a relic of the glacial period, which would also account for the large boulders seen below the bridge. Below Cwmpant Road is a large shale mound, now covered with fields and gardens, which is the result of tipping operations from an old mine-pit near by, known as Pwll Phil Rees. This pit was very shallow, being only about 19 yards deep, and worked on the balance principle, the veins and seam worked being the Rosser and Garw group. Passing near the bottom of the pit was a large water-course which drained a large number of levels and pits. This water-course ran underneath the old coke ovens at Ynysfach and entered the canal a little below Parliament Lock, but is now carried across by means of a concrete culvert. I was told by Mr. Jason Rees that the outer end of this culvert was made by his grandfather and that of Mr. Richard Maliphant. At the western corner of Ynysfach Yard was an old level known as Lefal Yard. Here the Gellideg or lower 4ft. coal seam was worked. This is the lowest workable seam in the coal-field, although there are two small seams—the Garw, and one at Galon Uchaf—which have been worked on a small scale.

Now we reach the cross-roads at Llwyncelyn Square. On our right is the southern end of the huge cinder tip, between which and the field there is an old road, which curved around and crossed the Heolgerrig Road near the Gethin railway crossing. When the Brecon and Merthyr Railway was constructed, the Devil's Bridge was made for the convenience of those using the old road, and especially those living at Upper Colliers' Row. The old road was subsequently closed beyond the bridge. Following the Llwyncelyn Road from the Square, we reach the old residence of Llwyncelyn, which was anciently the abode of a family of princely lineage. I have reason to believe that Wern Farm was part and parcel of Llwyncelyn, which was the patronal residence of the estate. In his "Notes on the Parish Register," Major F. T. James mentions that a Treharne lived there at a very early date. There is authentic evidence that in 1758, "John, son of David Rees of Llwyncelyn, was born on the 20th day of January, and baptised on the 4th day of February, by the Rev. Samuel Davies, dissenting minister." This reverend gentleman was the minister at Ynysgau, and, after the resignation of his father, the

Rev. James Davies, who later lived in retirement at Gwernllwyn, Dowlais, he was buried in the old Parish Churchyard, May 3, 1760. He was the minister of the church at Cwmyglo when the decision was made to remove the cause to Ynysgau in 1749.

Joseph Bailey—a nephew of Richard Crawshay, and to whom the latter left in his will a quarter share in the works—lived at Llwyncelyn when manager of Cyfarthfa under his uncle. Henry Kirkhouse came to Cyfarthfa about 1800 as manager of mines and collieries, and in due course lived at Llwyncelyn, and later was promoted to a more important position under Richd. Crawshay. He was the son of Bedlington Kirkhouse, of Neath Valley, whose family produced some eminent engineers. George Kirkhouse, brother to Henry, was chief engineer at Dowlais Works. Henry married the daughter of Thomas Llewelyn, who was responsible for building the first form of rolls at Cyfarthfa Works. Richard Crawshay, recognising his ability, entrusted to him the development of all the collieries and iron-mines, and made him his adviser on all important matters. For over 50 years he was chief engineer to the Crawshays, and under his supervision most of the pits at Cyfarthfa were sunk. Henry Kirkhouse left four sons—Bedlington, Thomas, Herbert, and Howel. Bedlington succeeded his father as engineer at Cyfarthfa, and died at Llwyncelyn, where he had been born 78 years previously. Thomas became manager of the collieries, and lived at Penycoedcae, Heolgerrig. The following is a story about Bed. and Tom when they were living at Llwyncelyn. One evening, the former made a scare-crow which he placed up in an apple tree. He then ran into the house, declaring that he had seen a thief up in the apple tree and was sure that he was still there. Instantly Tom said, "Let us take the gun out." Both decided on this plan of action, and crept cautiously into the garden. "There he is," said Bed. "Fire, Tom!" No sooner said than done. Down fell the supposed intruder, and both young men took to their heels, one blaming the other, and did not return to the house until very late.

On another occasion one of the hauliers called at Llwyncelyn, and asked Bedlington for a note to get a bucket, whereupon the latter remarked: "Why not take hold of the first one you can see?" The haulier, upon leaving, perceived a new bucket near by, and at once took possession of it, only to be hauled up next morning before Bed. for an explanation. He was let off with a caution.

Herbert became an eminent engineer, serving under Francis Crawshay, and was one of the first to suggest that coal-dust was a medium which played an important part in colliery explosions. He died in September, 1904, at the age of 72. Howel was appointed vicar of Cyfarthfa Church after the death of the Rev. John Howells (the first vicar) in 1868.

I have already dealt with the old Cyfarthfa Canal, which wended its way from the Llyn to Llwyncelyn, and under an arch which is still to be seen behind the signal box, and then through a field to the lower end of Upper Colliers' Row. That was before the B. & M. Railway was made in 1865—1866. Returning to the main road at Pen y Trip Mawr, we come next to Cyfarthfa Church and Vicarage, completed and opened in April, 1857. Its first vicar was succeeded by the Rev. Howel Kirkhouse. The latter, after serving the Church and his Master faithfully for 46 years, died in August, 1914, at the age of 75. On each side of the road above the Church there are huge cinder tips. Before 1870 this road was very narrow ; in some places the top of the old hedge can just be seen still. The road was widened and straightened from John Street up to the farm road, Heolgerrig, by the local authority ; it was also fenced and young thorns planted where required. About 60 years ago it was a sight to see the cinder-tip at the roadside on fire ; it was covered with blue, sulphurous flames, caused by the tipping of huge oblong blocks of molten cinders from the works, covered over by the ash from the coke ovens. Before reaching the stone bridge connecting the tips on each hand, we pass what was known as the Cinder Hall, so christened during the time when large outdoor miners' meetings were held, and addressed by labour leaders like David Morgan (Dai o'r Nant), the late Thomas Thomas, and others. It was in the old days a hollow in the surrounding tip which later excavation has much enlarged. Above the stone bridge, built in 1855, are the lime-kilns, which date from about 1870. Previously lime was burnt near Cefn Bridge, but, for the sake of convenience, new kilns were built here. Now we reach Cyfarthfa railway crossing, which was the site of John Cook's Lodge. John Cook was the gateman here 60 years ago, and a very original character he was. Possessed of a wooden leg and a picturesque, flowing and frizzly silvery beard, he was well versed in all the topics of the day. If any information was required, one had only to pop into the lodge and ask John, who promptly supplied it. Just here used to pass the old road from Llwyncelyn towards Swansea Road, Tranch Bach, Tai Mawr, and Pontycapel. A little way above is the old Cyfarthfa Canal and the Cwm Pit railway, and we pass under the B. & M. Railway bridge, which is constructed of iron supported by large blocks of limestone masonry and two massive tubular iron pillars. There are two bridges close together—one over the road, railway and canal, the other over the Gethin line only. After passing the bridge, we reach the site of two very old houses, just where now stand two rows of workmen's dwellings known as Pantygelynen, built in 1902. The two old houses were Nos. 1 and 2, Heolgerrig, respectively ; therefore at this point we enter Heolgerrig. They were known as Tai Mark Grai. The first party I can recall living in No. 1 was Isaac Lewis, a cobbler and miner. Timothy Williams, who was killed at Lefal Coedcae in 1864, also lived there at one time. Isaac Lewis was a brother of William Lewis, of Salvation Army fame, who lived a little higher up the road and became a market gardener. His son, William, still lives quite near this place, and carries on the same business. John Lewis was another brother, and all three worked as miners at David Beynon's Pit, which was behind the Six Bells. In No. 2 lived Susannah Rees and her daughter Hannah. There are descendants of "Sue" (as she was called) living in the neighbourhood at the present time. At the rear of these old houses runs the stream known as Nant y Gwenith. The present name, Pantygelynen, is very appropriate, as in front of the old houses there was a large amount of holly in the hedges, which were always neatly trimmed.

CHAPTER VI.

THE OLD TRANSPORT ROAD—UPPER COLLIERS' ROW—LEFAL AND PWLL COEDCAE—PENYCOEDCAE—OLD HEOLGERRIG FARM—TAI CANOL—PENYRHEOLGERRIG FARM—THE WILLIAMS FAMILY—THE OLD FACTORY—MORGAN WILLIAMS.

A LITTLE way above Pantygelynen there was an old tramway. Formerly this was the old road from Cyfarthfa to Cwmcanaid and Glyndyrus, and — as has been previously explained—was used for transport purposes, teams of horses and mules bringing the fuel or raw material to the works. Down the tramroad, somewhat later, were brought the building-stones from near Blaencanaid, to build Cyfarthfa Castle in 1825. Upper Colliers' Row, a number of workmen's dwellings of the old type (17, to be exact), is not far to the south of the main road. Lefal Coedcae, an old level where the 7ft. coal seam was extensively worked, is just above. Twenty horses were at one time employed there. The 7ft. coal was of excellent quality, with a good strong "roof" above it—the top coal, almost 2ft. 3ins. thick, the bottom coal of the same dimension, with a very strong fire-clay clod between, from 2ft. 6ins. to 3ft. in thickness. Some time ago, I had occasion to travel through the old level for a long distance. Proceeding along an old double parting, there was not to be seen a single post or piece of supporting timber, and the roof had remained intact for a considerable time. In later years, a great quantity of fire-clay, and the lower 2ft. 9ins. seam, was worked there by Edward Lewis and William his brother, colliery contractors. A little to the left of this level, and on the same side of the Cwmpant Brook, was the old Coedcae Mine Pit where, many years ago, a large number of miners were employed. Near the site of the pit there is the large market garden of Mr. William Lewis, who has recently built a fine bungalow within the garden fence.

After crossing the tramroad, we actually enter the Coedcae, which has given rise to the names—Pwll Coedcae, Lefal Coedcae, Pound Pwll Coedcae and Pen-y-Coedcae. It is sometimes known as Coedcae Llwyncelyn, but more generally the name of the occupant of Penycoedcae House is linked to it. This house was formerly part of a small farm, the lease of which was acquired by Anthony Bacon, afterwards passing into the possession of the Crawshays. During the riots of 1816, when William Crawshay had just taken over the ownership of Cyfarthfa Works (after his father's death) with his brother George, he left Cyfarthfa House to take up residence at Gwaelodygarth. Shortly after the removal, trouble arose at all the iron-works, regarding wages. The iron-masters took steps to arm their adherents with all kinds of pikes, made at the works, to protect the works and their masters' homes. The strikers assembled in great crowds, soon overpowered the pike-men, and the iron-masters fled. William Crawshay sought refuge at Penycoedcae, Heolgerrig, and remained in hiding there for some days. Gwaelodygarth was the residence of the iron-master until the Castle was built in 1825 at a cost of £30,000.

When Thomas Kirkhouse became manager of the collieries at Cyfarthfa, he resided at Penycoedcae ; so did his successor, Mr. Moody, who was manager at the time of the terrible Gethin explosions in 1862 and 1865. Then came a Mr. Bates, followed by Mr. David Abraham. During the tenancy of the latter many improvements were carried out in connection with the house and its surroundings. The brook, from Cwmyglo Road down the drive, was arched over for a distance of about 50 yards, and a shrubbery made, in which huge lumps of coal, which had come from various levels and neatly trimmed, were placed on walls and pillars. There were also various specimens of fossils found in the mines, mounted there for adornment. In one of the levels a live toad was found in the solid coal, and this curiosity was taken to Mr. Dd. Abraham, but I have no information as to what eventually became of it. The next to take up residence there was Mr. Tudor Rogers, who, previous to being appointed manager, had been a colliery surveyor. He brought to an end a long line of the old type of faithful company official, living in the Company's house and enjoying a number of privileges. Mr. W. J. Morgan, who purchased the freehold of the house and land in 1925, is the present occupier.

The freehold of the Coedcae was bought by Mr. William Jones in 1926, and during the transfer of ownership a right-of-way through it was secured. Near the upper entrance to the Coedcae, close to the path, there is a substantial well, sunk in the old days, to supply water for domestic purposes at Penycoedcae, before Taf Fechan supplied Merthyr with a pure water service. Near this spot is Moody's Pond, constructed during the time of the manager of that name.

Returning to the main road, we will take up our itinerary at Heolgerrig Farm, now of very small proportions. About 100 years ago it consisted of 24 acres. In 1842, according to old rate-books, Shon Dafydd Evan left the farm, and Evan William took possession. The latter was the father of Catherine Harris, wife of Henry Harris, commonly called "Harri Bach y Tanwr," who afterwards took possession after his death. Catherine remembered seeing the wheatfields of Nantygwenith previous to their being covered by extensive tipping operations. After her death, the farm still remained in the possession of the family until the Cyfarthfa lease expired in 1926. The original area of the farm was greatly reduced owing to tipping, quarrying and mining, therefore I believe certain land nearer the mountain side was given as part compensation to the tenants. This would account for the part known as Waun Shon Dafydd Evan, Shon being the farmer then in possession of the farm. The freehold of the farm as it now stands is in the possession of Mr. Morgan Davies, but the old farmhouse has been in ruins for years. When Anthony Bacon leased the minerals of this large estate, he had to buy up most of the farm leases before he could enter upon the land for works purposes. With the exception of those held by the more intelligent farmers, these leases were bought at an average of about £100 apiece. Wilkins, in his "History of Merthyr," does not state definitely the farm at the side of the Heolgerrig Road in which one of these shrewd intelligent farmers lived, although he mentions his name as being Evan Williams, living in a thatched-roof farmhouse. This would suggest that the farmhouse was no other than Heolgerrig Farm. The premises consisted of three dwelling-houses—Nos. 3, 4 and 5, Heolgerrig—one of these being at the rear of the farmhouse, the farmhouse itself, and a small thatched dwelling at the extreme end of the cowsheds. I can remember two old characters, called Shon and Shan, living there at one time, both of whom used to turn out in the morning with their stools to break stones at the roadside.

Now come in order the following: Farm Terrace, Rock Cottage, Castle View, and Coronation Terrace—all on the left of the main road and of fairly recent construction. At the rear of these are the new Council Houses—40 semi-detached dwellings, built about 1920, on fields that once belonged to Penyrheol Farm. They formed the Heolgerrig No. 1 Scheme, which has since been named Brondeg. On the right of the road are four very old houses known as Tai Canol Isaf. The first house, No. 6 Heolgerrig, was once the home of the late William Lewis, market gardener, of Salvation Army fame. In No. 7 lived Thomas Powell. No. 8 was once a public-house, and Thomas Jones (who later removed to Treorchy with his family) lived there. Then Jenkin Jenkins, one of the Ty'nycoedcae family, came to live there, but in 1873 moved to Nantgau, hence the name " Shinkin Nantgau." His second son, William Jenkins, who became a schoolmaster, died a few years ago at Cefn Coed, where he returned upon retirement. He served his pupil-teachership at the British School, Abermorlais. Jenkin Jenkins had three sons and two daughters. One of the latter, Margaret Ann, had charge of the first night-school at Heolgerrig about 1884. In No. 9 lived Will Dai (William Thomas), notorious for his rough habits. The brook passes close in the rear of these old houses, while opposite them is an entrance into Brondeg. On the left of the road again are Lewis Terrace, Herbert House, The Hollies, and eight new Council houses built in 1924. Previous to building the latter group, the road was very narrow, and three old houses, known as Tai Canol Uchaf, stood in front. These had to be demolished, to make room for road widening, and the tenants removed into the Council houses. A very old landmark thus disappeared. It is said that between the Hollies and Tai Canol Uchaf there used to be a gate on the main road, separating the lowlands from the mountain lands, or Gwaunydd. A little higher is Meirion Place, built for the late Rev. I. J. Evans about 34 years ago ; and then Dan-yr-Onen, the old ash tree from which the name was derived—is still to be seen. This is the residence of Mr. Richard E. Davies and his two daughters. Recently, six more Council houses have been built just above, at the roadside, thus making in all a total of 52 built by the local authority. The whole of the land at the rear, which originally belonged to Penyrheol Farm, has been bought by the Merthyr Corporation for building purposes.

The next place of importance we reach is what is known as Penyrheol. On the right side of the road and brook is the Penyrheolgerrig Farm, which has been for many years the largest of the remaining farms in the neighbourhood. Before 1842 it was a small and unimportant place occupied by William Price, a mine contractor, who kept a few horses and cows. Mr. Evan Evans, Six Bells, married Mary, the daughter of William Price. Price, being anxious for the match, Evan Evans wanted to know what the marriage portion was to be, and the former agreed that it should be a cow and a calf. The marriage was arranged, and eventually took place. Some time later, Evan inquired of Price when the cow and calf were likely to arrive, to which the latter replied: "Fy machgen annwyl i, 'rwyt wedi eu cael!"—implying, of course, his daughter. The son-in-law had to be content with this at the time; but according to an old rate-book, when Price left the farm, between April and September, 1842, Evan Evans took possession, and during his tenancy a considerable extent of waste land was added to the farm land, and a considerable brewing business was built up. When Evan Evans left, a haulier named John Davies, with Jenny his wife, lived there and looked after the farm. Their daughter married Mr. David Phillips, draper, and a former Mayor of Merthyr. Ann, daughter of Evan Evans, and mother of Mr. Richard and Mr. Tom Davies, also lived at the farm, where the latter were born. She removed to Gilfach Goch about 1873. Afterwards, William and Nelly Williams, who had previously been living at Penyrheol Farm, looking after the land and cattle for Mr. David Williams and, afterwards, Mr. Tom Heppel, came to live at Penyrheolgerrig Farm. Many bailiffs have since dwelt there among whom were — John Williams, Charles Prosser, and Mr. Low; but the name of the farm was known to most people as Six Bells Farm. Many years ago, the late Mr. Christmas Evans built extensive stables and carriage buildings at considerable cost. Later the farm was let to the late Samuel Davies, formerly of Penpound Farm, Cwmtaf, but who was born at Cwmdu, Heolgerrig. When the general sale of leaseholds of the various farms and tenements took place in 1926, the present owner and occupier, Mr. Henry T. Davies, son of the said Samuel Davies, purchased the farm. The total acreage of land sold in 1926 was about 242 acres.

On the opposite side of the main road is the very old Penyrheol Farm, which belonged to the Williams family. At one time its land extended from Cwmyglo Road to the Cwmpant Road. One of the earliest maps of this locality, made by Thomas Kitchen in 1755 and again in 1763, shows Penyrheol Farm as being the only one in this district. He also shows the old Heolgerrig Road —the only road on the western side of the river. Kitchen, however, confined himself to the roads and roadside farms chiefly. The old farmhouse of Penyrheol was converted into two dwelling-houses long ago. William Williams, the bailiff, occupied the one nearest the road, while Thomas Williams (a brother of "Billy Blaencanaid") and Shwan his wife, occupied the other. Shwan had the milking as well as the distribution of the milk to see to. The first person of whom I have any account of living in the old farmhouse was a certain Letitia, mother of Kitty, who was the wife of David Lewis, a blocklayer. Then there lived there also Margaret John and William Williams. The farm consisted of the old farm building, a large barn and cowsheds below, a fairly large residence with a verandah in front, surrounded by a green; there was also a large storeroom, and, near the brook, not far away, a factory. All these belonged to the Williams (or Williamses) of Penyrheol, a very intelligent family; and quite probably it was one of these Williams that Wilkins refers to as claiming more for his lease from Anthony Bacon than many of the other farmers. I have reason to believe that William, son of Lewis Williams, yeoman of Nantygwenith, lived here. His son William was, I should think, the father of the noted Morgan Williams. Lewis Williams died March 4, 1768, aged 56; and Mary, his widow, died at Penyrheol, May 10, 1789, aged 71. It is very likely that they left Nantygwenith Farm soon after its purchase by Anthony Bacon.

Now let us try and trace this noted family of Penyrheol. The first that we have any record of are William and Margaret Williams. William married a Miss Nicholas of Pant-Cad-Ifor, daughter of a smith of that place. According to Wilkins, Nicholas, the smith, was a descendant of Sir Dafydd Gam. When Mrs. Williams of Penyrheol was a young girl, John Guest was working his first furnace at Gellifaelog, about 1763. At that time the post was brought from Brecon via Pontsticill and Pant to Merthyr once a week by an old lady on horseback. She brought in her bag two newspapers with the letters—one for John Guest and the other for an important person in Merthyr. Those belonging to Guest were left at Nicholas' smithy to be taken over to Gellifaelog by the smith's little daughter. The latter well remembered John Guest, sitting on a stone near his furnace, waiting patiently for his newspaper, and his rewarding her occasionally with a few coppers for her little deeds of kindness. Mrs. Williams of Penyrheol (the former Miss Nicholas) was quite able, in after years, to describe John Guest as she remembered the great pioneer of the renowned Dowlais Iron Works. Both Mr. and Mrs. Williams were very intelligent people, and counted many eminent people in their circle of friends, one of these being Edward Williams (" Iolo Morgannwg "). Iolo stayed many a night during his travels through South Wales, at the old mansion of Penyrheol, and during these visits important topics of the day were earnestly discussed by Iolo and his host and hostess. To the children he was simply " Old Iolo." The famous poet's seat was usually a comfortably prepared arm-chair. He was always a heavy tea-drinker. Occasionally he would be offered a pot of broth: and no sooner was it placed before him than he would cast a swift glance to see if the contents were up to strength. Now the strength of the broth was measured by the number of " stars " or " eyes " on its surface. On a certain occasion, Iolo, perceiving the beverage not up to the standard, knelt solemnly before the table, and in a serious tone murmured : " O Lord, who hath sinned that this hath been born blind ! "

Six Bells Farm—or Penyrheolgerrig Farm as it is termed upon ordnance maps of recent years—was at one time part and parcel of Penyrheol. It was in 1842, when Evan Evans took possession, that the names Penyrheolgerrig Farm and Six Bells Farm arose. If this was the case, the Nantygwenith Brook ran through the Penyrheol Estate—the farm, mansion and factory being situated between it and the Cwmpant Bach Brook. The latter, in my estimation, was the ancient Nantygweunydd, which passed Penycoedcae and the Old Factory, whence the name Nant-y-Ffactri. Penyrheol may have been called Nantygweunydd. In the 1842 rate-books the rateable value of Nantygweunydd, held by William Crawshay, was £90. In a " History of Merthyr " compiled by William Edmunds, of Quakers' Yard, a list of farms and their occupants was given, in which the farm of Abernant-y-gwenith appears, the farmer being David Williams, who married a daughter of William and Margaret Williams of Penyrheol. They afterwards removed to the Greyhound Hotel, opposite the T.V.R. Station. David Williams was well acquainted with Plymouth Works, and I believe that he had some connection with it, as he was in partnership with Mr. Nixon at the Werfa Colliery, Aberdare. While licensee of the Greyhound Hotel, Mr. W. S. Clark, agent to the Marquis of Bute, called upon David Williams, asking him to recommend a good man to him as assistant engineer, seeing that he was familiar with Plymouth. There and then the name of young W. T. Lewis, son of Thomas W. Lewis of Plymouth Works, was mentioned, and arrangements were made for David Williams to interview the young man, to ascertain whether he desired the position ; if so, he was to call upon Mr. Clark at his office. Young Lewis accepted the offer, which proved to be the turning-point in his life. Later, by dint of perseverance and industry, he became the distinguished Sir William Thomas Lewis and, later, Baron Merthyr of Senghenydd. David Williams eventually left the Greyhound Hotel upon the death of his mother-in-law, and moved to Penyrheol to take possession of the farm and factory — at the same time keeping up his connection with Werfa Colliery. Towards the end of his days he became very feeble, and had to be constantly watched by his workmen, though the factory was kept going up to his death. He was succeeded at the Greyhound by his niece (daughter of Morgan Williams) and her husband, Thomas Heppel, who, after David's death, took over Penyrheol Farm. The factory was then discontinued and converted into cottages — the widow and her sister, who was a spinster, taking up their residence at the old mansion.

Now mention must be made of Morgan Williams, who was born at Penyrheol in 1813, and died August 27, 1886, at the age of 73. Morgan, when at the age of 12, remembered old Iolo Morgannwg at Penyrheol very well, and would listen attentively to the discussions upon the principles of democracy and other topics that took place between the famous bard and his father. When Morgan was 25, there was a great Radical movement in the country towards emancipation for the working classes. There were several stalwarts of the movement locally—David John, the smith ; his sons, David and Mathew John ; Morgan Williams ; William Gould, inventor of the ballot-box, which can be seen at Cyfarthfa Museum ; Henry Thomas, and David Ellis. One of their first public meetings was held near Penyrheol, the chairman being selected on the spot. The "Charter" (as O'Connell named it) demanded six points—vote by ballot ; abolition of property qualification to become a member of Parliament ; payment of M.P.s ; manhood suffrage ; division of the country into equal electoral districts ; and annual elections. The political movement was then termed Chartism. A section, desperate from excessive poverty, turned to the use of physical force to bring about their demands ; but the majority used more peaceful means—meetings, presentation of monster petitions to Parliament, or the circulation of a paper promoting their views. The Merthyr men believed in moral rather than physical force, and Morgan Williams was often selected to try and mollify the more turbulent sections at meetings held in other places. The agitators were known as the Chartists. On one occasion, a special design of Welsh flannel waistcoat was invented to be worn on special occasions by each of the local Chartists, the cloth being made at Penyrheol Factory. One of the first demonstrations of the Chartists took place on a Sunday morning at the old Parish Church, in a very simple manner so as not to attract much publicity. Each member was to attend church service in the morning in his specially designed waistcoat. Every available seat and all the standing room in the church was occupied, and the members were more than satisfied that everything had gone on so peacefully. Movements in Merthyr brought about Government suspicion, and a spy was told off to collect information. He called at the smithy of David John one day, and attempted to discuss with the honest old smith an easy way of casting lead bullets. Suspecting the character of his visitor, David John told him to leave the smithy promptly, or he would put his head under the hammer! The spy immediately took to his heels. When "Udgorn Cymru" ("The Trumpet of Wales"), the Chartist newspaper, was started about 1840, it was edited jointly by Morgan Williams and David John, and printed in the Glebeland.

On his return home from the last Chartist Convention, which he had attended as the representative of Merthyr, Morgan Williams was given a great public welcome. Thousands of his enthusiastic friends lined the highway, and he was borne shoulder-high, like a Roman hero, to the Market Square. But soon after his triumph he and some of his friends had to flee from their native heath to Newtown, Montgomeryshire—as a result, I should imagine, of their political activities. In the following " englynion " by Idris Ddu, composed in 1843, a description of Morgan and his mother is given :—

Attat wr mwyn, wr dymunol,—Deheu
Adewaist yn hollol ;
Mae it' blaid, rho naid yn ol
I dre, gwedda'n dragwyddol.

Mae dy fam ddi-nam, ddoniol—o'r herwydd
A mawr hiraeth ddyddiol,
A difrad siarad siriol
Fod ei mab arab ar ol.

Unig fab, cu-fab call,—Ow ! i Marged
Yw Morgan, wi'n deall ;
Ei fam dawel gwêl y gwall,
Try i anwedd tre arall.

Gwr o ddawn a gwr o ddysg—yw Morgan,
Mawr ei gais am addysg ;
Gweinydda i'r gwan addysg,
Clodfawr, gwr mawr yn ein mysg.

Later the fugitive returned to his native Merthyr and filled some important positions, one of which was the registrarship of births, marriages and deaths. The Williams family carried on the woollen factory for many years at Glanynant, on the upper side of the Cwmyglo Road and near the old mansion of Penyrheol, where the storeroom for the manufactured goods was completed. Motive-power was derived from a water-wheel suitably positioned in the brook. Just above the Old Factory a large pond was constructed in a field at the rear of Salem Chapel, to store water so as to keep up a continuous supply for the factory. It fell into disuse about 70 years ago. A small sample of the check Welsh flannel manufactured there can be seen in the Welsh kitchen at the Cyfarthfa Museum. After the conversion of the factory building into cottages, some members of the Williams family lived there for many years, the dwellings being known as Old Factory Cottages. Now the place is a small farm, occupied by Mr. and Mrs. David Davies. The old pond was filled-in when David Williams, Penyrheol was part-owner of Werfa Colliery—some of the Werfa workmen, during a period of slack time, being employed for the work.

CHAPTER VII.

THE EVANS FAMILY, SIX BELLS—PENYRHEOL HOUSE—SOME LOCAL CHARACTERS—LEFAL BENNI—CYFARTHFA TRAMWAY—PENCOEDCAE BRYNTEG—PWLL LEWSIN—JENKIN JENKINS, OLD TRAVELLER'S REST—THOMAS GRIFFITHS Y GOF—OLD QUARRY—THE FIRST INDEPENDENT CHAPEL—THE BREWERY—SALEM CHAPEL—HEOLGERRIG SHOP AND POST OFFICE — MR. THOMAS JENKINS, GREENFIELD HOUSE— —DAVID NICHOLAS.

EVAN Evans, Six Bells, came to Penyrheolgerrig from the Neath Valley, having been attracted to Merthyr—the metropolis of the iron trade then—when he was very young, in the same way as thousands of other adventurous young spirits who forsook farm life for a newer and more prosperous career. His parents lived for a short time at Gellideg. Like many successful men before him, he began at the lowest rung of the ladder, starting simply as a haulier, without the advantage of schooling or the knowledge of any trade. But the haulier grew bigger and stronger, then entered the grade of collier, and, after some years of slaving and saving, he at last became a contractor at some of the levels. He now started a public-house known as the Old Six Bells. I cannot say whether he built the house, but I have reasons for believing that there was a house at the spot previous to his launching the public-house business. In the 1832 map, showing the proposed new Parliamentary boundary, a block of buildings, surrounded by a garden, is shown. As the nearest survey of South Wales made previous to the map of 1832 took place in 1824, it would appear that Evan Evans, who was only 15 years of age at the latter date, could not possibly have built the house, although he did eventually add a brewing-house to the public-house. The malt for the business was supplied by John Williams (Felin Frâg). The Old Six Bells presented a very old appearance; the kitchen was very large and low, with massive oak beams stretching across the ceiling, from which large wooden hooks, made out of tree roots, hung. The windows were very small, and in front of the house was a neat little porch, with large stone slabs at each side. During the time he was contractor, his men were paid at the house—and, naturally, portook of the beverage. On pay-day, therefore, trade was particularly brisk, with the result that many a fight took place on the flat between the public-house and the factory pond, between those whose temperature had risen above the ordinary level. This place was known afterwards as "the bloody spot."

Some of Evan's fellow-workers took a directly opposite line in life socially, and became leaders of religion in the neighbourhood. By sheer determination, the contractor aimed at something above the ordinary when he settled down at Penyrheolgerrig. Soon after his 21st birthday, in 1830, he married Mary, daughter of William Price, who lived at the small farm, and for some years they resided at the Old Six Bells, the site of which is in the field opposite the present Six Bells. The brewing business expanded rapidly, and the venturous Evan decided to build more commodious premises to cope with the increasing trade. A new brewery was built at the side of the main road, alongside which very few houses existed at that time.

Upon the retirement of William Price from his farm in 1842, Evan Evans took possession. It was a very small farm then, but the latter began building additional stables, and cattle and wagon sheds, for the use of the brewery, as well as extending the farm boundaries by enclosing waste land and converting it into good agricultural land. So Evan prospered with his brewery, and succeeded in making an ample fortune. His labours were successful in all directions. A commodious new public-house, of the same name as the older one, was built alongside the new brewery, and all the business transferred from the old public-house to the new one. After many years, a new private house was built opposite Salem Chapel, where Evan lived in retirement, leaving the weight of the business to be borne by his son Christmas. In 1863 Evan Evans pushed his speculations further afield, purchasing the mineral rights of a large area at Gilfach Goch, in the lesser Ogmore Valley, and commencing operations on the No. 2 Rhondda Seam, which yielded very successfully. In 1868 he sank a shaft to the No. 3 Rhondda Seam, which also proved well, both seams possessing the best house-coal qualities. A large number of coke ovens were also built for the conversion of small coal into coke. These undertakings were known as the Dinas Main Collieries, and for many years was a good, paying concern. Mr. William T. Lewis (afterwards Lord Merthyr) came into partnership in the new undertaking, but soon sold back his interest to Evan Evans. Evan Evans, Six Bells, died March 19, 1886, aged 77. Mary, his wife, had predeceased him August 31, 1863, aged 53. Evan left two sons and one daughter—Christmas, Evan, and Ann. Evan (the son) spent most of his time in America, where he died December 26, 1905.

After his father's death, Mr. Christmas Evans took over the whole of the business. He sank two deep shafts to the steam coal seams at Gilfach Goch, known afterwards as the Britannic Collieries, but the venture was not very successful. Some years after Evan Evans' decease, Christmas purchased the old mansion of Penyrheol, together with the enclosed land and garden, which was getting into a rather dilapidated condition. The old building was pulled down, and a lovely modern mansion, which is one of the finest buildings in Merthyr, erected in its place. At the time of the purchase, the old residence was occupied by Mr. Thomas Heppel and his wife, Margaret (daughter of Morgan Williams), for whom Mr. Christmas Evans built a small house next to the old farm, and in which their son, Rowley, lives at the present time. Just when the rebuilding of the mansion was completed on April 11, 1888, a disastrous fire broke out in the brewery, which destroyed the whole of the building and its contents. The public-house—in which they then lived, and which was attached to the brewery—was in danger of ignition, so the roofing was disconnected. There happened to be a pond in the quarry at the rear, known as Pound Cwar, and a continouus chain of buckets of water was kept going by anxious helpers from the pond to the scene of the fire. Fortunately, as the new Penyrheol House was nearing completion, the furniture and other household goods were transferred there, and Mr. and Mrs. Evans lived here until the end of their days. Mrs. Evans died October 2, 1907, and Mr. Christmas Evans on March 23, 1909, aged 69. The marriage of Mr. Christmas Evans and Miss Annie Jones was the last that took place in the ruins of the ancient church at Vaynor; that was about 1868. The work of rebuilding the brewery was commenced immediately. Mr. Christmas Evans left six children—three boys and three girls. The mansion is now occupied by Miss Maggie Evans, who has remained there ever since the family removed at the time of the fire. The house carries the old name of Penyrheol House. Mr. Thomas Jenkins, of Greenfield House—who is now over 86 years of age, and who has grown white in the service of the family—acted as clerk and adviser to Mr. Evan Evans, then to Mr. Christmas Evans, and latterly as a father and friend to the children. His health gave way over 40 years ago, but, in spite of his infirmities, he has continued to carry on faithfully the duties of clerk and adviser to the children of the late Mr. Christmas Evans and others. For over 60 years he has served the Six Bells family with credit, not only to himself, but also to the recipients of his devotion. He is always ready and willing to give counsel to those in need of advice, and has gained the respect of the inhabitants of the neighbourhood in which he has lived so long.

I shall now return to the farm road, connecting Heolgerrig and Swansea Road at Gellideg. On the left hand side of the road is the site of two old houses down on a level with the brook, and on the other side of the brook are a number of houses known as the Cwm. Next we come to an old house built many years ago by one Owen Jones. His wife, Betsy, was the first midwife that I knew. The descendants of this old pair are still living there.

At the rear of the house there is a large cherry tree, three feet in diameter three feet from the ground, but which is now decaying On the right of the road is the Penyrheolgerrig Farm and stables. Further on is Mount Pleasant, a row of several houses built by Lewis Pugh. In one of these lived John Evans ("John o'r Darlwm"). He was a cripple from birth—having, unfortunately, a short and weakly leg, which necessitated his using a wooden one. Although thus handicapped, he worked as a miner underground. John o'r Darlwm was well-educated and a fluent speaker, and was known to his fellow-workmen at the colliery as "the Gladstone of Pwll y Cwm." He was the secretary of two large friendly societies, both of which held their meetings at the Six Bells for over twenty years. In appearance, he was very dignified, possessing a long white frizzly beard. He had taken a great deal of interest in the well-being of the children of the district, and, with some others, appeared before the old School Board over fifty years ago to urge the necessity of a school for the Heolgerrig children. He also advocated the widening of the road from Georgetown to Penyrheol. Both of these demands were ultimately granted and carried out. John Evans died in Pembrokeshire, December 8, 1888, at the age of 61.

In the same street lived another intelligent miner, Jacob Jones by name, who also occupied some official positions. During the time of Robert T. Crawshay, Mrs. Crawshay took great interest in the welfare of the Cyfarthfa workmen, and would occasionally take a walk up to Heolgerrig. Here she would arrange with Jacob Jones to meet other prominent persons for the purpose of discussing the establishment of a library for the benefit of the workmen, but nothing was done in the matter. A little higher up in the row are three houses known as Tai Morgan Shon Rees, named after their builder, who was a leader of men, possessed of strong will-power. He also had been secretary of one of the Six Bells friendly societies before John Evans. Possessed of very deep religious interests, he was one of the founders of the Independent cause at Heolgerrig in 1838.

After we have passed Mount Pleasant we reach the tramroad, which ran from the pits and levels to Cyfarthfa Yard. Branches of this tramroad from Cwmdu, Winchfawr, Pwll Lewsin mine pit, and various mountain-side levels, worked many years ago near Blaencanaid, linked up with the main tramroad. On the other side of it is the site of Lefal Benni, a noted old colliery, in which the Bute and lower 2ft. 9in. coal seams were worked extensively. The following are some of the names of men I have heard mentioned as having worked at this old level: David Thomas, manager of Werfa Colliery for many years; Elias Thomas, his brother; William Davies, manager at Coedcae Colliery, Porth, in the Rhondda

Valley; David Abraham, father of the late Rhys Abraham (who also worked there as a boy with his father); Rees Evans; Edward Griffiths; Lewis Phillips, Gelli Ddu, who was one of the hauliers there. Another interesting fact is that the tipper at one time was a woman, the late Elizabeth Robert Jones. Then there were the brothers Isaac, John and Thomas Davies; Morgan Webber and John his son; Edward Morgan; Thomas Davies, nicknamed "Twm Glomen"; Rees Price, manager at Werfa; Morgan Manner and Philip Howel (flue-man). The only one of these surviving is Lewis Phillips, now on the brink of his eightieth birthday.

Nearby is Tai Shinkin, most of these houses having been built by Thomas Jenkins, whose son, Jenkin, married a sister of Billy Blaencanaid; the houses were known as Tai Shinkin, Melin Cwrt. In this particular neighbourhood there are huge shale tips, relics of the old mine pit known as Pwll Lewsin, named after Lewis Richard Jenkins, one of the Ty'nycoedcae family. It was Twm Shon Gruffydd who was the first contractor in the pit in 1830. Lewis came afterwards, and died April 19, 1866, aged 74. After him, David Beynon became contractor, hence the name Pwll Dafydd Beynon. Most of the mine veins below the coal seams were worked at this pit. Not long ago I received a letter from a Merthyr boy, born at Georgetown, who had emigrated, and filled many important positions in Queensland, Australia—Henry Llewelyn by name. He was the son of Henry, brother of Peter Llewelyn, of Pencae'r Wern, and had worked when a boy with his father at this pit. During the General Election in 1868, he remembered his father asking one of his fellow-miners at work one day: "Have you voted this morning, William?" To which the latter, after some hesitation, replied: "Yes, Henry, I have voted. But it is very different to what it used to be. When I had no vote, there was plenty of bread and cheese and beer; but to-day, when I have a vote, there is nothing to be had!" This Election was the first after the extension of the franchise to the householder. Henry Llewelyn is now 74 years old.

Near the old pit is Pencoedcae Brynteg Farm, which is not very big. The first people of whom I have any account as living there were Morgan and Peggy Davies, whose daughter married William Davies, late manager of Coedcae Collieries, Porth. Now we must return to the main road once more, and begin at the Traveller's Rest, now a private house. The inn was built in 1833 by Jenkin Jenkins, and afterwards occupied by his son, William. The old premises were behind the site of the later Traveller's Rest. Old Jenkin was very queer in his habits, and attracted many a noted character to his house, among whom were Rowley Llanbradach (Idris Ddu), Bili Dafydd Richard, Jimmy Bach yr Archwr, and Rees Lewis (Rees Lodwick) from Abernant. One day, Lodwick and Jimmy met there, and in course of a general discussion Jimmy asked the former if he could say what was the distance from that spot to the moon. " No, indeed," replied Lodwick, " I have left all that for you to find out. You are light enough to be carried there with the wind, so you may go and see for yourself ! "

Jenkin Jenkins, the publican, died between 1833 and 1834, and on the morning following the day of his decease, Idris Ddu, when on his way to Aberdare, called at Gwrhyd Fach, Blaenynant, the home of Rees Lodwick, to convey the sad news, as Jenkin was a bosom friend of his. Rees gave a start of surprise, and, after collecting his thoughts, said philosophically : " Well ! well ! I could afford to part with many better than Shanco ; he has only fled before me ! " The rateable value of the Traveller's Rest and croft in 1842 was £12 15s. William, the son, then became owner and occupier. Mrs. Ann Davies, daughter of Evan Evans, Six Bells, lived there for a while. Then came William Williams, Pencae —the eldest son of Morgan Wm. Williams, of Wern Farm. Others who followed in the business were David Edwards and Roger Pugh.

The next place of interest is the site of a small house known as Tŷ Thomas Gruffydd y Gôf, named after Thomas Griffiths, who lived there with Ann his wife, and who had two sons and one daughter. One of the sons was the Rev. Richard Griffiths, minister of Tabor, Cefn Coed ; while the other son, David (known as Dafydd Thomas y Gôf), worked at the same trade as his father, both being smiths on the railbank at Cyfarthfa. The old people were exceedingly religious, but David the son was not. On one occasion a boring match was arranged between David—who, upon the closing of the Cyfarthfa Works, had gone as a collier to Werfa Colliery—and John Thomas of Clwydyfagwyr. The match was to take place on a Saturday afternoon, after the day's work, at the " face " of the colliery. The boring was to be done by hammer and chisel only, to a depth of 2 feet 6 inches into the coal, the loser to pay for a 4½ gallon cask of beer. William Rees Morgan was appointed referee, and when everything was ready the match started, amidst lusty cheering, and the hammers rang merrily on the chisels. The holes were driven without stopping, the chisels being marked in such a way that the referee could see how the boring progressed. The finish was intensely keen, but the younger man, John Thomas, gained the victory : but there was only a margin of somewhat less than an inch between the two. This was just one of the many old customs in the mines many years ago. Old Dai Tomos y Gôf took an active interest in various sports as well, and excelled himself at pitching quoits, even when advanced in years. His quoits were not heavy, and only from four to five inches in diameter. Many of his descendants were also good quoit players.

Now we reach the road leading to the quarry, at the corner of which is the massive structure known as the Six Bells Brewery, rebuilt, after the fire of 1888, by Mr. Christmas Evans, and from which many thousands of beer of barrels were despatched all over the surrounding districts. How can we reconcile the fact that at the rear of this brewery was built the first schoolroom or chapel in which the Congregational cause was established in the neighbourhood ? This room was only 30 feet by 18 feet, so the accommodation was very limited. Before this, the religious meetings had been held in a private house, " Yr Hen Dŷ," since 1838 ; but the building erected was the first one used specially for the Sunday and week-day meetings as a chapel, and it cost £120. Bethlehem, as it was named, was opened for worship in June, 1840. Soon afterwards the building was utilized for another important purpose, namely, as a day-school for the children. The first schoolmaster was John Williams, who was succeeeded soon afterwards by William D. Richards (Billy Dafydd Richard), whose bardic name was Ceredig. The school accommodation, according to a return made, was 108, but the actual number on the roll was only 38 at that particular time. The total amount in fees received from the children in the year was £31, which was all the master received for his trouble. After serving its purpose, the need came for more ample accommodation, as the population of the rapidly growing district increased, and its use was discontinued. New additions were built, and four dwelling - houses formed in its place.

The old quarry, in which the 9ft. coal seam crops to the surface, is close by. Over a hundred years ago, the Cyfarthfa people worked an old level here, known as Lefal Cwar ; but the brothers David and Thomas Peters have also been working a level here until a few years ago. Overlaying the coal seam is a very strong rock, which has been quarried for building purposes. At this spot, too, the Six Bells family had their private level for supplying coal for brewery and domestic purposes. About 1845 there were very few houses in the locality, but, later, people began to be attracted to the village by the sinking of pits, opening of levels, and the big iron-works at Cyfarthfa. More houses had to be built, a bigger place of worship was necessary, so the members of the tiny Bethlehem sought a site for a more commodious building. The spot they chose was a waste piece of land between the factory pond and the main road, on which the new chapel was built, the name given to it being Salem. This took place in 1855—1856. The first old chapel, Bethlehem—the site of which had been given by Mr. Evan Evans, Six Bells, at a rental of only one shilling a year—after a period of 16 years useful service, was sold back to Mr. Evans, to be converted into dwelling-houses.

The opening meetings of the new Salem Chapel, Heolgerrig, took place on May 26 and 27, 1856, the officiating ministers being the Rev. Thomas Rees, D.D., of Swansea, and the Rev. John Thomas, D.D., of Liverpool. The cost of building the edifice was £368 8s. 7d. During the time of its building, the church sustained a very severe blow by the death of one of its foremost stalwarts in the person of Llewellyn Llewellyn, known as "Llewelyn yr Archwr." He had been one of the strong pillars of the church from its inception in 1838, and was a faithful member of the church at Bethesda for many years; he was also the grandfather of the late Llewelyn Davies, printer and bookseller. Although the church had been under the care and ministration of the pastor of Bethesda since its commencement, in 1861 Mr. Samuel D. Jones was ordained as minister of Salem alone. Before him the Rev. Daniel Jones (1840—1845) and Rhys Gwesyn Jones (1845—1858), both of Bethesda, had attended to the spiritual needs of the flock at Bethlehem, and later at Salem. When Samuel Jones relinquished his charge, he was succeeded by Mr. Daniel Jones, a very able man, but who soon left. In 1871 Mr. Isaac John Evans was ordained as minister, having pursued his studies at Bala-Bangor, and for 38 years—a period in which there were many industrial troubles—he guided his congregation along the Christian path. His was a very saintly character, which gained for him the highest reverence on all hands. He retired from the care of the church on account of ill-health, and died January 19, 1914, at the age of 75, at Iron Bridge, Salop, whither he had gone to stay with his brother and sister-in-law, Thomas Daniel Thomas (Tydfilfab) and Letitia his wife. The burial took place at Cefn Cemetery, Jan. 24, 1914.

Mr. George Evans, B.A., who had studied at Brecon College, was then ordained, and during his ministry the church flourished. During his stay he studied hard and secured his B.D. He married another unflinching worker in the cause of his Master, in the person of Miss Jennie Oliver Jones, of Tai Mawr. To the great regret of the church, which he had served so faithfully and so well for 13 years, Mr. Evans left to take up the pastorate of Tabor, Penygraig, November 25, 1923. The present pastor of Salem is the Rev. W. Hopkin Jenkins, who was ordained to the care of the church September 6, 1928, and is doing very well.

When the new chapel was built, in 1856, there was a small schoolroom underneath, used for the weekly meetings of the church as well as for the instruction of the smaller children of the Sunday School. The school-master, William D. Richards, moved his day scholars from the old building to the new one; and even after his days, others kept school at Salem, among them being "Mac Ebrill," "Mabonwyson," and William Hitchings. This took place before the old School Board started functioning, and many took advantage of this rudimentary type of education. When Salem was rebuilt, in 1871, the schoolroom was done away with.

Opposite the chapel is the Heolgerrig Shop and Post Office. Years ago, this was the only shop in the district, and was first kept by W. Kernic and Gwennie his wife. The latter was the daughter of Mr. Evan Evans, Six Bells. Following these came William and Martha Hitchings, and then two old maids — the daughters of John Powell. Then Mr. and Mrs. Joseph Davies came to the shop, and in 1889 a district branch of the Post Office was opened as well, under the supervision of Mr. Joseph Davies. Some years later the name of the branch was changed from Penyrheolgerrig to Heolgerrig. After the death of Joseph Davies, Mr. and Mrs. J. J. Thomas took over the business. The work of the Post Office has been considerably increased as a result of the extended facilities to the general public, and our genial postmaster has always carried out his duties courteously and satisfactorily. It was within a few doors of this shop that the writer first saw the light of day, 67 years ago.

Now we reach Greenfield House, the residence of Mr. Thomas Jenkins, one of the most respected residents in the district. Of a very kindly disposition, a scholar, he is well-informed and has a good recollection of matters in general, but more particularly of those pertaining to the neighbourhood. In his younger days, some 60 years ago, being fond of his gun he developed into a good shot, and many a crow fell, a victim to his gun, from the tall poplars which lined the Cwmyglo Road behind the old Penyrheol House. I remember Mr. Jenkins amusing himself and the children with his galvanic battery. He would get the children to form a circle, and, after joining hands, he would switch on the current so as to pass round the circle. He was very fond of children and would amuse them in all sorts of sport. When nine years of age, he started as a stoker at Ynysfach, then went to the fitting-shop at Penydarren Works. Afterwards he entered Lloyd's School, where he subsequently became an assistant teacher. Above Greenfield House is a large field known as " Cae'r Shop "—one of the fields enclosed from the waste land by Mr. Evan Evans for his farm ; this was done before the building of Greenfield House, hence its name of " Cae'r Shop." On the other side of the road was the Factory Pond, which was filled-in about 1860, and two fields on the same side were fenced-in and added to Penyrheol Farm : these were known as Williams' Fields. Now we reach the residence of Mr. David Nicholas, who has taken a keen interest in the welfare of the neighbourhood and has always had the good of the village at heart. He had an inclination towards Unitarianism, but is a faithful attendant at Salem Congregational Chapel and Sunday School and a staunch supporter of the good cause. In discussion at the school or elsewhere, he does not attempt to introduce foreign thought of a controversial nature. He learnt his Welsh at the Sunday School, and his Welsh is worthy of a Welshman. At the first night-school held under the School Board, he began to study English, and soon became interested in the works of Dr. Channing, Emerson, and others. Previous to becoming a fireman he worked underground in various capacities. For 25 years he occupied the positions of fireman and overman of the Cyfarthfa mountain levels, and is an authority on old workings and water-courses from the Canaid Brook to the outcrop. There is one specially outstanding act to his credit which places him in the class of the gallant heroes of the mine. On June 19, 1899, which was the Tuesday following Mabon's Day, it appears that both the night and day firemen arranged to make the morning inspection together, as they knew of a dangerous place in the return airway of the drift at Cwmdu, where occasionally an accumulation of firedamp would surely be found if there was any interference with the air current. On reaching this place, where a fall had previously occurred, but a passage made over the top of it, they found that they could not pass through the gas that had accumulated there. When they tried from the other side they were still unable to pass, so they returned to where the air entered. One of the firemen, Mr. William Roberts, who knew the position well, climbed the fall with Mr. David Nicholas following closely behind. As it was impossible to use their lamps at the top of the fall, David Nicholas held out his light as near as he dared, while William Roberts stretched over the top down to the other side of the fall to try and find out what had blocked the air-passage. Nicholas, finding his calls unanswered, realized that something was wrong, and immediately found that Roberts had been overcome by the gas. No time was to be lost. Nicholas sprang forward, scrambled over the fall, heedless of the noxious gas, and, gripping firmly the feet of his unconscious companion, tugged with all his might, but was unable for a while to move him. After a supreme effort he got him free, and proceeded to drag him back over the fall to a place of safety, where he soon regained consciousness. But for this prompt and courageous act, his colleague would undoubtedly have succumbed from the effects of the gas. Both are still alive and well although well over 70. David Nicholas is a direct descendant of the noted Shôn Llewelyn of Cefn Coed, who was admitted into membership of Cwmyglo Church in 1713, at the age of 22. Shôn was born in 1691, just when Cwmyglo Chapel was built, and three years before Edward Harri of Gyrnos was born at Cwmyglo Farm.

Shôn Llewelyn's daughter married Harri of Garwdylau, formerly of Pontycapel. Harri had three sons—Shôn, Gwilym and Edward. Gwilym Harri was the great-grandfather of Professor

Dan Price, Dowlais. Edward's daughter, Margaret, married Thomas Shôn of Cefn, and there were seven children of the marriage. Shôn Thomas Shôn, the eldest, was a great tenor, and succeeded in taking the prize at Abergavenny Eisteddfod. He was also choir conductor at the old chapel, Heolgerrig. Of the seven children, the youngest was Ann, who later became the mother of David and Margaret Nicholas.

CHAPTER VIII.

PISTYLL-Y-WAUN—NANTYGWEUNYDD—DAFYDD MEURIG, RED LION—JOHN AND MARY SIMON, BELLE VUE—THE NEW SCHOOL — DAVID ABRAHAM—THE NEW BAPTIST CHAPEL — WILLIAM GEORGE — OLD TRAMROAD—THE SQUARE—CASTELL RHYS Y CRYDD—YR HEN DY.

ABOUT a hundred yards above Salem Chapel, and opposite the home of David Nicholas, there is a lane between two fields known as Heol Pistyll y Waun, at the far end of which is the old Cardiff Corporation puddle or clay field, better known as "Y Patch Clai." On reaching the brook, which I believe to be the original Nantygweunydd referred to in the maps, a flight of stone steps is seen, surmounted by a fence which can be easily negotiated. Formerly there was a stone stile at the top of the large stone steps. A few yards above was the "pistyll," at one time a very noted spot in the neighbourhood, and from which a great deal of water was carried for domestic purposes, especially during periods of drought, previous to the installation of an efficient water supply from the reservoirs. After crossing the stile, we enter the Gwaunydd known as Waun y Cwmni and Waun Penyrheol. A portion of the flat meadow here has been for many years the playing-field for children on the occasion of their day or Sunday school treats. It was customary to ask permission from the owners, but there never was a refusal to allow young or old to divert themselves, and the old "pistyll" came in for much attention from the more thirsty picnicers on hot summer days. During the last forty years this flat meadow has been excavated considerably by the Cardiff Corporation for the purpose of procuring boulder clay for use at the Cwmtaff Waterworks. It was first opened about 1886 or 1887. The clay at this spot is a strong, dark-blue material, of good quality for puddling purposes, but very stony. The thickness of the bed is from 14 to 15 yards, being undoubtedly clay and stone drift deposited during the glacial period. It is interesting to study the stones, for intermingled with the clay are old red sandstone from the ramparts of the Breconshire Beacons, fragments of mountain limestone and millstone grit, and big conglomerate boulders, all of which underlie the coal measures in their geological sequence. Thousands upon thousands of tons of these rock fragments are to be seen intermingled with clay, shale and ironstone, and, upon close examination, scratches can be seen on the surfaces of many of them, due to the scraping during their transit at the base or edges of the ice flow.

During the building of the latest reservoir at Llwynon, Cwmtaf, the engineers considered the clay too stony, and therefore changed their field of operations. Before the working of the clay, this part of the meadow was practically flat, and when the Merthyr Volunteers first came into existence, about 1800, they sometimes met here to drill, under the captaincy of Watkin George; occasionally, too, the Aberdare contingent, under Captain Tom Rees, of Werfa Farm, would meet the Merthyr men on this flat ground near the Factory Pond. One can just imagine the usefulness of Pistyll y Waun on such occasions in quenching the men's thirst on hot summer days after the fatigue of laborious drilling and inspections. The Volunteers of those days were disbanded in 1812, and sterner regulations came into force regarding their reorganisation. In 1842, Cwmyglo Uchaf and Waun Penyrheol were rated together at £35 10s., the occupier being William Crawshay.

The next place of note is the Red Lion Inn, owned and occupied many years ago by David and Mary Meyrick—David, I believe having built the premises. The pair were known locally as "Dai a Mari Meurig, Red Lion." David was the son of Dafydd and Mari Meurig, who lived at one time at the Old Six Bells, but afterwards built a small house for themselves on the mountain side near the top of Waun Penyrheol and just off the main road to Aberdare. This house had an earth-and-lime floor, and was known as "Trap y Defaid," from which they subsequently moved to Tranch Bach. While living here, a son of theirs, named Richard (Dick Meyrick), was suffocated on the old tramroad between the smith's shop, Penyard, and Swansea Road, in 1865. There is an old story concerning Dick, when the family lived at "Trap y Defaid," to the effect that when working at the Forty Colliers' Level, which was close by his home, he continued to work for three whole weeks, day and night, with the exception of mealtimes in the morning and at night; and this feat was followed by a period of there weeks' carousing. Dick was a brother of Dai Meurig, Red Lion, who was the eldest of a large family and worked at Werfa Colliery. Dai was a natural rhymer in his native tongue although unable to read or write. His rhyming was spontaneous, and he was possessed of very witty poetic instinct. For example, one day when the room was full of visitors, and noticing the tomcat seated comfortably in front of the fire, he burst forth :

Wel, dyma gwrcyn hynod !
O flaen y tân myn e fod,
Yn pobi ei lyged
Yn lle dala llygod.

On another occasion, there being no work at the colliery, Dai and his friends on the way home partook rather too freely of the strong ale at the wayside inns. Upon reaching the Red Lion, who should be waiting but Mari, ready to shower upon him a woman's wrath. When the outburst had ended, Dai seized his chance and broke forth :

Dyma Dafydd Meurig enwog,
Yn dod tua thre heb ennill ceiniog ;
Ni bydd Mari fel y gôg,
Ond 'sgyrni fel 'sgyfarnog.

One morning, at the Werfa Colliery, Dafydd Meurig was about to proceed to the workings with his fellow-workmen. It was the custom for someone to have a ride on the back of Ned, the donkey, every morning from the stables at the pit bottom to the "face." On this particular occasion the privilege of a ride fell to the lot of old Dafydd Dafis, and on passing Dafydd Meurig, the muse of the latter was immediately kindled, and turning to his friends with profound seriousness, he said :

Wel ! wel ! dyma Dafydd Dafis digri',
Pwr ffelo ! wedi ffeili.
Bydd Mr. Evans ddim yn gros
I rido asyn Iesu.

The Mr. Evans mentioned was the minister of his place of worship. The Red Lion has been kept by various people since the death of David and Mary Meyrick, the most noted of whom were William Jones (Will Jones, Patchwr) and Mary his wife.

Next we reach another public-house, the Belle Vue, built many years ago, and kept at one time by John and Mary Simons, afterwards of Brynteg Farm. They took possession of the farm from William Richards in 1842. Mary was the daughter of Hywel Giles, who lived at Pencoedcae Brynteg, and both—as has already been mentioned—hauled small boats along the old Cyfarthfa Canal. John and Mary Simons had three sons—Howel, who lived at Cefn Coed ; Rowley, who lived at Tai Mawr ; and John, who lived and died at Brynteg. There were also three daughters—Cecilia (or " Sis Fach "), who kept the Belle Vue after her parents and died at Brynteg, May 12, 1914, at the age of 80 ; Ann, and Margaret. John Simon Jones, of Cefn Coed (who is now 74) was Cecilia's eldest son, and Evan Jones (the present owner and tenant of the Belle Vue) was the second son. A little way above, on the right of the main road, is the Winchfawr Road, known in the past as Heol Bwdlac. On the left of the main road is Heolgerrig Mixed School, opened August 29, 1907. Just above the school is Calfaria Baptist Chapel, built in 1901—1902, the opening ceremony taking place August 24, 1902. I shall deal more fully with the history of the school and of the Baptist cause when dealing with Horeb.

The first dwelling-house on the main road after passing Heol Bwdlac is occupied by Mr. Lewis Pugh, the only one left of the Pleasant View family. In the next house lived some noted families, the first of which I can recall being that of Evan Jones (Brecon) two of the sons of whom entered the ministry. In 1862 Evan Jones wrote and had published a history of Salem Church and the locality, and later the family removed to Troedyrhiw, about 1870. Another who dwelt there was Edward Edwards (Cilhepste), who became one of the Latter Day Saints, and the family went to Salt Lake City, Utah, U.S.A. Afterwards Mrs. Mary Morgan and her aged widowed mother, Mrs. Mary Nicholas, lived there. The former was the mother of Rees, Nicholas, Tom and Obadiah Morgan, and several daughters. Mrs. Mary Nicholas was also the grandmother of Mr. David Nicholas, previously mentioned. Nearby lived Philip Howell and Jennet his wife, both of whom were buried in Seion Churchyard, Twynyrodyn. Philip was a brother of William Howell, of Georgetown, who adopted and brought up the late Mr. Evan Lougher. In the same house afterwards lived William and Hannah Evans, Ty Mawr. William worked as a miner at the Winch Fawr Pit, and had lived at Ty Mawr—a house at Cefn Isaf, Pontycapel Road. We now reach the house in which the late William Walters, the guard, and his family lived many years ago. Afterwards they moved to Hendrefawr Farm, where William died on October 21, and Ann his wife on October 23, 1911, both being interred on the same day at St. Mellons. Then Mr. and Mrs. Rd. Evan Davies, Six Bells, took possession, after William Walters left Heolgerrig, and lived there until Danyronen was built. Mr. Richard Davies filled the important position of traveller for many years under his uncle, Mr. Christmas Evans, of the Six Bells. Mr. John B. Jones and his wife, Rachel, occupy No. 94, Heolgerrig, where they carry on a bakery and grocery business. Three doors above lived Richard and Hannah Williams. The former was contractor of one of the mountain-side patches. In the old days, it was customary to employ girls to do the collecting, filling and tipping of mine at the patches. Jennet, the eldest daughter of Richard Williams, was one of those thus employed, and one day was injured so severely by a fall that she succumbed on reaching home. A sister of the deceased, born after her death, was given the same name, and is still alive in the person of Mrs. Jennet Owens, of the Market Tavern. The accident happened in August, 1866, Mrs. Owens being born on October 10, 1866. Morgan Williams (Mocyn Philip Howel) was also a son of Richard and Hannah Williams and a grandson of Philip Howel. Morgan was a famous quoit-pitcher of the old school. In his time the custom was to hold both quoits, one in each hand, and then to throw them alternately from a fixed position. He was successful in most of the numerous matches in which he participated. On September 28, 1887, he emigrated to Washington State, U.S.A., and died there on February 4, 1889. It was the custom in the out-of-the-way mining camps, such as those of Burnett aud Carbonado, for friends or relatives to dig the graves : so the work of preparing Morgan's last earthly resting-place was carried out by his brother-in-law, W. H. Pedler, and Thomas Havard, a friend—both natives of Heolgerrig.

In the same house — 96, Heolgerrig — lived another family noted for the part it has taken in assisting the religious cause in the neighbourhood ; this was the family of David and Catherine Abraham. David, born at Llansamlet, was the son of Rhys Abraham, who eventually brought his family to Merthyr and opened some of the Cyfarthfa levels on the mountain side, one of which has always been known as Lefal Rhys Abraham. David Abraham worked underground until he was 80 years of age. He was small in stature, but possessed strong mental powers ; in manner he was quiet and unassuming, and was, unfortunately, very deaf. His brother was Billi Rhys Abraham (Abraham Fardd). David married Catherine Lewis, who, when a young girl, was one of the members of the first Independent church at Heolgerrig in 1838. Kitty Abraham continued to be a member until her death on January, 4, 1880, at the age of 62. David, her husband, died on February 25, 1895, aged 82 years. They had seven children—Ann, Rhys, Thomas, Samuel, David, Ivor and Gwen. Ann married Richard Williams, a collier ; but afterwards they carried on a grocery business at Penywern, Dowlais, and at Georgetown, and took up their residence at Hill House, George Street, Georgetown. Rhys Abraham died at 10, Abermorlais Terrace, on December 8, 1926, aged 79. He was well-informed, quiet, and very unassuming. For some years he occupied official positions in some of the collieries of Japan. He was a glutton for knowledge. The outward journey to the Far East was made via the Mediterranean, the Suez Canal, and the Indian Ocean ; while on the homeward journey he crossed the Pacific Ocean, the American Continent and the Atlantic Ocean. Thus he had encircled the globe completely. When a lad, Rhys had worked with his father at Lefal Benni and afterwards at Blaennant. He had received but scant education, and his success in after life was entirely due to his own efforts and perseverance. He was appointed a clerk at one of the Rhondda Valley collieries, and while there he was advised to apply for a colliery post in Japan, which he was successful in obtaining. After his return home he found that his health had been somewhat impaired, so he never entered the mine afterwards. He was a faithful member of Salem Chapel, in which he filled many important positions. Until he went away in 1873, he had been precentor and choir-master. Some time after his return he was appointed secretary of the church ; and, on the death of his brother-in-law, Mr. Richard Williams, he was made treasurer—a position he held for 18 years, until he was compelled to relinquish it, on the grounds of ill-health, after long and faithful service. In 1900 he was made a deacon of the church. In 1892 he wrote a "History of Penyrheolgerrig," and pointed out the pressing needs of the village ; and this essay was very highly complimented by Mr. Ebenezer Williams (Gwernyfed) for its high standard of composition. In 1908 Mr. Rhys Abraham read a most interesting paper on the progress of the Independent cause at Heolgerrig from its commencement in 1838. He had gone to a great deal of trouble to collect information for his paper, and the records which he succeeded in getting together were invaluable to the church, and his memory will always be cherished by its members.

Thomas Abraham was very pious. Unfortunately, he lost the sight of one of his eyes whilst engaged as a striker with the blacksmiths at Ynysfach Works.

Samuel Abraham was a tenor of distinction. I remember him singing " Chwifio'r Cadach Gwyn " very effectively. He married Mary, daughter of David Daniel Thomas, Cwmyglo, and sister of Thomas Daniel Thomas (Tydfilfab). During the 1881 " National " at Merthyr, Samuel was lying seriously ill in bed, and requested that the bed be moved as near the window as was possible so that he could hear the choirs singing at the Eisteddfod at Penydarren Park. He died on November 11, 1881, aged 28 years.

David L. Abraham (the third son) has been endowed with a deep sense of religious instinct, largely inherited from his religious mother. When only 23 years of age he was made a deacon of Salem Chapel ; and when his mother heard of his appointment, she addressed him thus : " Now, my boy, you have been appointed to a very important office. Your life must be a pattern to others. You must serve your God and Master and your church in the best way you possibly can." I am of opinion that he has carried out his mother's advice to the letter and nobly fulfilled her fondest wishes. He was precentor and choir-master at Salem for some years. In 1900 he moved to Skewen to take up a position as colliery under-manager under Mr. George Dawkins, who was the manager. The latter hailed from this neighbourhood, and had lived at Coedcae, Brynteg and Llwynyreos, and had married the daughter of Lewis Williams of the Wern. After 19 years' faithful service at Skewen, where again he was a strong pillar in his church, David Abraham returned to Merthyr and was placed in his former position as deacon of Salem Church, Heolgerrig.

Ivor Abraham possessed a rich bass voice, and was of great service to the church and various concerts. He settled down in a bakery business and as sub-postmaster at Penydarren. When Merthyr was granted its Charter of Incorporation in 1905, Mr. Ivor Abraham was elected one of the members of the new Borough Council, and afterwards was made an Alderman for the Penydarren Ward.

Gwen Abraham was married to Samuel Evans, son of Howel Morgannwg, and both went to America. All the boys had worked underground in various capacities.

In the next house above lived Thomas and Cecilia Jones. Thomas was a miner and carpenter, while Cecilia was a midwife. Both were very religious and staunch members of Salem, Thomas serving as deacon there for many years. Being a carpenter, he would carry out many small jobs for his church. For instance, he made a slicing-board, furnished with a large knife, for cutting bread and cake at tea-parties, which is still in use after 50 years' service. The family lived about 60 years ago at Tai Canol Uchaf, and Thomas worked as a collier and fireman at the level known as the "Forty Colliers." At present there is living in this house one of our most noted local bards in the person of Tom J. Jones (Telor Tâf). His "englynion" flow with ease, and on many of my tramps I have had the pleasure of his company. He enjoys them immensely, and his muse is every ready to break forth into appropriate verse, much of which has appeared in the local press.

On the other side of the road, above Calfaria Chapel, there is a field and a block of nine houses, the field belonging to Mr. David Peters. The first house in the block was built by William George, who was one of the first to open patches on the mountain side, therefore he built stables for his horses near his house. In due course he left the district for Gilfach Goch, selling his interest in the property to Morgan Isaac Morgan, of Cefn, who built additional houses and converted the stables into dwelling-houses ; and henceforth the court was called Morganstown. The most noted who lived in the largest house were David and Margaret Williams. David was the son of "Billy Pencae," son of Morgan W. Williams of the Wern. He worked many years at the Werfa Colliery, and was afterwards contractor in many of the Cyfarthfa levels and pits.

Before leaving Morganstown I should like to mention a most original old character, by name John Shôn Rees, who lived there for many years. He had worked all his lifetime in the Cyfarthfa collieries, was quite illiterate, but became very religious, and for a long period acted as door-keeper of the Sunday School at Salem. John was a regular attendant at all church meetings, and when addressing his Creator in prayer, would always refer to the great blessings bestowed upon the children of men, and that the greatest of all was " y perl gwerthfawr " (the precious pearl)—the soul. In prayer he was very earnest, and in conversation very original. He would introduce into his prayer something like this: " Os na ydyn' ni'n byw yn ddigon da wrth Dy fodd, newid ni fel newid gaing "—the custom being with the miners, when a wedge had become well-worn, to take it (" y gaing ") to the blacksmith's shop to get a new one in exchange. When the work of rebuilding the Six Bells Brewery was in progress, after the fire, John was told that they were putting in a very large boiler for brewing beer; so he said: " Nid oes eisiau iddynt gael un mor fawr er fy mwyn i; bydd tebot yn ddigon mawr i fi." John, however, liked an occasional glass of Six Bells XXX, known as " Cwrw Six." On one occasion, when seriously ill, his son John asked him if he would like a drop of beer. " Ydw'n wir," said the father, " cera i 'mofyn hanner peint o'r XXX." Whereupon the son said in a serious tone: " Nhad, mae un X yn ddigon cryf i ddyn fel chwi, siwr o fod! " If one should meet John on a winter's morning and address him thus: " Shwd y'ch chi heddi, John? Mae'n sharp iawn, on'd yw hi? " he would instantly answer: " Wel, mae'n rhaid bod yn sharp gyda hi! " He was very ready with his answers at all times. John Shôn Rees was made a deacon at Salem in 1900, and died on July 8, 1904.

On reaching the crossing of the old Cyfarthfa Tramroad, a large open space is seen. This is now the 'bus terminus, and there is ample space for the 'buses to turn. Fifty years ago all the house-coal supplied to the Cyfarthfa workmen living in the upper part of Heolgerrig was weighed here. In the centre of what is now called " The Square " was the " Lodge Fach " used by the weighers. One night during the 1875 strike, when people were in dire need of coal, a number of men decided to enter the old level nearby, known as Lefal Rhys Abraham, which had been discontinued. Meeting on the Square and discussing the matter, it was decided to make an inspection of the lodge before the men entered the level. On entering the lodge a match was struck, and to their surprise they found two policemen—Bell and Coombes—there. Needless to say, the raid was cancelled.

The first 'bus service that ran to Heolgerrig was started by Mr. Thomas Simcox ten years ago. The start was a very modest one, the vehicle being a small Ford car, afterwards fitted with a hood, which plied for hire between Victoria Street, Merthyr, and the Square, Heolgerrig, and occasionally Winchfawr. Later, the inauguration of regular 'bus services by the Merthyr Corporation from Victoria Street to the Square proved a valuable boon to the residents of this district. The Square is about 939 feet above sea-level, and the distance from the Iron Bridge is about a mile and a quarter, the difference in altitude between these two points being about 385 feet. On the left of the Square is the road leading to Cwmdu and Blaencanaid. This takes us to Pwll Cornel-y-Waun, Pwll Cwmdu, the old Drift at Cwmdu, and the present Cwmyglo Drift. About 100 yards from the Square there was an old house known as "Yr Hen Dŷ," rebuilt about five years ago by Mr. John Davies, who did the whole of the work himself, as he is a mason by trade. The alteration has been creditably carried out, and the name of the house is now Gernant, the brook which passes by being Nant-y-Gweunydd. The old house was built over a hundred years ago, and the people who lived there were Modryb Pali Dafydd, and Shôn—known as "Shôn Shishwn," a nickname he gained from his employment entailing the use of the shears at Cyfarthfa Works. Both were deeply religious, and it was at their house that the first religious cause was commenced in 1838. The cause at Heolgerrig was not mooted by one particular sect. There were three—an Independent, a Baptist, and a Wesleyan, all being members of different churches in the town of Merthyr, but living in this neighbourhood, concerned in the founding of a common meeting-place. They decided to hold the weekly meeting at "Yr Hen Dŷ," the home of Shôn and Pali Dafydd, and many others joined the movement, and soon a Sunday School was held there. Step by step the numbers increased, irrespective of sect, but the majority were the ones who were members at Bethesda. Every one who joined the cause at "Yr Hen Dŷ" was asked as to which church he or she would like to enter. Very soon the membership became too numerous in comparison with the accommodation; therefore the little meeting-house, called Bethlehem, was built at the rear of the Brewery, and was opened in 1840. William and Marged Evans also lived later at "Yr Hen Dŷ."

On the right of the Square is a plot of ground known as Waunfach, which was until recently an open playing space for local children, but now it is enclosed by a fence. The oldest house in this locality is Tŷ Lawrence, built about 1850 by William Williams (Yr Hen Will). Lawrence and Diana Peters lived there for many years, and David (their son) still lives there. Next comes the house of "Henry'r Teiliwr," built in 1873. Henry was the first tailor in this district. In the large garden at the rear of this house was the "Cobbler's Castle" or "Castell Rhys y Crydd." Years ago it was the custom for some people to build their own houses, although they were far different to the modern type of dwelling. Such, for instance, was "Trap y Defaid," with its earth-and-lime floors, built by old Dafydd Meurig. Rhys y Crydd built another of these houses for himself and family. Rhys, and Ann his wife, had two sons—Rhys and William. Rhys married, and moved to Dowlais, before the building of the "Castle" by the old cobbler. This Rhys was a notorious spinner of yarns. Upon paying a visit to his companions he was asked: "Wel, shwd mae'n dod 'mlân yn Dowlesh, Rhysyn?" To which he replied: "O, ma' lle pert yn Dowlesh. Ma' shwdwrs ym mhob cwtch yna, a ma' 'yna un hen general mawr: mae e'n cwato yn y dydd ac yn cered pob man yn y nos." "Wel," meddai un o'i gyfeillion wrth Rhys, "beth y'ch chi'n pido troi mâs gyda'ch gilydd, fel un llaw, yn y nos?" "Dyna beth netho ni," ebe Rhys, "a daliwyd yr hen walch, a rhwymwyd rhaff am ei wddwg ef, a chlymwyd ef mewn twlc mochyn. Fe dorrodd y rhaff, a chiliodd yr hen fochyn." "Wel, tebyg i beth oedd y gwalch?" gofynnai un o'i gyfeillion. Meddai Rhys: "Gallwn i feddwl wrth ei weld nad oedd dim coesau ganddo. Ma' nhw yn galw '*bugs*' arni nhw, a mae'n debyg ma' hwn oedd y '*Big Bug*.' Yn y bore yr oedd pawb yn cymryd wilbar a rhaw i glirio'r rhai a laddwyd yn y frwydr yn ystod y nos!" "Rhysyn," meddai un o'i gyfeillion, "dyna un o Nhw eto."

When the "Castle" was finished, Rhys and Ann Williams, together with their son William, and Catherine his wife, moved into the new house. The house was very small, measuring but five yards by three yards inside, with two windows and one door. The walls were thick; the fireplace large, with wide hobs, while one could easily climb through the chimney; the floor was very rough. At one end was a bed, while the other part was used as a kitchen and a workshop. Above was a small loft, the height of which was only about five feet, and covered over with a thick thatched roof. William and Catherine occupied the room upstairs. This was the "Cobbler's Castle" or "Castell Rhys y Crydd," as people humorously dubbed it. Rhys and Ann were very religious folk. Both attended services in town before the Baptist cause began at Heolgerrig. On Sunday both would turn out together. Ann would be wearing a dark gown, an old-fashioned cloak, and a white cap covered with a wide-brimmed hat. Rhys would be wearing heavy boots (of his own make) with buckles, a pair of coloured stockings, yellow breeches, a calf-skin waistcoat of many colours, a dark-green tail coat with brass buttons, a handkerchief around his neck, and a tall hat upon his head. Rhys was small of stature and possessed a full, frizzly, white beard. Thus arrayed, they would walk arm-in-arm to their place of worship, and always carried with them a large green whalebone umbrella. Truly a most quaint pair!

One Saturday, a little girl called at the "Castle" with a pair of boots to be repaired, and asked Rhys when they would be ready. "O, yfory, merch i," said the cobbler. "Na, na; mae'n ddydd Sul yfory," intervened the pious Ann. "Ydy, Wir Dduw," said Rhys. And turning to the girl, he added: "Wel, trynydd, merch fach i!"

Rhys had hanging up in his house a horse-pistol, which filled children with horror when they gazed at it. When Rhys was annoyed, he would threaten terrible things with this weapon. But there was another weapon in his possession more terrible still to us children than the dreaded horse-pistol, this being "dryll gam Rhys y Crydd." This wonderful fire-arm was able, it was said, to shoot around corners even, so one could never be said to be safe unless right out of range. Rhys and Ann were very fond of singing, often taking part in a duet at penny readings and small concerts at Horeb Chapel. Ann would sing the bass part, while Rhys—who had a thin, slender voice—would sing the treble. Many of the old people used to sing together in this way, among whom were Meyrick Rees and Griffith Hall and their wives.

CHAPTER IX.

THE BAPTIST CHAPEL — ELEMENTARY SCHOOL — WATER SUPPLY—PATCH PEN-Y-WAUN—GWENNI'R MEISWN—HYWEL MORGANNWG—THE FIRST POLICE STATION—TAI'R GILFACH —TAI TOMOS SHON—CORNER HOUSE INN—WATER TANK — CWMDU COTTAGE — ALFRED WILLIAMS—PLEASANT VIEW.

AT the beginning of 1872 some of the Baptist brethren living in the district, who were members of Ainon, Tabernacle, or Ebenezer—the Baptist chapels in the town—thought that the time had arrived to institute a church of their own at Heolgerrig. Consequently these enthusiasts founded a Sunday School in a long room at the rear of the Corner House Inn, the premises being occupied by Thomas and Jane Nicholas. The following were among the first who met to worship here :— Evan James, one of the prime movers in advancing the Baptist cause ; John and Benjamin James ; John Thomas Rees ; Thomas and Jane Nicholas. Very soon others joined them, and within a few weeks the Rev. John Vaughan, minister of Ainon, Georgetown, was invited to preach at the new Baptist school-room. He accepted the invitation, and on Sunday, February 4, 1872, the first sermon of the Baptist cause at Heolgerrig was delivered, the minister taking for his text the 16th and 17th verses of the 3rd chapter in the Book of Malachi. The Sunday School was held in the morning for the convenience of the Rev. John Vaughan, who preached the sermon at the afternoon service, and thus the cause was firmly established. In a very short period, the school-room was unable to accommodate the increasing number who came there to listen to the Word of God, so these good people sought more commodious premises. Not far away was an old chandling-house, which had been used for the making of candles and was now vacant. There was a dwelling-house attached to this building, and the whole of the property was for sale. The Baptists thought that this would suit them admirably, so they bought the property from Mr. Austin L. Jones for £95. Mr. Jones had married Mary, the widow of Thomas Lloyd, who lived in this isolated dwelling. Her daughter, Mrs. Hicks, now of Thomastown, and who is about 70, informed me that her father, Thomas Lloyd, died when she was only nine months old and the youngest of four children. Mr. A. L. Jones then married her mother, and bought up the small dwelling-house as well as sufficient land to build a chandlery. He also kept a small grocery business in Wellington Street, which was supervised by Mrs. Jones after the chandlery came into being, while he looked after the chandling operations. When the chandling business ended, the place was offered for sale. The new owners cleaned out the building, white-washed the walls, and fixed some benches for seating accommodation, and the place became a decided improvement on their former meeting-place.

The first sermon was preached in the new place of worship by the Rev. John Vaughan on November 8, 1872. But one of the prime movers in the young church was not destined to see the realisation of his fondest hopes, Evan James dying in September, 1872, this being a terrible blow to the cause. The first baptism by immersion in this district took place on Sunday afternoon, July 7, 1872, when Rees Jones was baptised by the Rev. John Vaughan in Winchfawr Pond before a large concourse of people, the minister taking as his text John i. 25 : " Why baptisest thou them ? " After the ceremony a thunderstorm raged, and rain fell in torrents. Within a year or so of commencing worship in the new building, it was decided to carry out some improvements in the way of fixing new seats, providing a pulpit and an immersion tank, and suitable decorations—the total amount expended, including the purchase price, being £300. After the renovation, the opening ceremony took place on September 21, 1873, when the following ministers took part in the proceedings :— Rev. John Lloyd, Merthyr ; Rev. David Davies, Dolau ; Rev. J. Parish, Abercanaid ; Rev. O. Waldo James, Merthyr ; Rev. T. D. Mathias, Bethel, and the Rev. Thomas Owen, Penydarren. Although the members only numbered eight at the commencement, at the time of this re-opening the membership was 58. The Rev. J. Vaughan of Ainon Church continued to minister at Horeb, as the chapel was called. The following are mentioned as being deacons : Philip Howell, Griffith Hall and Henry Jones. The Baptist cause flourished for some years under the ministry of the Rev. John Vaughan, then something happened which proved very painful to the members : their ardour was damped and their faith almost shattered at this turn of events, with the result that they disbanded and the cause collapsed.

In 1897 the church was re-established after a few months of house-to-house meetings. On October 24, 1897, they returned to Horeb, and, after satisfactory arrangements had been arrived at between the owners and the School Board, the church was reconstituted on January 6, 1898. The four deacons appointed were : Griffith Hall, Thomas Williams (Patch), Henry Harris and Thomas Richards. The first baptism in this reconstituted church took place on March 6, 1898, when twelve people were immersed, among them being George Llewelyn and R. H. Richards. In the following May, Evan Davies, who later became one of the strongest pillars of the church, was baptised. The need now arose for a more substantial place of worship, and this materialised in the erection of a fine chapel on the main Road some 200 yards below Horeb. The new chapel—which cost £1,210 and was opened on August 24, 1902—was named Calfaria; and on April 28, 1903, the Rev. Thomas Davies (Treforest) was instituted minister. The ordination of Mr. Richard H. Richards at Calfaria took place on February 28, 1916. He was followed by the Rev. Noah W. Hopkins (April 22, 1917), who accepted an invitation to shepherd the church and attend one Sunday in the month.

In 1876 a deputation, representing Heolgerrig and Clwydyfagwyr, appeared before the School Board, pressing the need of schools for the children of those localities. The deputation consisted of the Revs. John Vaughan and I. J. Evans, and Mr. John Evans (John o'r Darlwm). They so impressed the Board of their needs that steps were taken to find suitable accommodation. After some correspondence, a letter was received from the Rev. John Vaughan offering, on behalf of the Baptist church, the use of their chapel and vestry at Horeb (the old chandlery) at the Board's own terms (£12 per annum), and an agreement was reached. The school was opened on August 13, 1877, the number on the register being 73. This was the beginning of the Heolgerrig Mixed School. The first headmistress was Miss Thomas, daughter of Supt. Thomas, and she was assisted by two pupil teachers—Miss Margaret Thomas and Miss Margaret Davies. On the same day Clwydyfagwyr School was opened with 62 children on the roll, the headmistress being Miss M. A. Rees. On April 17, 1878, Miss Watkins was appointed headmistress at Heolgerrig at a salary of £65 per annum, but in 1882 this was increased to £70. In 1883 the school was improved by the addition of the old dwelling-house and its conversion into a classroom at a cost of £230. Miss B. Morgan was appointed head of the Infants' Department at a salary of £45 per annum. In May, 1888, the School Board got into legal difficulties concerning the rent of the school property, but they satisfied the court as to whom they were obliged to pay the rent once the owners established their legal right to the property.

On November 9, 1888, the school was lent gratis by the Board for evening school purposes, the supervisor being Miss M. A. Jenkins, Nantgau. Many happy hours were spent there, and I could mention many names of old and young persons keenly interested in the movement. Miss M. A. Williams was appointed head of the Infants' Department on March 26, 1890. On October 11, 1895, the evening school was recommenced under the direction of Mr. R. G. Price, who was then senior assistant at Abermorlais, and at this time it proved to be one of the best evening schools under the Board. Mr. R. G. Price became headmaster of the day school on January 22, 1897, upon the appointment of Miss Watkins (who had served the Authority faithfully and well for 19 years) to Caedraw. The evening school was still directed by Mr. Price and an able staff of men teachers.

On October 9, 1903, Mr. W. T. Williams was appointed headmaster at Heolgerrig, upon the removal of Mr. R. G. Price to Gellifaelog, from which he went to the largest school under the Board—the Dowlais Central School. About two years after Mr. Williams was appointed to Heolgerrig the Board decided to build a new school, which was opened on August 29, 1907. It was built by Mr. D. W. Davies, Cardiff, at a cost of nearly £4,000. The opening ceremony was performed by His Worship the Mayor, Coun. F. S. Simons (the second Mayor of Merthyr). It was a mixed school, with accommodation for 250 scholars, while the old Horeb School became the Infants' Department. Upon the retirement of Mr. Jenkin Jenkins, Mr. W. T. Williams was appointed head of Abermorlais Boys' School on October 3, 1919, after a fine record of 16 years' faithful service at Heolgerrig. Both he and the late Mr. R. G. Price took a very active interest in the welfare of the village. During their respective headships they resided in the district and took a deep interest in the social life of the community, and both were masters of the Welsh language, which was a distinct advantage to them in their labours. Their names will always be cherished by those whose school careers came under their masterly guidance, as well as by those who had the pleasure of working with them for the public good.

Mr. Williams was succeeded by Mr. Tom Thomas, another very conscientious worker during his brief stay (4½ years), but who did not reside in the district. On the removal of Mr. Thomas on February 26, 1924, Mr. D. L. James became the new headmaster, but his stay again was very brief (4½ years). In August, 1928, the present head, Mr. Josiah Lewis, was appointed to the school.

The following are the names of the heads of the Infants' Department :— October 7, 1884—Miss B. Morgan (£45 per annum) ; March 26, 1890—Miss M. A. Williams ; April 16, 1898—Miss H. T. Bowen ; July 6, 1900—Miss B. Rees ; 1907—Mrs. E. Denny (14 years) ; 1920—Miss Gertrude Jones ; 1924—Miss Margaret Evans ; 1927—Miss Alice Gordon, who was the last headmistress. On May 24, 1928, the old school was closed and the children transferred to the Mixed School under the care of Mr. Josiah Lewis.

Attached to the old Baptist chapel are three houses known as Horeb Cottages, the one adjoining the chapel having been built for the convenience of the Rev. J. Vaughan. Under this house was a well, known as Ffynnon Mari Lloyd after Mary Lloyd who occupied the old house previous to the erection of the chandlery. Before her, Thomas and Ellen Jones—parents of William Jones,

Patchwr—had lived there. A great deal of water was carried from this well for domestic purposes ; and when the first of the three houses was built, the well-water was conveyed to the road-side by means of pipes for the convenience of the consumers. In 1887 a typhoid epidemic broke out in the district, and scarcely a household escaped the consequences of its terrible ravages. The water of Ffynnon Mari Lloyd was suspected by the Medical Officer of Health, and was immediately condemned, the spout being done away with. The first victim of the typhoid scourge, D. W. Jones, who lived at Horeb Cottages, died on January 31, 1887. It was argued that a field above the well, after being manured, would in wet weather drain into the well, thus causing pollution. Subsequently the water was conveyed into the covered brook close by.

The whole of the upper portion of Heolgerrig was dependent for its water supply for domestic use upon wells and water-spouts, such as Ffynnon Cae'r Williams, Ffynnon 'Rhen Dŷ, Pistyll Cwm-du, Pistyll y Gwter Felan, Ffynnon Mari Lloyd, Ffynnon Calvart Winchfawr, Pistyll y Ffos Las, and others. Later, the Board of Health deemed it advisable to extend the public water supply as high up as was possible, and a stand-pipe and tap was placed at the roadside opposite the site of the old Horeb spout. Just at this spot a temperance hotel was built, about 1876, on the left of the main road, by a working man named David Ben Lewis, but the speculation proved a failure. This was later named Park View, and the Rev. J. Vaughan rented the house and lived there pending the erection of the house adjoining Horeb. A little way above is a house built in 1871 by Dennis Perrin, a contractor who had opened several levels on the Cyfarthfa side of the mountain, and had previously lived at the Old Six Bells. Dennis Perrin met with a fatal accident at Blaennant Old Pit.

On the right side of the road and at the rear of Horeb is a block of four houses known as Tai'r Garnant or Jones' Terrace. The first house was built by John Williams (afterwards of Pont-storehouse), and he was succeeded there by Edward Morgan, William George, and Richard Williams. John Williams, Llifiwr, as he was called, was one of the founders of the Independent church at Yr Hen Dŷ, and his widow, Mari Treharne, lived many years ago in a small house below the Travellers' Rest. Then William and Margaret Jones, Garnant, bought the property from John Williams —and Mrs. Jones (who is now over 83) still resides there. The daughter of William and Nellie George, she came to Merthyr from Cardiganshire when very young. Her parents and those of Mr. Henry Owen, valuer and auctioneer, were closely related. Mr. Henry Owen and Mrs. Jones being cousins. William George came to the district first, and opened mine patches at Pantywaun, later spending a short time at Cyfarthfa Ironworks. He then opened a patch on the mountain-side above Heolgerrig, and sent for one of his daughters to assist him by carrying messages and performing small jobs. Margaret was the one who came, and she remembers carrying tools from the patch to be sharpened at the smithy while her father was at work at the patch. She must have been about seven years of age before she could be of any assistance to her father. Eventually the whole family came and lived at Twyn-yrodyn, where William was staying. If we assume that Margaret came here about 1853 at the age of seven, we can also assume that the patches were commenced before 1853. Richard Thomas and William George opened adjacent patches at the same time, the one belonging to the former being next to the road and to the right of it. After some years, William George sold his interest in the patch to David Owen of the Glove and Shears, and opened another patch more to the north. The patches of Rd. Thomas and David Owen were afterwards worked into one, and, later, Richard Thomas worked another on the south side of the road. Some years afterwards William George's son-in-law, William Jones, joined him in this underatking, which in due course became known as Patch William Jones y Patchwr. The mine, used for the production of iron at Cyfarthfa, was brought down from the patches along an incline which crossed the main road near Beiliglas and then joined the Cwmdu tramway near Cornel-y-Waun.

Now William Jones, Garnant, was a son of "Shon o'r Garnant" of Cwmtaf, who settled in this neighbourhood when William was quite young. I have been informed that Shon was a cousin of David Williams of Penyrheol Farm, and by whom he was employed as his farm bailiff, living in one of the Old Six Bells houses. William remembered going about over the Penyrheol land with his father in company with David Williams, who was also at this time part owner of Werfa Colliery. William worked at the Werfa for many years, mostly as a haulier, and was one of the workmen previously mentioned who helped to fill-in the Factory Pond about 1860. He died February 6, 1921, aged 79 years.

The next place of note is what is known as The Patch. Here are two small houses remarkable insofar as they were built by a woman named Gwenni, who justly gained for herself the title of "Gwenni'r Meiswn." She had built other houses—one near Winchfawr Pit, and another on the present site of Twyn Carmel and known then as Tŷ Shon Tai Cypla. Gwenni was a remarkable character. In her manner and her actions she was to all outward appearance more man than woman. It was only her attire that betrayed her sex. She smoked and drank just like a man, was rough in her ways, and able to do a hard day's manual labour.

Proceeding further into The Patch, we come across a small cottage together with a new house built on the site of an old thatched dwelling formerly known as Penywaun. I gather that the original Penywaun was a little to the north-west of this place. The owner and occupier was Richard Edwards, another of the founders of the Independent cause at Yr Hen Dŷ. The surrounding land was Waun Shon Dafydd Ifan, hence the name Penywaun. Some years afterwards a small house was built nearby, in which lived Thomas Williams and Letitia his wife, the daughter of Rd. Edwards. Thomas Williams, who came there from Gellideg, was a Baptist, and his uncle, Thomas Jones, was one of the founders of the local Independent cause in 1838. The former was very innocent in his ways, but this did not detract from his being a very staunch supporter of the Baptist church at Heolgerrig. I remember an incident that happened when Thomas was applying for his old age pension. After his application form had been filled-in, he took it to the office of the pensions officer, where he was questioned thus :

" A fuoch chwi yn America, neu allan o'r wlad hon erioed ? "

" Naddo, yn fy ngwir," said Thomas, meekly.

" Wel, a fuoch chwi yn y carchar erioed ? " asked the officer.

" 'Nes i ddim erioed a fu'n achos i bolisman ddodi ei law ar fy ysgwydd, fy machgen i : naddo, yn fy ngwir," was the innocent reply of the saintly old gentleman.

The present owners and occupiers of the new Penywaun House are Mr. and Mrs. James Thomas. James is one of my tramping companions, and is greatly interested in many of the things we come across. His bardic descriptions of our tramps are most interesting and amusing, especially where he refers in one to the crossing of the Taf Fechan River near Gurnos Quarry, where he failed to get a firm footing and had to execute a pole jump backwards to the bank. In this old patch the 6ft. coal seam crops to the surface, and has been worked in the patch and a level nearby.

Coming back over the brook to the main road, we come next to a house owned and occupied by John R. Lewis, fruiterer. This was built by Howell Evans (Hywel Morgannwg) over 60 years ago, and was occupied by him for many years. Previously he had lived successively in two small houses just above, from which he had the name of Howell Tŷ Bach. Howell was a learned man and a bard of no mean standing, having many noteworthy bardic efforts and literary compositions to his credit. He was employed as a weigher at the Upper Blaennant Pit. For some years he was deacon and secretary of Salem Church, and also secretary of certain friendly societies. He took part in many eisteddfodic competitions, and I have read the essay he sent in to the Adulam Eisteddfod in 1867, the subject being " Y fantais sydd gan ferched i ddarostwng Meddwdod, a'r lles deilliedig iddynt o hynny yn y Sefyllfa Briodasol." The following "englynion" are two chosen from an imaginary letter from a young man to his dearest love:

"Breuddwydio yn brudd ydwyf—yn dyner
Am danoch pan gysgwyf;
Mae'm calon union ynwyf
O'r gwraidd dan glafaidd glwyf."

"O na chawn yr hyn wy'n chwennych,
Hyn ofynnaf i chwi'n fynych—
Dyma yw: eich cael yn briod
Yn ddiwyrni rhyw ddiwrnod."

"Ydwyf, I—— Jones, Rhif 1af, Heol Gobaith,
Yn Nyffryn Gostyngeiddiaf Cariad,
Swydd Unigedd."

In response to these tender appeals, Gwen, the object of his affections, proposes certain conditions upon which the match can be arranged, somewhat after this style:

"After having a wife, are you prepared to do your duty by her, respect her, and be faithful to her in all circumstances? Are you prepared to be a total abstainer? as I am determined to have a sober husband or not one at all." These conditions were absolutely essential ere tying the nuptial knot, so Gwen replies, referring to the blessings in store:

"Mae'n ffaith nas gwelwyd yn y byd
Anwylach deulu'n byw yng nghyd;
Duw'n hawddgar a'i darparodd,
I'r eithaf mae wrth fy modd.

"Nid oes planed ysblennydd,
Na lleuad wen, na lliw dydd,
Holl ser, na Gwener gwiwnef,
Na dawn ail i hon dan y nef."

Howell's house was the first police station at Heolgerrig, although there had been parish constables long before the days of P.C.s Bell and Coombes. Not very long ago I saw one of the clubs which they carried, belonging to old Rhys y Crydd. Lawrence Peters had also been a special parish constable. The clubs bore the initials V.R. P.C. Phillips was the first policeman to live in the police station, followed by P.C. Bowen, who, after a short stay, left for Gilfach Goch. Then came P.C. Bowens, and his successor, P.C. Thomas, was the first to live at the new police station in Meirion Place. Afterwards P.C. Stephens was in charge, and upon his retirement from the force, P.C. T. Davies took up residence there, and is still the officer in charge of the district.

Next we come to a block of undoubtedly very old houses, although alterations have recently been carried out in the two lower ones. The third house had a stone roof, whereas the others were thatched and very small in size. The stone-roofed house was owned until recently by the Cyfarthfa Company, and may have been erected as a shepherd's dwelling, or possibly as a residence for one of the mine officials ; it is an older and larger house than any of the others. I remember John and Mary Jones living there, and also William and Mary Nicholas living in the top house. Billy was an official at the levels and patches, and was known as " Billy Buttons." At the rear of these houses is Plas-y-Darren, a very old house in which lived, many years ago, Rees Williams (Gwenddwr). His widow married her brother-in-law, Wm. Rees Williams (Gwenddwr), who was a brother of Rees, Richard and Ann Williams. Later, John Thomas Owen rebuilt the house, and Mathias James lived there for a while. Then Thomas Hopkin, a working man of unusual strength and ability, bought up the property and built additions to it. Thomas was commonly referred to as " Yr H " (meaning Hopkin), and also "Y Left," because in debate he always swung his left arm when the argument became a bit heated. His son-in-law and grand-children still live there. A little way behind is Pantynhowell, a block of four houses built over 70 years ago by Griffith Griffith y Gof, and in which Benjamin Samuel, a fireman at the Werfa Colliery for many years, lived long ago. These houses are built in a large hollow in which the 6ft. coal seam crops to the surface. Near this place there was a small house built, one of its walls being the outcropping rock, and Howell Morgannwg lived there for some time. Returning to the right of the main road, there are to be seen three houses built by the Thomas Shon family. Here lived Evan Dafydd, as well as Henry and Sarah Jones, who occupied the middle house. Henry was one of the main pillars of the Baptist Church at Heolgerrig, of which place of worship he acted as secretary, and was also a deacon for many years. Two of his children—Mrs. Eleanor Jones-Hudson, at one time one of our leading singers, and the Rev. W. R. Jones (Pelidros) — have distinguished themselves in the musical and literary world. Thomas Jones, Hendrefawr, also had lived in this house previously. Next door lived, successively, John Morgan, Benjamin Brace, and Benjamin Griffiths (Ben yr Hitchwr). It is interesting to note here that in this small area there lived at least six members of Caradog's memorable choir, which competed at the Crystal Palace in 1872 and 1873, and won the coveted cup and a thousand guineas. These were Benjamin Griffiths, Robert Watkin Jones, John Howell Evans, John Watkins, Samuel and Rhys Abraham, and Samuel H. Evans. Some years after his great triumph, I remember Caradog paying a visit to Salem, Heolgerrig, to take part in a concert in aid of Robert Watkin Jones, who was in poor health.

On the southern side of the road are Tai'r Gilfach, built by John Thomas (John o'r Gilfach), who had come with his parents, when John was very young, from a farm in the Neath Valley called Y Gilfach—hence the name John o'r Gilfach. Fifty or sixty years ago the sport of cock-fighting was greatly indulged in locally, and John, together with Will Dai, Wat Twm Williams, William Richards and others, were keen enthusiasts. While working at Blaennant Pit in 1871, John o'r Gilfach met with a serious accident, fracturing one of his legs, from the effects of which he did not completely recover, and died September 10, 1873, aged 59. In a part of the bottom house in Tai'r Gilfach, Rhys y Crydd had lived before he built the "Cobbler's Castle." One day, William, the son of Rees, met with an accident at work, and it fell to the lot of one Thomas Twmi to convey the sad news to the old cobbler. Now the bearer of the news was a very jocular old chap, and upon reaching the house of Rees he told the latter that his son Will had been badly hurt about the head. "How much has he had?" inquired Rees, eagerly. "Well," said Thomas bluntly, "I think he must have had his head off!" Whereupon Rees looked very glum, and Thomas Twmi took his leave. Some time later, Will met with another accident and was borne home on the shoulders of his fellow-workmen. His father met them at the garden gate, and, turning to his injured son, asked: "Faint wyt ti wedi gael, Will?" Someone whispered: "Mae e' wedi torri ei glun, siwr o fod." Upon hearing which, Rees turned sharply towards the luckless Will and said: "Wel, ma' arna' i want dy ladd di, Will!" On another occasion the old cobbler and Ann his wife quarrelled, with the result that she and Will decided to part from Rees. Will and his mother hired a donkey and cart to take away their belongings; and, after the loading was completed, the old cobbler came to the door with his gun and calmly fired point blank at them. The shot, a blank one, was probably intended as a parting one.

Margaret Thomas, widow of John o'r Gilfach, and known locally as Pegi'r Gilfach, died in January, 1909, being about 80 years of age. John, her son (who is now over 70), and Elizabeth Thomas, her daughter-in-law (who is nearly 80), still live in Tai'r Gilfach. Mrs. Thomas, who is a widow, has been a faithful church member all her lifetime, and has a son in the ministry—the Rev. David Thomas.

Close by is Plas-y-Gog, an old house in which lived David Jones Walters. His mother, Mari Thomas Shon, came of a very old local stock, and was one of the religious enthusiasts at Yr Hen Dŷ; and David himself became one of the deacons. Morgan, his son, was a contractor at Blaennant. In this locality, a hundred years ago, there were very few houses above the Six Bells. The chief were Plas-y-Gog, Cwmdu Farm, the old Cyfarthfa house at the roadside, Plas-y-Darren, the house of Thomas Lewis, at the top of Waun Shon Dafydd Evan, Ffos Las, the house of Howell Rees, and a few beyond Winchfawr Pit. Near Plas-y-Gog was a very old level—Lefal Cornel-y-Waun—where the yard and 4ft. coal seams were worked extensively, as can be judged by the huge tips which were the result of its working. About 200 yards south of the level was another level—Lefal Thomas Lewis—working the yard seam. Here, many years ago, David Thomas of Werfa, and William Thomas, Brynawel—both conspicuous figures in the South Wales coal industry—were employed for some time. Cornel-y-Waun Pit is also quite near to Plas-y-Gog. This pit was sunk, throught the coal seams to the mine, but, for some reason or other was not extensively worked. Both the Cwmyglo and Canal Levels (working the 9ft. seam) passed here. The last banksman or lander who worked this pit was David Thomas of Gelli-Ddu, Cwmyglo; and after the pit was closed, he went to work at Gethin Pit, being employed there at the time of the explosions in 1862 and 1865. His daughter Jane was employed as a tipper at Cornel-y-Waun Pit when it was closed. She is now over 80, and, with her husband, Lewis Phillips (also over 80), resides at Pencoedcae, Cwmyglo. Lewis has a wonderful memory of local incidents in the mines of the neighbourhood.

Returning to the main road, we reach a row of houses originally built as stables by David Owen when working at the patches, but afterwards converted into dwelling-houses. Many years ago, Margaret and Edward Thomas Shon lived here, and afterwards Kitty, widow of Benjamin Jones; then Robert and Elizabeth Jones lived there. Elizabeth had been a faithful member of Salem Church since childhood, and, in her younger days, being a fine singer, on many occasions assisted the choirmaster. She died on January 3, 1928, at the advanced age of 87.

Next, the Corner House Inn is reached. Attached to the old inn are several houses, built about 1855 by Thomas Nicholas. Timothy and Ann Davies first kept the public-house. Then William Jones, afterwards bailiff of Wern Farm, kept it for some time—his sons, John and William, being then quite small. John and Rachel Passmore then moved in; but in 1874 the public-house was discontinued. It was at the rear of this house that the Baptist cause was initiated at Heolgerrig. In one of the adjoining houses lived

James and Letitia Meyrick. "Shams," as he was called, was a son of Dafydd Meyrick, Trap y Defaid, and a brother of Dafydd Meyrick, Red Lion.

Just here, but on the other side of the road, is the Corporation water tank, built in 1906 to ensure a continuous water supply to the more elevated parts of the district. At night the water flows quite easily and keeps the tank full, and is capable of supplying the intended area for upwards of four or five days by means of a return pipe. The water supply for Winchfawr comes direct from the main at a point a hundred yards below the tank.

Following the main road, we pass Nant-y-Gweunydd and the Old Incline down which the mine was conveyed from the patches to Cwmdu tramway. The surface on the right becomes very broken just here. To the left are Beili Glas House, built by Wm. Harris, and Tŷ Dafydd o'r Wern, the latter having been built by Dafydd. The present occupier is Tom Tong. A little to the south are Tai Herbert Lloyd, where Evan James, the founder of the Baptist cause, lived and died in 1872. William R. Morgan also lived here, and died on March 6, 1881. Another noted person who lived in this spot for many years was Alfred Williams, who died July 3, 1907. Originally the family belonged to Sennybridge, then moved to Aberdare, and finally settled down in Merthyr. Alfred Williams was very intelligent and had received a fairly good education. He worked at the Plymouth Collieries, but, being rather ambitious, he determined to gain all the knowledge possible, studied and succeeded in gaining a first class colliery manager's certificate. He served in the capacity of manager at various collieries, held the secretaryship of certain friendly societies, and for some years was checkweigher for the mountain levels, Cyfarthfa. Being of the Catholic faith, he attended the Catholic Church at Merthyr. His wife, Margaret, was a daughter of Dafydd and Mari Meurig, Trap y Defaid, which was not far away. From Tai Herbert Lloyd to Pleasant View there are no houses, the mountain-side being rather bleak, bare, broken and uninteresting. Pleasant View, at the summit, was built in 1858 by Lewis Pugh, who was a contractor at Blaennant and also at Cyfarthfa. He was a man of much practical knowledge, and died on January 4, 1905.

CHAPTER X.

FROM THE WATER TANK TO WINCHFAWR — THE WATER-COURSE—WINCHFAWR POND—FFOS LAS—TAI'R POWND — WINCHFAWR PIT—LEFAL GEORGE—TRAMWAY—TAI'R MYNYDD — TAI'R CWM — LEFAL MYNYDD—WINCHFAWR DRIFT.

FROM the Corner House there is a road branching off to Winchfawr, and just above and running parallel to it is the water-course known as Y Gwtar Felan, thus named because of the yellow texture of the clay bed from the main Heolgerrig road to the Winchfawr Pond. The water which is drained into the water-course feeds the Winchfawr Pond. Above the water-course the 4ft. seam crops to the surface, and the yard seam below. Many years ago the patch tips were so high and the pressure was so great that, in many places, owing to the slippery clayey foundation, they slid for considerable distances—in one part right to the edge of the water-course, a distance of about 100 yards. Before reaching the pond, we pass a very old house which is a little distance above the old house of Penwaun Shon Dafydd Evan. It is uncertain as to when or by whom it was built, but it is evident that it existed before the sinking of Winchfawr Pit in 1825. The first people of whom I have any account living there were named Edwards, Mrs. Edwards being the sister of Thomas and David Owen, of the Glove and Shears; but later they went to Blaenllechau. Afterwards, Thomas Lewis, contractor—father of Kitty Abraham and of the first wife of Dafydd Lewis of the Cwm, near Penrheol Farm—came there to live. Then William Jones, Patchwr, lived there when he was working the patches above, and reared a large family of boys and girls. One of his sons was the late Rev. Thomas Gwilym Jones, of Bridgend, who died on June 11, 1929. After relinquishing the pastorate of the Bridgend English Congregational Church, he became the principal of the Bridgend Commercial and Preparatory School. Until he had passed the age of 20 he worked as a collier; but, bent on bettering his position in life, he commenced attending preparatory schools, spending three days a week at school and working during the other three at a level near his home. He thus equipped himself with sufficient education to enter the ministry. At Carmarthen College he gained high honours during his course, and subsequently paid a visit to America, where he graduated as B.D. at Yale University. When the pastorate of Market Square Church, Merthyr, fell vacant, he was a candidate for the post along with the Rev. D. Eurof Walters.

To deal fairly with the subject of the distinguished sons of Heolgerrig, there would be necessary some additional chapters, but as space is limited I must curtail my accounts.

After William Jones, David Edwards, Tai Mawr—a descendant of Edward Harri of Gyrnos and Cwmyglo—came there to live, and during his occupation the house was rebuilt. Previously he had occupied the Travellers' Rest Inn. The present owner and occupier of the property is Mrs. Mary Jane Pugh, the widow of William Pugh of Pleasant View. A few yards further on, near the pond, was a small thatched-roofed house known as Tŷ'r Pound, in which the famous runner, Hywel Jacki Dafydd, lived. "Hwlyn," as he was called, was the son of John Davies (Jacki Dafydd) and a native of Clwydyfagwyr. He was a miner by occupation. In his time, foot-racing was greatly indulged in, and there was intense enthusiasm and excitement over a big race. When "Hwlyn" ran a mile race at Penderyn with another champion called "Bedwas" (as he hailed from Bedwas), and was defeated by a narrow margin, it is said that the people of Clwydyfagwyr, Cefn, and Heolgerrig, who had backed their local champion to win, lost very heavily. Even pigs were wagered by some of the Clwyd people upon the result. In another race, he met Meredith, a tailor, of Aberdare, who conceded him 10 yards start in 200 yards ; but Hywel was the winner, and could have beaten him on level terms. In his last race in this country he defeated John Forry of Aberdare quite easily. Hywel Jacki Dafydd was born in 1817 and was an all-round sportsman, delighting chiefly in running, jumping, and quoit-throwing. In 1857, with his friend Sam W. Powell, he went to Australia, from which country, some years later, he sent home a gold ring to be competed for in a race by his old companions. Rowley Simon, Brynteg, won the coveted prize. Later, Hywel was accidentally drowned in a lake.

In 1872 William and Mary Morgan lived at this place. It was here that Griffith y Glo was living at the time of the tragedy at Clwydyfagwyr, and I believe that his family was the last to occupy the house before it fell to ruins. Nearby a house was built in 1870 by Edward Paul Griffiths, and just above, below the patches, were a few small cottages. The first of these was built by one Thomas Shon over a hundred years ago and was known as Y Ffos Las. Thomas Shon had married Margaret, daughter of Edward Harri ; and Ann, their daughter, was only three years old when her parents went to Ffos Las, which had not then been completed. As Ann was born in 1820, the house must have been built in 1823. Afterwards more houses were built close by. The following are known to have lived there :— Thomas and Margaret Shon, Wm. Williams, Thomas Owen, Morgan Shon Rees, Thomas Dandle, Ben and Kitty Jones, John and Betty Tinker, Henry Davies (Cwmdu), and John and Margaret Daniel. The children of the latter couple still live there, and David (the son) told me that when carrying out repairs they found the date 1756 carved on an old door. I don't think this has any bearing upon the date of building the house, but there may have been an earlier building of some kind. The name Ffos Las was discontinued many years ago, and now the spot is known as Cwm Hwnt.

Now we reach Winchfawr Pond, which is quite near the old Winchfawr Pit, or Pwll y Mynydd, and which has been the scene of many drowning tragedies. Many years ago, Rees, son of David Evans, was drowned there. Another fatality took place when Mathew Webber, son of Morgan Webber and brother of John, Rees and Morgan Webber, was accidentally drowned on September 20, 1872. He was a haulier in the "six-feet" level nearby when Dafydd Jones (Briddy) was contractor, and, as was customary after his day's work was over, took the horse to the pond to have its feet washed. The horse, however, proceeded too far into the pond, and, failing to turn him around, Mathew got off his back and tried to make for the bank. Had he remained on the horse's back he would have been safe, for the animal swam right across to the other side. On March 10, 1886, another tragedy took place here, a young lad named Lawrence—grandson of Lawrence Peters and a nephew of David and Thomas Peters—being drowned as a result of the ice breaking under him.

Winchfawr Pit, or Pwll y Mynydd, was the first pit sunk for Cyfarthfa, in 1825. There were some levels working in the neighbourhood before this date, but most of the cottages were built after the sinking of the pit. Henry Kirkhouse was the engineer responsible for the sinking, and it was in his time that most of the Cyfarthfa mine and coal pits were sunk. Some are of the opinion that Rowland Thomas (Idris Ddu) carried out the work, or at least had a hand in the sinking operations; but as he was born in 1789, I doubt whether he was not too young to undertake such a big task. There is evidence, however, that he worked there between 1840 and 1850. He was an exceptionally intelligent and experienced miner, as can be gathered by his evidence placed before a Commission in the House of Commons on February 19, 1849, on the question of explosions in mines, and also from the Treatise which he wrote on the South Wales Coalfield in 1835 and again in 1853. The depth of the pit was 100 yards, passing through all the coal seams below the "six-feet," which cropped out at the surface just here. At Penydarren there was another Winchfawr Pit sunk at the same time by Homfray. A winch would mean a windlass worked by hand, water or steam-power, with cranks geared to a drum around which the hoisting-rope or chain was wound. Afterwards the pit itself came to be called a winch or winge. Richard Rees Walters—grandfather of Mrs. Mary Williams, Blaencanaid—sank Graig Pit, or Pwll y Witw, on the Graig Estate. David Tasker sank Pwll Tasker, Glyndyrus, and also Gethin Pit. Mine levels had been worked in the direction of Winchfawr long before the pit was sunk, and it reflects much on the ability of Henry Kirkhouse as a surveyor when we find that, after making a survey above and below ground, he made a circle in chalk on the roof of the mine level at the very spot it was intended to bore the shaft. So accurate was the survey that the shaft and the chalk ring coincided. During the sinking operations, the raising and lowering of the workmen and material was effected by means of a whim or windlass, the power being supplied by a horse traversing a circular beat. After its completion the pit was worked on the water-balance principle, which has been previously dealt with, and a great quantity of water was required for its operation. In 1830, just before the Merthyr Riots took place, times were very bad, and, according to Wilkins, "at one pit near Penyrheolgerrig, which had only recently been sunk, there were 60 or 70 persons employed, and all but three were receiving parish relief." This pit was Winchfawr Pit. On July 22, 1845, it was the scene of a terrible accident in which four men were sent to their doom through the breaking of a winding-chain. It happened on a Tuesday morning, when the miners were being lowered to proceed to their daily toil. The following lost their lives in this disaster: Watkin Jones (aged 61), Lewis W. Powell (31); Dafydd Dafis (27), and Thomas Jones (23). Samuel W. Powell, brother of Lewis, had gone back just before the descent of the cage, to get some candles which he had left in the lodge at the pit-head, and this incident saved his life. He was the companion of Hywel Jacki Dafydd on his trip to Australia. As the cage descended, the chain broke somewhere in the shaft, and the four poor miners were hurled to the pit-bottom.

I have been told that Mary Nicholas lived in the little thatched house at the southern end of the pond, known as Tŷ'r Pownd, before the pit was sunk. For some years she was employed at the pit-head, later marrying Billy Nicholas, a miner who afterwards became a mines official, and both went to live in the old farmhouse at Cwmyglo, which was the residence of the sub-official of mines. Previous to going to Cwmyglo, the pair had kept a public-house between the Iron Lane and the shop of Herbert Lloyd in George Street, Georgetown, and afterwards they kept the public-house at Jackson's Bridge. Mary Nicholas was born about 1797, and died at the advanced age of 95 at 89, Heolgerrig, on April 13, 1892. She remembered the pit disaster very vividly. When Billy and Mary left the old house by the pond, their daughter Mary, and William Rees Morgan, resided there for the next 23 years.

It was at this house that the changing of garments took place during the baptismal services held by the Rev John Vaughan in 1872. Billy Nicholas was of very small stature, and his grandson, Rees Morgan, told me that one day he tried to put on the old man's coloured tail coat which had been carefully preserved by his grandmother; but alas, he was unable to get even his hands into the sleeves!

Rowland Thomas (Idris Ddu) lived at Winchfawr between 1821 and 1831, and there three of his children—Aneuryn, Mari and William—were born. It was during his stay there that the pit was sunk, although I have been unable to find in his writings any reference to the sinking. He had worked in some of the levels before the opening out of the pit. Amongst his manuscripts there were dated copies of his pay-sheets, and these give us an idea of quantities and prices so that we can compare them with mining figures of the present day. The output is that of Rowley and his helper monthly:

MOUNTAIN PIT (WINCHFAWR).

	£	s.	d.
May 4th, 1844.			
Mine: 34 tons at 6/4 per ton	10	15	4
Coal: 32 tons at 1/5½ per ton	2	6	8
Total	13	2	0
Deductions	9	4	9
	£3	17	3
June 1st, 1844.			
Mine: 30 tons at 6/4 per ton	9	10	0
Coal: 7 tons 1 cwt. at 1/5½ per ton	0	10	3
Stones	0	0	9
	10	1	0
Deductions	5	10	9½
	£4	10	2½
July 27th, 1844.			
Mine: 24 tons at 7/1 per ton	8	10	0
Coal: 26 tons at 1/7 per ton	2	1	2
4 yards at 5/- per yd.	1	0	0
	11	11	2
Deductions	5	3	6½
	£6	7	7½

These statistics show the very low wages prevailing in Rowley's time. The quantity of mine reckoned is that sent down periodically from stock, then it was weighed monthly. It is interesting to note that coal and mine were worked together, and that the amount of the deductions from wages monthly amounted to about half the total earnings of the miner and his helper.

Near the pit was a ventilating shaft, sunk many years after 1825. The level which passed under the pit was known as Lefal Tomos Morris, and commenced near the long arch, near the mountain level screen, over which the B. & M. railway passed. It provided a certain amount of ventilation, but the air shaft was sunk in addition. It passed through a tremendous thickness of coal, the result of the overlapping of the 9ft. and 6ft. coal seams, due to some disturbance of the strata, the thickness of the coal being from 20 to 24 feet. As this shaft was not sunk to the level of the pit-bottom, wooden tubes were utilized to connect the shaft to the pit, but this method of ventilation did not seem to have been successful. The flueman attending to the furnace was William Dafydd, who lived close by. The 6ft. seam was also worked in a level between the pond and the house of Will Hopkin. This house (the one nearest the pit) is another built by Gwenni'r Meiswn. Winchfawr Pit fell into disuse in 1877, and in 1924 it was completely dismantled. On the other side of the road is the site of another old house, later rebuilt by William Thomas (Wm. Shenad), in which lived one of the victims of the pit accident, Lewis W. Powell, who was a son-in-law of Watkin Jones. Mary and Isaac Jones afterwards resided there before moving to Tŷ'r Pwll, from which they went to the Green Dragon Inn at 76, Heolgerrig. Behind Tŷ'r Pwll is another very old house, that of Howell Rees. Now at the time of Hwlyn's famous race, this house was wagered and lost upon the result! In it a large family was reared, and the majority of the children lived to a ripe old age.

Just at the turn of the Winchfawr Road is the site of a noted old level known as Lefal George, where the 9ft. and 6ft. seams of coal were extensively worked. The road passes between the stables, which belonged to the level, and the rubbish tip. South of this level there has been a geological dislocation of the underlying rocks, thus making it difficult to locate the various seams. These were some of the colliers and hauliers who worked at Lefal George: Wm. Rees Morgan, John o'r Darlwm, Dai Phil Harri, John Shon Rees and Phil Bach (his son), William Davies (afterwards manager of Coedcae Collieries, Rhondda), Wat and Morgan H. Rees, Dai Morus, Thomas and Hopkin Hopkin, Evan Hopkin (father of the preceding, who was killed at work in their presence when Thomas was eight years old), and John Morgan. At the earlier period of its working, female labour was employed in the tipping operations. Margaret Hopkin and Mary Nicholas doing this work. This was a feature of local industrial history which seems almost incredible in these days. Here is an incident concerning some of the workmen in this level. One morning, when ready to enter for their day's work, they heard the yelping of hounds hot on the scent, so a number of them, relegating coal-hewing to the background, decided to join in the sport. John Shon Rees and his son Phil, after following the pack for some hours, gave up and decided to go nutting at Penmoelallt, where, unfortunately, they fell into the clutches of the keeper, who told them he would have to report them for trespassing. "All right, do as you like," said John as he made off. Next morning at the level, Dai Morus, the haulier, when changing John's tram, handed John a sheet of paper which had been folded carefully. "Beth yw hwn, Dai ?" asked John. "Gŵr boneddig mas wrth wddwg y lefal ofynnodd i fi am fynd ag e i John Rees," answered Dai. "Darllen e, Dai," continued John. "Na, na ; i ti mae e, Shon," said the haulier, and added, "Ble buoch chi ddo ?" "Mo'yn cnau," was the answer. "Wel, gwelodd rhywun chi ?" asked Dai. John had to admit that the keeper had caught them. "Wel," said Dai, "*summons* yw hi, siwr o fod." Turning to his son, the old fellow addressed him thus : "Dere, Phil bach, crynho y twls 'na. Awn lawr trwy Gwmnedd ar unwaith ag i'r America." And to the haulier he said : "Ffarwel, Dai. Dyma'r pip diwetha arnat ti !" And forth they went. But Shon was at work next morning, as usual, undoubtedly thinking that his crime did not after all warrant such a lengthy trip as the one proposed.

Quite near here is the old house of Thomas and Mary Rees. Mary's mother, Gwenllian Williams, died at the very ripe age of 103 years, and had been a church member for over 80 years. Next comes the house of Evan Hopkin, one of the old colliers of Lefal George, and in this house was reared a large family of robust sons and daughters, one of the latter being Margaret, who had lived in this small place all her lifetime. She died, at the age of 83, on April 8, 1925. The girls, in their younger days, worked on the tips and in the patches. Now we reach the old house of Daniel Jones, father of Rees and Isaac Jones. Rees, who was very religious and a very witty character besides, was baptised in Winch-fawr Pond in July, 1872. Once, Rees and his friends with their sweethearts went on a day trip to Bristol, and while there, much to the consternation of the party, Rees' young lady got lost. In his anxiety, Rees approached a policeman and addressed him thus : "A welsoch chwi ferch â gŵm glas yn rhywle ?" Rees was built on small lines and was known as Rees Bach Jones o'r Mynydd, so we can just imagine the perplexed look on the face of the big man in blue on being asked.

The most westerly house at Winchfawr is that of Thomas Morgan (Rhigos), and one could write half-a-dozen pages in relating reminiscences of this family. One day, the late Dr. Biddle, called there on business, and tried to bargain with Mari Rhigos for a certain cockerel. He offered her half-a-crown, but Mari, not understanding English, thought that he was trying to get the better of her, so she said : " Na wnai i, yn wir. Ydw i wedi cael cynnig pymtheg (1/3) am dano yn barod, a chaiff e ddim mynd am lai na hynny ! " An old tramroad, now disused, leading to the patches and levels which have been yielding house coal under the direction of John Harris, then his sons Richard and John, and —at present—Thomas Lewis, passes near here. All the coal seams crop to the surface in this neighbourhood. Carn-y-Frwydr is within a few hundred yards of this spot. After passing the old stables at the bend of the Winchfawr Road, a row of houses is seen on the left, in which the Lewis family, of Cwmdu, lived. William Lewis, with his sons—David, John and Rees—and three or four married daughters, lived in this neighbourhood. The former was one of the early members of Clwydyfagwyr Church. Rowland Thomas also lived in one of these houses between 1821 and 1831. William Shon Powell, a very enlightened Christian and a deep thinker, also lived quite near and reared a large family. On the right of the road lived the parents of Councillor John Williams—Thomas Williams, his father, being one of the early members of the Baptist cause at Heolgerrig. Another son, Wm. Williams, who had been employed at the Waun Level, went to America on May 22, 1888, and became a minister of one of the churches there. Thomas Williams was at first an iron-worker at Cyfarthfa, later working underground at Blaenllechau, and was in the pit at the time of the explosion in 1867. He died at Winchfawr, January 10, 1908. Others who lived here were William Toulds, William Rowley, Daff Dafis and a number of sons.

The next place we come to is The Cwm, which undoubtedly is one of the oldest places in this district. There were ten houses in all, near each other, known as Tai'r Cwm (3), Tai Becca (2), Tai William Rowley (4) and People House. The latter was very small and in a very bad state. Dr. Edward Davies had occasion to call there one day, and, on entering, vented his wrath upon the occupants. " Do you call this a house ? " he said. " It is more like a cow-house. A post here and a post there. D—— such a People House ! " Just below is the old house of David Evans, a mine official, who was secretary of the Clwydyfagwyr Church for over 40 years. Nearby is the old Lefal Mynydd, driven in a southerly direction through the cross measures, starting on top of the Gellideg Rock. It was either from here or from Lefal George that a large block of coal, weighing 4 tons 3 cwts, was conveyed to Cyfarthfa Castle on January 6, 1850, having been taken from the district in which Sam W. Powell was working. The latest undertaking in this district was the Winchfawr Drift, worked under the direction of the following in turn: William Harris, J. Lewis, W. Edwards, and Thomas and David Peters.

CHAPTER XI.

JOHN BRYANT, THE TANYARD—WILLIAM STEPHENS, THREE HORSE SHOES—KIRKHOUSE MEMORIAL HALL—NATIONAL SCHOOL—COURT OF REQUESTS—TAFF VALE BREWERY—OLD CANAL HOUSE AND DOCKS—DR. DYKE'S REPORT ON THE WATER SUPPLY—DYNEVOR ARMS—OLD CATHOLIC CHURCH—BETHEL CHAPEL—AINON CHAPEL—GEORGETOWN — BEN JONES (MERTHYRFAB) — PONTSTOREHOUSE BRIDGE—CHAPEL ROW—CYFARTHFA CHAPEL—WAGON SHED AND DOCK—OLD OFFICE SCHOOL—NANTYGWENITH ST.—TURNPIKE GATE.

LET us now return to the Canal Bridge, Penry Street, and continue along the northern side of Aberdare Road. The old road crossed the brook between the Canal Bridge and the Corner House Inn and followed the right side of the brook, but the making of the Glamorganshire Canal altered things entirely. At the Corner House, afterwards known as The Woolpack, in the angle formed by the junction of Dynevor Street and Aberdare Road, lived the Bryant family, who carried on the Tanyard business for many years. John Bryant was High Constable of Merthyr in 1859. Mrs. Anthony, an old resident, remembered skins being carried from the Tanyard to be dried in the sun in a field above the site of the present Cyfarthfa Church. That must have been before tipping took place upon that particular spot. Close by is the old hostelry known as the Three Horse Shoes, kept for many years by that quaint old personality, William Stephens, who was greater in girth than he was in length. Will Stephens, as he was popularly called, was, in spite of his extensive waistline, a great all-round sportsman. He hunted hares and rabbits with his dogs for many years over the land of the Cyfarthfa Company. The entrance to the stables of the old hostelry, at the side of Aberdare Road, took the form of a big stone arch, which does not fail to attract the attention of strangers passing by. What could have been the purpose of the building at the head of the flight of steps which rises alongside and over the archway? This is a very unusual sight. William Stephens died December 29, 1884, aged 61, and his wife predeceased him December 3, 1868, at the age of 42.

Next we come to the Kirkhouse Memorial Hall, a fine building erected in memory of the Rev. Howell Kirkhouse, M.A., late Vicar of Cyfarthfa Church. The hall was opened by Mr. Henry Parfitt on February 5, 1923, during the vicariate of the late Rev. E. R. Davies, B.A. It was built on the site of the old Cyfarthfa National School, built in 1843, with accommodation for 300 children, in Dynevor Street. The school pence, the fees paid for the children's education, were deducted from the wages of the workmen at Cyfarthfa Offices. St. David's, a Church of England school, built in 1845 in High Street, was a similar school.

The next place of importance is Mr. Coffin's house, where at one time were held the Courts of Requests, which functioned somewhat like the more modern County Courts, but on a much smaller scale. The Clerk of the Court was Mr. Coffin, and the Stipendiary Magistrate was Mr. Bruce Pryce, who was later succeeded in this capacity by his son, Henry Austin Bruce. The latter became M.P. for Merthyr on the death of Sir John J. Guest, and, in 1873, upon his elevation to the peerage, became the first Lord Aberdare. Coffin's house is a prominent building and stands at the corner of Coffin's Court, Dynevor Street. During the 1831 riots it was the scene of severe disturbances. At the rear there was, in 1800, a large field known as "Yr Ynys."

On the opposite side of the street there was an old public-house, known in the old days as "Y Briw-ws Bach," a very popular house of call in the flourishing period of the canal, which passed quite near. Between the canal and the River Taff was the old Taff Vale Brewery, owned for many years by Mr. David Williams, who came to Merthyr when a boy and became High Constable of Merthyr in 1878.

In this neighbourhood several wells were sunk in the old days. In 1850, Dr. Dyke, the Medical Officer of Health, made a report of the town's water supply. In this he mentioned that the water for public consumption was derived from wells, springs, brooks, ponds, and the River Taff. The public wells, he stated, were twelve in number, from which a plentiful supply could be had for payment, but the quality of the water was very bad. After this report upon the very unsatisfactory state of the town's water supply, preparations were made to promote a Water Bill in Parliament. The Act passed in 1858 conferred the necessary powers for the construction of a waterworks, and in 1859 the Pentwyn Reservoir was commenced. This undertaking was completed in 1863. Water, however, had been taken from Taf Fechan to supply Merthyr in 1861. There were four wells sunk in the neighbourhood of Georgetown, these varying in depth—one in Coffin's Court, the water being raised by a pump; one in Vaughan's Garden, between the canal and the river; one in the yard of the old Taff

Vale Brewery ; and one in Canal Square. The latter well, when measured, was found to be 120 feet deep. This was the one near the old Malt Mill. Possibly there were others besides these. There were also numerous springs and spouts, which were very useful.

Near Vaughan's House, between canal and river, were very important docks for loading and unloading material from Dowlais and Penydarren Works, as well as lime-stone from the local quarries. There were also covered places for loading and unloading provisions and other classes of goods consigned for the great stores at Pontstorehouse. To-day we have no conception of the volume of traffic and the immense tonnage that was dealt with at this busy quarter.

Between the canal and Dynevor Street and quite near the bridge there stood the residence of one of the canal officials. The part of the canal between the two locks was recently purchased by the Merthyr Corporation and filled-in. Upon the site garages have been erected, serving as the Corporation Bus Depôt. Nearby, on the opposite side of Dynevor Street, is Ainon Chapel, built in 1859 by some of the Baptist friends who patronized High Street Church. The services here have more than once been entirely Welsh in character : but when the needs of the English Baptists required more room, they would arrange with the Welsh Baptists for a change of chapels. Bethel and Ainon are carried on in this way to the present day.

The Dynevor Arms is a very old public-house occupying a very prominent position in Dynevor Square at the top of the street of the same name. For many years it was occupied by Mr. and Mrs. Davies. In 1855 the old Philosophical Society, which had been disbanded after having been in existenec for many years previously, was reorganized. The surviving members, with the addition of new-comers, met regularly at the Dynevor Arms for their lectures and discussions. The Rev. Owen Evans, Mr. Morgan Williams, and the Rev. J. Jones, Aberdare, often lectured to the Society. Later it became attached to the Merthyr Library, to which institution all the instruments were transferred. Some of these are now in use at Cyfarthfa Secondary School. After the time of Mr. and Mrs. Davies, the house was rebuilt (about 1881), and then occupied by Mr. and Mrs. E. Nicholas, of the Lamb Inn. Behind the Dynevor Arms is the Red Mine Tramroad, which, if followed southwards, leads us to the old Catholic Church, built in 1857. Father Bruton was one of the first priests ; he was also a member of the first School Board. I think that it was during the ministry of Canon Wade that the Catholic Church was removed from Georgetown to the neighbourhood of Penydarren Park.

Bethel Baptist Chapel, which is close by, was built in 1809 by the General Baptists on the flat field known as "Yr Ynys." It was rebuilt in 1826. The first minister of Bethel was the Rev. W. D. Nicholas. All the local Baptist churches at that time held their services in Welsh, with the exception of a small gathering which had met at Tai Cochion since 1807. These members formed themselves into an English Baptist church, and the blind preacher, Daniel Davies, ministered to them. He also preached to the Welsh Methodists, which caused some irritation amongst their members. The result was that the English Baptists acquired Bethel Chapel, but I do not know what arrangement was made with the existing Welsh Baptists. English services were commenced in 1813, at which date Mr. Daniel Davies had retired from the ministry, and Mr. Faraday took over the care of the church. In 1840 the English Baptists built High Street Chapel, and I presume that upon their departure to their new spiritual home, the vacant Bethel was re-occupied by the Welsh Baptists. In 1859 something happened in the affairs of High Street Chapel which resulted in Ainon being built. After some years an interchanging of chapels was made by the English and Welsh congregations, but after a further period things were restored to the original state of affairs.

Georgetown is a very populous district. It was named after George, a grandson of Richard Crawshay. William, the son of Richard Crawshay, had three sons—William, George and Richard. William, the heir, became one of the greatest iron-masters of his time. George was part-owner of the Cyfarthfa Works with his brother, and the district then rapidly developing and numerous houses being built, gave rise to the name Georgetown. It comprises that area between Aberdare Road on the south, Nantygwenith Lane on the north-west, Dynevor Street and Nantygwenith Street on the east. George Street and John Street, which intersect at right angles, are the main divisions. The former, a perfectly straight road from Cyfarthfa Church to Dynevor Square, is about 250 yards long, although its upper end is very steep. John Street, at the base of the Big Hill, is also a straight road, 300 yards in length, from Aberdare Road to Nantygwenith Lane. With the exception of the lesser cross-roads, all this area has been built upon.

Before leaving the southern side of Georgetown, I should like to refer to the late Benjamin Jones (Merthyrfab), who lived at 84, John Street, and died July 9, 1928, aged 72. "Ben Jones the Postman," as he was familiarly called, was a Welshman to the core, a very intelligent person, and a bard of no mean attainments. He worked strenuously to further the interests of various societies in his native town of Merthyr, but more especially the

Cymreigyddion, the Sons of Temperance, and the religious cause at Salem Congregational Church, of which he had been a most faithful and active member for many years. Possessed of a great deal of local as well as general knowledge, which he was able to impart in a most amusing and happy way, his literary contributions to the Press were always interesting and instructive. For many years he was postman for the Heolgerrig and Clwydyfagwyr districts, and was one of the most genial personalities one could encounter.

Let us retrace our steps to the Bethesda Street bridge and follow the canal again at the huge store-sheds known as Pontstorehouse. Under the canal bridge there branched off a counter canal which passed between the Stores and the river, but on a lower level than the main canal. Above the Stores, the red hematite iron-ore, brought up along the canal from Cardiff, was unloaded, and then it was taken in trams to Ynysfach and elsewhere. The soil at the place of unloading still bears the reddish tinge of the ore, and the tramroad was known as " Y Ddramroad Goch." Following the canal, we come to Tai'r Capel (Chapel Row), where the eminent musician, Dr. Joseph Parry, was born on May 21, 1841. He was the son of Daniel and Elizabeth Parry, who were both faithful members of Bethesda Church. Bet, as his mother was familiarly called, was a good musician and could sing very well, so young Joseph was brought up in a musical sphere. When still a boy he worked for four years at the puddling furnaces, but in 1854 the family emigrated to America. Joseph was then 13 years of age. It is said that at the age of 17 he knew not a note of music, although he had been singing in certain choirs before leaving for America. He had had scant education as a boy, but his mother made up this deficiency with what she had learnt at Bethesda Sunday School, and was able to guide him into the way of knowledge. At the age of 19 his musical powers began to develop, and Joseph Parry won his first prize for a musical composition. This paved the way for better things: people of note began taking keen interest in the young genius, and he was admitted to the Royal Academy of Music, London. After three years' study he returned to the United States, where he directed a school of music, but in 1880 came back once more to his native land, having accepted the offer of a professorship of music at Aberystwyth. After being at Aberystwyth for some time, he accepted an invitation to become organist of Ebenezer Church, Swansea, and in 1888 was offered a professorship of music at Cardiff University. He had gained the highest distinctions in the musical world, being a Mus.Bac. and a Mus.Doc., and his compositions were very varied in character and very popular at one time. He died on February 17, 1903.

In Chapel Row also lived P.C. Charles Bell, one of the earliest of the Cyfarthfa policemen. He came here from Penderyn, and was constable in charge of the Cyfarthfa district for many years. His son, Mr. Richard Bell, was for many years General Secretary to the Railwaymen's Union, and represented Derby in Parliament, afterwards being succeeded by the Rt. Hon. J. H. Thomas, M.P.

Adjoining Chapel Row is the old circular chapel of Cyfarthfa, built as a chapel-of-ease at Mr. Richard Crawshay's own expense. Here the then Rector of Merthyr—the Rev. Mayberry—would come to preach to Mr. Richard Crawshay and others on the Sabbath. The iron-master paid £100 annually towards the ministry and the upkeep of the chapel; but when Mr. Mayberry left the district for Swansea some years later, this grant was withdrawn and the chapel was closed. The date of closing is not certain, but as Richard Crawshay died in 1810, it must have been some years before this date. There was a Sunday School held in connection with the chapel, and Mr. Crawshay extended an invitation to Robert Raikes, of Gloucester—the founder of the English Sunday School (and whose centenary was observed last year)—to come and organise the school. It was held there until the building of the English Wesleyan Chapel at Pontmorlais, which was opened June 18, 1797, and the school was then transferred to the new edifice. If the Cyfarthfa Chapel was closed in 1797, it must have been opened for worship about 1788. The building, which is strongly constructed and massive, has a conical roof supported by a number of iron pillars encased in wood. The pillars are connected, near the top of the wall, by iron girders, and in all the recesses in the wall there are semi-circular windows. The diameter of the building is about 45 feet. It has been used for over 50 years as a carpenter's shop, but when the writer last saw it the place was used as a storeroom. This old chapel is worthy of a visit.

Following the canal bank, we pass through a large fitting-shop furnished with various kinds of machinery, then enter the huge saw-mills and the old rail-sheds where the blacksmiths finished-off the rails as required before they were loaded into the boats. After crossing the canal above the old chapel, we come to the wagon-shed, an enormous building 146 feet in length and 39 feet in width. I do not know for what specific purpose it was originally built, but the iron framework at both sides, and the long curved spans in the upper portions of the walls, seem to suggest that it was intended for some special use. There is one very interesting record concerning it. On May 21, 1846, a great ball was held there, at the expense of William Crawshay, to commemorate the marriage of his son, Robert T. Crawshay. There is at the Cyfarthfa Museum a print of this ball — taken at the time — with full particulars concerning it: and one can hardly believe that it is one of the sheds belonging to the works, in its festive transformation. When passing the shed there is to be seen, on the left hand side, lying at the side of the wall, an old mill-stone—one of the best examples of a mill-stone I have seen—and it is in excellent condition. I have tried to persuade Mr. Holder (the curator) and Major F. T. James (chairman of the Museum Committee) to try and preserve the stone somewhere near the Museum, and I trust that it will eventually be done.

Next we come to the old Dry Dock where boats were repaired, and quite near are the shops of the blacksmiths and carpenters who carried out the necessary repairs. When we glance at these old buildings and know something of the use to which they were put, what scenes we can conjure together of the busy days of the past! We are now nearing the head of the canal, where in our boyhood days we delighted in seeing the great bubbling of the water into the canal. Between the road and the canal were the offices and stores; but when the new offices were built on the other side of the river, the old building was converted into a boys' school. That would be about 60 years ago.

We now return to the old Cyfarthfa Coalyard, in Dynevor Square, from which thousands of tons of coal were distributed annually among the company's workmen. Nantygwenith Street, which connects Dynevor Square with Swansea Road, is broad, always clean, and one of the finest streets in the town. On the right is a long row of workmen's dwellings, forming a gentle curve from one end to the other, and it reminds one of Regent Street in London. I wonder if the present King and Queen, during their visit to Merthyr on June 27, 1912, noticed the similarity to Regent Street when passing this way. Anyhow, they did halt in the centre of this street, and, after alighting from their car, went into one of the workmen's dwellings to see what a workman's home was like, and were very pleased with what they saw. There are 30 houses in this long continuous row. At the back there is another long row of a similar type, known as Cyfarthfa Row. On the left hand side of Nantygwenith Street there are many business premises. At the corner is the site of Herbert Lloyd's grocery. Next is the old chemist's shop of Mr. V. A. Wills, J.P. Mr. Wills has been a staunch Catholic all his lifetime and an active member of that religious body. He was also a very useful member of the old School Board, continuing to serve that body up to the time when its duties were transferred to the Borough Council. Besides this, he had been a member of the Urban District Council, of which he was chairman in 1898, and during that year he was also elected High Constable of Merthyr. When Merthyr became a

County Borough, Mr. Wills became a Justice of the Peace. Mrs. Wills also has participated in social work, and has been a member of the Board of Guardians for very many years.

Howell Street, which is passed next, was very likely named after the Howells family, who occupied the Patriot public-house, upon the site of which the present grocery establishment of Messrs. William Harris stands. It was here that the local Cymreigyddion met on St. David's Day, 1822, to hold their first eisteddfod. The public-house was then kept by William Howells, uncle of Philip and William Howells. The latter became the guardian of our worthy and patriotic friend, the late Mr. Evan Lougher, who lived most of his lifetime in Patriot Row, Nantygwenith Lane, at the house into which William Howells moved when he left the old Patriot. Mr. Evan Lougher died November 11, 1929, aged 74. On this side of the street there were several public-houses. At the Full Moon lived at one time William Morgan, the father of the noted miners' agent, David Morgan (Dai o'r Nant). The premises were afterwards taken over by Mr. Herbert Lloyd, who erected the brewery at the rear in Nantygwenith Lane, on top of the rise at the north end of Iron Lane. Mr. David Braddick some years ago took over the premises as well as the brewery, but the latter has not been used for brewing for many years. The Prince of Wales public-house is a commodious building and was greatly patronized in the prosperous times of Cyfarthfa Works. At the top of Nantygwenith Street is the site of the Nantygwenith turnpike gate. The gate, which was demolished in 1896, was on the county road between Merthyr, Neath and Swansea. At this point also the road from Llwyncelyn and Cwmpant crossed the county road to Cyfarthfa and Gurnos. A branch road, starting near the gate, went north-eastwards, crossed the river at the ford to Caepant-tywyll, and joined the Gwaelodygarth road.

CHAPTER XII.

NANTYGWENITH FARM—LEWIS WILLIAMS—DR. THOMAS WILLIAMS—DR. DAVID DAVIES—DR. EDWARD DAVIES—THE FIRST FURNACE—CYFARTHFA HOUSE—THE CYFARTHFA TRAGEDY—TY'R MECHANIC—PONT Y CAFNAU—PEN LEFAL TRANCH BACH—TAI MAWR—PENRHIW—PONTYCAPEL.

NEAR the old turnpike gate was the old Nantygwenith Farm, one of the first farms taken up by Anthony Bacon for works purposes. Before the ironworks came into existence, this farm was a very flourishing homestead, comprising about 200 acres of well-cultivated land. This extended along the low expansive flat between the river and the great Cyfarthfa Rock upon which White Row and Cyfarthfa Lane, Georgetown, have been built. Cyfarthfa Church has been built at the top of the Rock. The boundaries of the farm would then be: the River Taff on the north-east, from the junction of Cwmpant Brook with the river near the old Iron Bridge, to the Cyfarthfa Rock on the Swansea Road. This is near the sharp bend in the river and not far from the furnaces; the Cwmpant Brook on the south; a line approximately following the Old Incline over which cinder and slag were conveyed from the works to the huge tips. Here the Nantygwenith lands adjoined in turn the lands of Gellideg, Heolgerrig and Penyrheol Farms. There are various traditions concerning the old homestead which may contain a substantial amount of truth. According to one of them, the family that occupied Nantygwenith in the 17th century had two sons, and during the Civil War (1642—1649) one son sided with the Royalists, while the other threw in his lot with the Cromwellians and Roundheads. Both were lieutenants in the rival armies. The Roundhead was referred to as Lieutenant Coch, but it is rather difficult to say what the family name was, as records are so bare. "Coch" was only a nickname. Some are of opinion that their name was Edwards, others again maintain that it was Vaughan, and that they were both Roman Catholics. Anyhow, the action of the brothers caused a great deal of dissatisfaction. Another tradition is that the farm lands extended to the western boundary of the parish. The main farm building had a very firm earthen floor. The ruins of the old farm could be seen some time ago inside the big stable yard, and when I paid it a visit to see what remained of the old place, I found some traces still left. In the meantime, Messrs. Thomas and

Evans have converted the place into a mineral water stores. My attention was first of all drawn to the large oak beams lying about there, some of them being 13 inches square. Over the fire-places also there were beams eight or nine feet long set in the wall. The walls were thick and mostly built of rubble-stones of various kinds which seemed to have been picked from the neighbouring river bed.

There was a family by the name of Williams living at Nantygwenith in the early part of the 18th century. Lewis Williams, a yeoman of that place, was born at the farm about 1712, and died March 4, 1768, aged 56. His relict, Mary, died at Penyrheol on May 10, 1789, aged 71. They had four sons and two daughters. Thomas, the third son, became a surgeon to the Cyfarthfa Works, and died September 28, 1814, aged 58. It is very probable that William, elder brother to Thomas, moved with his mother from Nantygwenith to Penyrheol; and it is known that his son, also named William, was father of Morgan Williams, the Chartist. Morgan's grandfather, William, died April 30, 1811—two years before the Chartist was born. Now, Thomas Williams was the first surgeon to Cyfarthfa, but also served other works besides. David Davies, one of the Garth family, was appointed assistant to Dr. Williams, and, upon his decease, succeeded him as surgeon to the works, and took up his residence at Ynysfach House (the present Cyfarthfa Surgery). His son—afterwards the noted Dr. Edward Davies, of Cyfarthfa—acted as his assistant. Edward was born in a house adjoining the Crown Inn, in 1800. When a young man he was apprenticed to his father at Cyfarthfa, then, going to London, studied and practised at Guy's Hospital, finally qualifying as apothecary and surgeon in 1822. Following up his studies, the young surgeon gained fame as a skilful operator; and upon his father's retirement, in 1832, he was appointed to be his successor at Cyfarthfa. Dr. Edward Davies practised there until 1850, then resigned, and travelled a great deal, thus gaining considerable experience. When he returned to Merthyr he practised as a consulting surgeon in Bethesda Street, and married Sarah, eldest daughter of Mr. Lewis, Canal House, Aberdare. In personal appearance, Dr. Davies was tall, handsome, and erect in carriage. Physically he was well developed and muscular, and, when walking, had a long and easy stride. He had keen blue eyes, a fair complexion, and his face alwaye bore a bright intelligent expression. One peculiarity of his was that whenever he was out walking he carried his walking-stick on his shoulder. An old resident of Penry Street, Mrs. Anthony (then 85 years of age), described him to me one day. In doing so, she picked up a walking-stick, placed it on her shoulder, and paced the room, holding herself erectly, with long, considered steps, as if she were a young woman of 20. This interesting character, Dr. Davies, died at the Court House, Merthyr, in 1880, aged 80, and was buried in the churchyard at Vaynor. His successors at Cyfarthfa Surgery have been dealt with already in Chapter V.

Having wandered a little from the subject of Nantygwenith Farm and its occupiers, I will now take up the thread of the story again. After Dr. Williams, Mr. Hallatt, the farrier, lived there. The last occupier was John Pask, a shepherd employed by the Company, and then the old farmhouse fell into ruins. Between the old farm (the lands of which were gradually covered by the huge tips) and Nantygwenith Lane, the company built a boys' school to replace the old Office School. This would be, I should think, about 50 years ago. In 1907 the Borough Council purchased the school and land, and built a modern school, consisting of three departments, there, to meet the needs of the surrounding populous district. The new school was opened on December 6, 1907, by the late Alderman J. M. Berry.

Now, how did this place come to be called Nantygwenith? and where is the "nant" or brook? In my personal estimation, it is the brook on the northern side of the Heolgerrig Road. Before the Cyfarthfa Canal was made and the huge cinder-tips came into existence, the course of the brook was from Heolgerrig Old Farm, passing behind Tai Mark Gray, near the present railway bridge, and continuing in nearly a straight line to Nantygwenith Lane. The exact point of entry into the lane would be at the southern corner of the boys' school playground, to the rear of Cyfarthfa Church, where water has been running out ever since the tipping finished. A little way to the north, above the stables, there was many years ago a well from which many of the local people drew their water supply. Pipes were also laid, before tipping took place at the spot, to the Cyfarthfa stables, so as to ensure a continuous supply of water from the well. Some years after Herbert Lloyd built the brewery in Nantygwenith Lane, he placed a tank at the base of the tip and at a little distance from the road, just where the water of the old brook issued, and then laid a pipe-line to convey the water to his brewery. Anyone standing near the north end of John Street, where it meets Nantygwenith Lane, could visualize the course of the brook onwards to the Taff; it would pass through the Georgetown "flat," in front of Patriot Row, to join the Cwmpant Brook near the Cyfarthfa Surgery, then the combined brooks would continue their rippling journey until they entered the main river near the Old Iron Bridge. Along the low-lying ground (anciently called "Yr Ynys") stretched the rich cornfields on either side of the brook, and on the ridge in the background was situated the old homestead, overlooking some of the best agricultural land in the valley.

If we follow the Cyfarthfa road towards the works, we pass the Old Hospital Field on the left, partly covered with tips. It was here that horses that were unfit for work were turned out to graze, hence the name. About 55 years ago the Volunteers used to drill in this field under the command of Captain Lewis, who was later promoted major and eventually colonel. Next we come to the old Cyfarthfa House, a very imposing building, built about 1770 by Anthony Bacon, the first iron-master to venture his fortune at Cyfarthfa. The first land taken over by Bacon was that at Rhydycar in 1763. In 1765 that memorable mineral lease of Cyfarthfa was obtained, and the same year witnessed the erection of the first furnace at Cyfarthfa. The iron plate that was on the front of the furnace, bearing the date 1765, is at present in the Cyfarthfa Castle Museum. Mr. Brownrigg then entered into partnership with Bacon. The Cyfarthfa Estate extended from the Canaid Brook to Nant Ffrwd, and from the parish boundary on the west to the River Taff. Soon after the erection of the first furnace, the Cyfarthfa Mansion was built, on the bank of the Taff, there being a fine lawn and shrubbery in front of the house. Like all old mansions, it also had its eerie story. Soon after the house was built, a murder was committed there. It seemed that one of Mr. Bacon's maid-servants had a love affair with a young man named William Owen, who, on one occasion presented her with a pair of silver shoe-buckles and a black silk neckerchief. The young folk attended Cefn Fair annually. It was the centre of attraction in those days, and continued to be so long afterwards. One fair-day, however, William Owen noticed that his sweetheart did not show him the usual signs of affection ; and when he saw her dancing with Benjamin Harry, obviously another suitor, poor Will was downcast. To crown his discomfiture, he saw his rival wearing the fancy buckles and the very silk neckerchief he had presented to his beloved ! Filled with bitterness and sullen anger towards his former sweetheart, who had treated him so shabbily, he decided to see her and get an explanation of her conduct. The following Sunday evening he attended divine service at Ynysgau Chapel, and afterwards proceeded to Cyfarthfa House for the interview. When the pair met, William declared how faithful and true he had been to her at all times, and surely did not deserve such treatment at her hands. He accused her of unfaithfulness, which charge brought a hasty retort to the lips of the maid. Heated words must have passed between them until William, goaded to madness by her biting tongue, drew out a knife and plunged it into her bosom. She managed to get into the house, and with painful steps climbed the stairs to join the other maids. As she ascended the stairs, faint through loss of blood, she rested her bloodstained hand on the wall for support. The tradition is that whatever paint or colouring was put on that wall afterwards, the shape of an open hand was to be seen through it. On July 8, 1926, in the company of two friends, I paid a visit to the old mansion and inspected the mysterious hand. We were guided through the building by a kind lady who lived next door and who had charge of the keys. We ascended the staircase to a square landing, where the mysterious mark was pointed out to us. There certainly was a similarity to the shape of a hand in the stained blotch upon the wall. It is thought that, after running into the house in great agony, with her hand trying to stanch the blood from the wound, she became so exhausted on reaching the landing that she stretched out her hand to the wall for support. I have been informed that one of the two lovers was buried in the Old Churchyard at Aberdare, and that the particulars of the murder were inscribed on the tombstone. Should the stone be located —as I anticipate it will be in the near future—and the essential particulars obtained, it would be most interesting to confirm the main points in the story.

On reaching the upper landing, we entered a spacious room which was rapidly decaying. On the front of the mantelpiece was Bacon's coat-of-arms—a pig, carved in a panel of wood of special quality. This has been rescued, fortunately, and is now in the safe custody of Mr. Holder at the Cyfarthfa Castle Museum. The following lived at this house : Anthony Bacon, Cockshutt, Richard Crawshay, Joseph Bailey and Watkin George. William Crawshay purchased Gwaelodygarth House, and lived there until Cyfarthfa Castle was built in 1825. It is said that Anthony Bacon built a smith's shop about the same time that he built the furnace at Cyfarthfa, but the roof fell in some years after it was opened. One day, when the workmen were busy at their work, a country-woman passing by with some fruit for sale, chanced to pause at the entrance, and thus attracted the workmen, who admired her basket of plums. With the exception of two, all the workmen left their work and crowded round the saleswoman and her wares, outside the shed. While they were being served, the roof of the shed suddenly gave way, killing the two who had remained inside at their work. The workmen outside were struck with horror at what had happened. The basket of plums was the means of saving many lives.

About 1785, during the time of the celebrated engineer Watkin George, a great water-wheel was built in accordance with plans and instructions of the engineer, to be used for blast purposes. The wheel was made mostly of cast-iron, and was 50 feet in diameter and six feet in breadth. The gudgeons around the wheel, into which the water fell, were made of cast-iron and weighed in all 100 tons. The total cost of it was £4,000. To set the wheel in motion water was conveyed by three streams discharging upon the wheel, one above the other. Not far from the water-wheel, and near Pwll Wat, is a very ancient house known as "Ty'r Mechanic." It is said that a manager named Thomas Treharne lived here during the time of David Tanner. Here also lived the grandparents of the late Lord Rhondda. Before he came here to live, in the early days of the iron-works, his grandfather had been a farmer, but it is not stated where his farm was. Soon after the works started, he was employed as a haulage contractor and kept a large number of horses for the purpose of hauling wood, coal mine and lime-stone. The contractor had three sons—Samuel, John and David. Samuel became the owner of the Ysguborwen property, on which he opened several collieries, and afterwards extended his mining operations to Clydach Vale, Rhondda. Samuel was the father of Mr. D. A. Thomas, who represented Merthyr in Parliament and later became Lord Rhondda. John Thomas died of consumption at an early age. David, the other son, became an eminent divine. Until 1827 he was a clerk in London, but, after a course of training at Highbury College, he became pastor of Zion Chapel, Bristol. In 1842 he was appointed to the pastorate of Highbury Chapel, Bristol. In 1865, at the end of his chairmanship of the Congregational Union, he delivered such a powerful and effective address that the mover of the vote of thanks said: "We should offer up our thanksgiving to God that we have been privileged to hear an address so touching and spiritual in its character." The grandmother of "D. A.," after her husband's death, removed with her children to Pontstorehouse.

Just below "Ty'r Mechanic" and Pwll Wat is the great Merthyr Church Fault, crossing the River Taff. No local mining or geological student should miss the opportunity of examining this interesting spot. At this point there was a road coming down from the direction of Gellideg, passing Tranch Bach, crossing the old Tai Mawr Road, and leading down to the ford across the river. If we follow the river bank we soon come to the extreme end of the works premises—the forge, the pattern-shop, the site of the old brickworks, and Pontycafnau, at the end of which was the police station, occupied by P.C. Coombes at one time. The bridge is constructed of cast iron, and over it the water was conveyed in cast iron troughing to the works below. On the outer side of the bridge water was also conveyed in large cast iron pipes from Cyfarthfa Lake to the works. It was over this bridge that limestone was brought from the Gurnos Quarry, and lime from the kilns near Cefn Bridge. The stones used for building Cyfarthfa Castle in 1825, and brought from Blaencanaid, also were taken over this important bridge. Very near the bridge is the Cymmer, the confluence of the two rivers—Tâf Fawr and Tâf Fechan, hence the name Cefn-Coed-y-Cymmer, which signifies " the wooded ridge in the apex between the two rivers."

From Pontycafnau (the bridge of troughs) a path winds up towards the locomotive shed and passes under a feeder conveying a stream of water from a point near Pontycapel Viaduct to the works. A weir had been constructed across the river to divert river water into the feeder. There is a very early record of Bacon obtaining the necessary land for making this water-course. In 1768 Anthony Bacon rented three fields at an annual rental of £5 10s., and was granted permission to construct the feeder. The place was known as Coed Evan Maddock. The locomotive shed at the top of the path was the place where the colliers used to get their train (the " cwbs ") when working at Cwm, Gethin, or Castle Pits. On the left was a short but steep incline used for taking down material for works purposes to a lower level. This incline crossed the feeder below just at the point where water was diverted to turn the large water-wheel below. Just above the feeder, near the incline, there was a house (if not houses) many years ago, known as Pen Lefal. It was there that the eminent engineer, Mr. T. Llewelyn, lived, who built the first form of rolls at Cyfarthfa in 1788. His daughter married Mr. Henry Kirkhouse, father of Mr. Bedlington Kirkhouse. On leaving Cyfarthfa Mr. Llewelyn was presented by the workmen at Pen Lefal with a copper box containing many guineas. In 1797 it is known that Edward and Ann Hudson lived at Pen Lefal, and in 1803 William and Phœbe Rees resided there. William Morgan, when manager of the boiler-makers, is another one who stayed there, and when he left for Rhymney was presented by his workmen with a gold watch and chain.

We are now on the site of the great Cyfarthfa Yard, where in olden days numerous pits (or long barrow-shaped mounds) were operated for the conversion of small coal into coke, and they were a sight to see when in use. These were replaced by long rows of coke-ovens, but these again were supplanted by a modern type, built by a Belgian firm, and were known as the Belgian Ovens. With the latter was built a very large and lofty coal-washing machine for the purpose of preparing the small coal used at the coke-ovens. The great dingle of Nantgau was arched over and filled in as the works progressed. Just at this spot passed the old Tai Mawr Road, coming from the direction of Llwyncelyn, then crossing in turn the Heolgerrig and Swansea Roads. It then proceeded from Penrhiw'r Tranch down to the brook at the rear of the old Tranch Bach, and afterwards crossed Nant-y-Wern at the north end of Tranch Bach. Both brooks met below, in front of the old houses. Between the brooks ended the land belonging to Nantgau Farm, but things have changed since then. A little further on the old road was cut by the construction of the B. & M. Railway in 1865, so the old Tai Mawr Road was closed and a new road made on the other side of the railway line. The old houses at Tranch Bach had to be vacated as tipping operations took place, and on the site afterwards a modern brickworks was erected. It is a matter for regret that just at the time when the town of Merthyr was most in need of bricks for building purposes this undertaking came to an end, and supplies now come from elsewhere.

Between the police station—on the Swansea Road—and Penrhiw'r Tranch was a straight flat stretch called the "Cant Llath." This would be just where the Gellideg Road joined the old Tai Mawr Road. It was here that the long iron rods, which were used as guides in the balance pits, were made. They were usually 100 yards long, so the "Cant Llath" gave the smiths employed in making the rods plenty of room to work. On reaching Penrhiw, the old road called Heol Ddu came down from Gellideg by the side of a large field known as Cae Jenny. At the corner was a house called Penrhiw, occupied about 60 years ago by Thomas Jones (Cross), and afterwards by John Price, a locomotive driver. The old Tranch Bach was a long row of company houses of a very early type; they were 29 in number and quite near the works. I should think they were in existence about 140 years ago, but I cannot say definitely why the place was called Tranch Bach. In the Parish Register there are eleven different entries referring to the place; there are entries of burials and christenings between 1782 and 1803, and in each case the place is called Trench Bach. Possibly in the early days a ditch or trench was made in connection with the iron industry. The lands of the three farms—Gellideg, Nantgau, and Tai Mawr—met in front of Tranch Bach, so the Nantgau property did not reach the river.

Tai Mawr will next attract our attention. Before reaching it we come to a gentle ridge, and looking back from there over the railway cutting we can easily see where the road was cut. There are many traditions concerning the old buildings at Tai Mawr, and there is no doubt that the farm dates back to a very early period and has played a very important part in its time. I have reasons for believing that the original farm was sub-divided many years ago into three separate holdings, these being Tir Tai Mawr Isaf, Tir Tai Mawr Canol, and Tir Tai Mawr Uchaf, and that the first farm was called Tŷ Mawr. In the Parish Register the name appears in 1741 as Tai Mawr, and this is the name it has borne ever since. About 20 years ago, when painters were cleaning the old joists in the the old buildings on the lower side of the road, which were then occupied, they came across the date 1436 carved in a beam. If this marks the date of its building, Tai Mawr is truly one of the oldest of our local farms, being thus about 500 years old. According to one tradition, there existed a Roman Catholic Chapel at Tai Mawr, and that Cwm Chapel derives its name from this place of worship. A priest was supposed also to have come over from Brecon to celebrate mass at this and other out-lying farms during the time of Catholic persecution. Creidiol in his "History of Vaynor" supports another tradition, which stated that "the chapel from which Pontycapel and Cwm Capel derived their names was on a field near Mr. Sutherland's house, near the north end of the viaduct, and that the two small farm lands in that locality were known as Tir Pontycapel and Tir-y-Capel."

The lower Tai Mawr consisted of two separate buildings, the one nearest the road being the smaller of the two. In the eastern end of the smaller building there are two arched entrances, one at each corner. The arches are semi-circular and are in keeping with some particular style of church architecture. The lower house was much larger and bore traces of some decoration. A bit of excavation about this old building might reveal some more objects of interest. It is conjectured that many years ago a relative of the Nantygwenith family, by the name of Edwards, lived at Tai Mawr. Wilkins, in his "History of Merthyr," when dealing with Edward Harri, who was born at Cwmyglo in 1694,-states that he was not on good terms with Edwards, the yeoman of Tai Mawr. Possibly there was some family connection between the two farmers; if so, the families of Nantygwenith, Tai Mawr and Cwmyglo were branches of a common stock. The Edwards of Cwmyglo were known to be Puritans and staunch Nonconformists, whatever the other families may have been. We read about the rival lieutenants of Nantygwenith during the Civil War, and it is likely that there were two factions in the local families. Early in the 18th century a certain Lewis Edwards was owner and tenant of Tai Mawr. "Of Lewis Edwards," narrates Wilkins in his "Tales," "not much is known, but that he was a staunch Roman Catholic, and owned a considerable portion of land and other property, and was of importance in his day and generation. He had one daughter who married the heir-expectant to the Dynevor title and estate. Lewis Edwards thought more of his religious ardour than of his worldly riches. Very little did Lewis think that there was immense wealth underlying some of his tilled land which extended to the top of the mountain. Lewis Edwards of Tai Mawr was buried in the Old Parish Churchyard prior to 1780." A few weeks ago I was shown his tombstone, but no inscription could be traced. There had been a plate fastened with lead plugs upon the tomb, but now only the plugs can be seen. Many years ago the following inscription was to be seen on the stone: " Preye for ye sowle of Lewis Edwards."

During the last century many families have lived at the old farmhouse. William Thomas Edwards and his wife lived there, and one of their children was Thomas Edwards. Idris Ddu, writing an account of him in 1855, mentions that when Thomas was employed at Penydarren Works he was involved in an accident, his arm being severed from his body, and that Dr. Martin had waited upon him most patiently during the most critical stages. Shan and Ann were two sisters of the injured man. Afterwards Rees Edwards occupied the old building, and was succeeded by John Davies and his sons.

At Tai Mawr Uchaf, as we shall now call it, lived another family by the name of Edwards, who were direct descendants of Edward Harri (Edward ap Harri) of Cwmyglo and Gurnos. Edward Harri had an only son, David Edward, who was a bard and scholar, and who died November 7, 1818, aged 77. David had five sons and two daughters. Edward, the eldest son, was the father of David Edwards of " Gilfach Glyd," Llanwonno, who was born at Gurnos, so Edward Edwards was the last of the family to live at that farm before it was purchased by Mr. William Crawshay. Another son of the bard was the David Edwards, or " Daff," who married a daughter of John Rheinallt (Reynold) of Coedmeurig, and who lived at Tai Mawr. This was the first of the Edwards family of Gurnos that lived at Tai Mawr. They were the parents of William Edwards, who, with Kate his wife, lived there afterwards. Another son of David Edwards—or " Daff " as he was called—was Edward Edwards (" Ned Daffi ") of Penllwynderi, Swansea Road. William and Kate Edwards had three sons, the eldest of whom, David, occupied the farm after his parents. Some time after this the three lands of Tai Mawr came under one tenant. When this David Edwards left, Margaret, the daughter of Edward Edwards, Penllwynderi, and her husband, Rowland Simon, occupied Tai Mawr. Therefore the farm was in the possession of the Edwards family for very many years. After her husband's death Margaret left the farm, and is now living at 1, Hanover Street, Merthyr, having attained the advanced age of over 80 years. She is a direct descendant of Edward Harri who died at Gurnos in 1800 at the very mature age of 106 years. Mr. and Mrs. Jones, late of Cae Mari Dwn, have been the tenants of Tai Mawr for the last 20 years; and the lands, during the last three years, have been divided. In front of the farm there used to be a bull-ring years ago, where oxen were baited by dogs before being slaughtered.

From Tai Mawr a road branches off in the direction of Clwydyfagwyr and Winchfawr, crossing the Swansea Road at Mile End.

Continuing along the road towards Pontycapel, a bridge is seen on the right hand side, under which passes an accommodation road leading to some fields below the line. A little way below the bridge there is a large spring issuing beneath a sandstone rock, which yields an excellent supply of water. It is known as Ffynnon y Galon Ddu. Following the road we come to Penrhiw Cwm Capel, and on the left there used to be an old house called Penrhiw Cwm Capel. Here the noted musician Morgan Rhys Williams o'r Ffrwd (Alaw Brycheiniog) was born. The descent from Penrhiw to the Cwmffrwd Bridge is very steep and rough. On the right appears the southern end of that beautifully constructed and wonderful example of the bridge-builders art, the Pontycapel Viaduct, across the Tâf Fawr. It is one of the finest masonry constructions in the country. As it is partly within the Gellideg Hamlet, I shall give a few particulars concerning the viaduct. It was built in 1865—1866 by Savin and Ward, contractors. The height from the foundation pillar in the river to the parapet wall is 122 feet. The arches, 15 in number, each have a 40 feet span. The first arch was locked on May 12, 1866, and the fifteenth on August 27, 1866, by Mrs. Sutherland, wife of the engineer. The first locomotive went over the bridge on October 21, 1866, and the railway line was opened for traffic before the end of the same year. Therefore the viaduct has been in use for 63 years. A few yards above the bridge, at the junction of the Ffrwd with the main river, the three parishes of Merthyr, Vaynor and Penderyn meet. On the southern side of this angle there is a number of old houses known as Tai Cwm Capel.

Retracing our steps to the railway crossing at Swansea Road, we come to the house of Catherine Williams (Kitty Ffe). Her sons are now nearing the age of 70. Kitty, like her mother before her, was born in this house. A little distance above is the old police station, but now it has no connection with the law. Opposite this place was the great stank on which the trams of coal that came up from the pits on "carriages," as they were called, were dealt with.

CHAPTER XIII.

PENYARD CYFARTHFA—GELLIDEG—CWM MWYN—TIR HUGH MORGAN—GELLIDEG FARM-HOUSE—GWILYM GELLIDEG—CAPEL GELLIDEG—WILLIAM RICHARDS, NANTGAU—THE TRAVELLERS' WELL — MOUNT PLEASANT—BRYNTEG—LEFAL PREGETHWR—REV. RICHARD GRIFFITH—REV. LEWIS JACK EVANS.

ON the left hand side of the Swansea Road, near the stank, is the site of the mountain levels screen, where all the coal brought down from the mountain-side was weighed and then tipped into wagons. The mine that was brought down many years ago was weighed a little below this place. A short distance south of the screen is the entrance of one of the nearest mine levels to the works, and in which were worked some of the lowest mine veins in the district—the Rosser and Garw groups. It was known as Lefal Tomos Daniel, and served as a horseway to Pwll Dafydd Beynon. Thomas Daniel was a brother of David Daniel, Cwm-yglo. The arched entrance to the old level is in the retaining wall of the railway embankment, near the north end of the long arch-way under the B. & M. Railway. The skilful workmanship displayed on this arch is worthy of a visit by those interested in such work. Near the other end of the long archway (" The Dark Shell ") is another level—Lefal Gwter—in which the Gellideg seam of coal was worked as far as the Aberdare boundary. The tips of these two levels formed the western part of the huge cinder tips below, upon which the engine-house at the top of the Incline was built. Both levels had been worked before the construction of the B. & M. Railway and the long archway.

Following the tramroad, constructed on the site of the old transport road to the works, we reach the entrance to a large quarry which overlies the Gellideg coal seam—the lowest seam in the district that is workable. Stones were quarried here for building purposes at the works. A little way above there was another mine level—Lefal Rosser, William Price. William Price was the farmer and contractor who preceded Evan Evans at Six Bells Farm.

We now come to the railway bridge over the Swansea Road, which is another fine example of masonry workmanship that we do not come across very often ; and those passing this way, who have not noticed the fine work on the bridge, are advised to do so at the first opportunity. On the right wing of the bridge, on the lower side, is the date 1865, which was the year of its erection. After passing the bridge, we are at the junction of the new Tai

Mawr Road with the Swansea Road. Road and railway have cut the large field, called " Cae Jenny," into two—one part being above the road and the other below the railway. In the upper part are the old buildings of Gellideg, which were converted into workmen's dwellings when the works commenced. The old farm that was here must have existed for centuries. It was on land belonging to Gellideg Farm that Bacon built his first furnace and smithshop (1765), for the holding extended along the southern side of the Nantgau Brook as far as the Taff, and joined the Nantygwenith land near the great bend in the river. Very little is known about the history of the old property. According to the MSS. of Rowland Thomas (Idris Ddu), it appears that before 1742 the land of Gellideg (or Tir Huw Morgan) was held on lease by William Richard Watkin. At the expiration of this lease (1742), a new one was granted by Lord Talbot and Hensol to Richard Williams (Richard ap William), who sold his lease to William Leysion in 1758 for £20. In 1769 David John (Dafydd Shon) was granted a lease of three lives—those of himself, his wife, and his son John (then six years old)—of the land of Gellideg. On September 4, 1786, David John granted a sub-lease of Gellideg to William Richards of Glyndyrus, who in turn leased the property to Richard Hill, agent first for Anthony Bacon and afterwards for the Bacon family. Richard Hill surrendered his lease to William Richards on May 30, 1794, but on condition that Richards should pay an annual rental of one peppercorn to Anthony Bacon (probably the son of the ironmaster), if called upon to do so. In the same year (1794) William Richards rented and took possession of Brynteg Farm, which had been held previously by John Williams and John Walters respectively. He also rented Nantgau, where he went to reside after leaving Glyndyrus. Thus we can see that William Richards held considerable property in the hamlet of Gellideg and must have been a man of importance in his day.

The cultivated land belonging to Gellideg Farm extended to the top of Cyfarthfa Rock (or Craig y Llyn). The lowest field of all—later the site of the blacksmiths' shop in the works—was called Cae'r Bryn. The great rock curved round in a crescent, and on the flat stretch below everything was left to grow in a wild state, as the owner could not utilise it for farming purposes. It was known as Gwern Loder or Ynys Isaf, Gellideg. Seeing that the place was not of much value in the estimation of the leaseholder of Gellideg, Bacon had very little trouble in coming to terms with the owner of the land in order to build his first furnace.

I have endeavoured to find out when the Merthyr Parish was divided into hamlets, but without success. I wonder whether the old farm of Gellideg was in existence when the division was made, and, if so, whether the hamlet took its name from this particular farm. Did the Garth Hamlet, again, take its name from the Garth Farm? Gellideg means "a fair grove," and the name at once conjures up a vision of a peaceful, rustic, woodland scene in a setting of smiling cornfields. But the eyes of the iron-master were not concerned with the beauty of the surface so much as with the wealth that was to be got from beneath that surface; and with the ruthless advance of industry the landscape was rendered scarred, ugly, and in places, desolate. I am of opinion that the coal seam called the "Gellideg," which was worked by the Cyfarthfa people about 160 years ago, obtained its name originally from its proximity to Gellideg Farm, which was only about 100 yards from the place where it was first worked.

Some years ago I read of a certain farm servant, named Siams Hywel Rhys, who lived at Craig-y-Gilfach, near the Aberdare entrance to the G.W.R. tunnel, and who was working on the farm at Blaencanaid during the Civil War (1642—1649). When Siams was told that the military authorities were conscripting all the young men they could find in the district, he disappeared from the locality and was never heard of afterwards. But in a pocket of a coat he had left behind was found a small sheet of paper upon which the following verse was written:

"Ffarwel, Blaencanaid gryno,
'E ddarfu Siams ymado;
A'r Gellideg, tra yno'n chwith,
Ni anghofiai byth mohono."

If this story be true, it goes to prove that Gellideg Farm was in existence early in the 17th century, and that Siams had had some associations with it. I can just imagine him standing on the ridge above Blaencanaid, before taking his final leave, gazing in the direction of Merthyr with a pang of regret at his heart, and then his eyes would alight on the buildings and land of Gellideg away to the left, and the tears would well in them, for he knew that he would not see them again.

The old farm building was fairly large, but low. The walls were very thick, and the floor was a strong earthen one, about nine inches thick, but worn to such an extent that the surface was as smooth as glass. Some massive beams are still to be seen there. I have been told that the bottom house in the row of dwellings was at one time a public-house. This is much smaller than the farmhouse. Its land having been commandeered for industrial purposes, the farm premises were converted into dwellings to house the workmen employed in the levels, pits, or works. Of late the new owner of the property, Mr. Wilson Beach, has built a fine house there.

Many persons have risen to distinction in life from the neighbourhood of Gellideg, and their names will be treasured in the memory. The first I shall mention is William Morgan (Gwilym Gellideg), who, although not born there, lived most of his life in Gellideg. He was born in Carmarthenshire in 1809, but when he was still very young his parents removed to Rhymney, where he afterwards was engaged in the iron-works. During his stay there he kept a Welsh grammar school during the winter nights, and it is said that some of his students became eminent literary men. Later he moved to the Merthyr district, where he spent most of his life in one of the thatched houses at Gellideg, being employed as a miner at Cyfarthfa. In 1837 the order of bard was bestowed upon him at Abergavenny by Rhydderch Gwynedd, Cawrdaf, and Tegid. That Gwilym Gellideg was a very able bard and singer is proved by the large number of prizes he won at eisteddfodau. One day Gwilym went to a meeting at Aberdare, and on the road met two of his old friends, Alaw Goch and Ifor Cwmgwys. Knowing of Gwilym's ability as a bard, they welcomed him in true bardic fashion as follows : "Gallu da yn y Gellideg," began Alaw Goch. "Na," said Ifor, "Gallu dau yn y Gellideg." "Na, na," said Gwilym triumphantly, "hwn yw'r gorau—'Gallu Duw yn Gellideg.'"

In 1846 Gwilym published a small book containing his literary compositions under the title of "Cerbyd yr Awen," in which one of his best efforts, "Myfyrdod Can Mlynedd," was included. At the Swan Eisteddfod, Merthyr, in 1833, the bard won his first prize for the best "penillion" composed on the subject, "Dyn o'i Grud i'w Fedd." Rhys Evan, son of Edward Evan of Ton Coch, in his adjudication referred to the winning composition thus :

"Darllenais drwy allu union—a llwyr
Yr oll o'r penillion ;
'Gostyngedig,' o ddigon,
Yw'r brawd a bia'r wobr hon."

The last years of the able old bard were, sad to say, very unhappy, as he went on the downward grade—pursuing his personal cravings, wandering from one public-house to another, composing verses of poetry and singing them for the amusement of the company there assembled. He died in Mill Street, near the Old Parish Church, on May 29, 1879, aged 70, and was buried at Cefn Cemetery, where his friends placed a memorial stone later to mark his grave.

Another who lived at Gellideg was Billy Dafydd Richard, one of the first schoolmasters at Heolgerrig, who kept school about 1840, and to whom Wilkins refers as being "a versatile song-writer." Ceredig (which was his bardic name) was a contemporary of Idris

Ddu, who treasured some of his work amongst his MSS., and both attended Cymreigyddion meetings together. William David Richard was also at one time secretary of one of the Six Bells clubs.

The following are some of the old people of Gellideg: John Webber, grandfather of J. Webber, the musician; Thomas Jones, one of the founders of Salem Church, Heolgerrig; David Lewis, known as "Dai'r Cantwr"; Isaac Richards (Isaac o'r Felin), who was born at Felin Ganaid; Morgan, William and Gomer Richards, sons of the foregoing; John Morris, of the Travellers' Well; Thomas Morris, and John his son; Morgan Webber (father of the musician), who, when 80 years of age, met with an accident at Gellideg, being knocked down by a marine-store cart on January 25, 1913, and succumbing from the results of the accident on January 28, 1913; Ann Williams, sister of the above, now over 82; Ann Richards, who is also over 80; William Jones, now at the advanced age of 85. The three mentioned at the end of this list are still living at Gellideg, and it goes a long way to prove that this small place is situated in a healthy spot. Fifty years ago very few people lived beyond the allotted span, but here we have three octogenarians living very near one another. Then there were Evan Evans, Six Bells, who lived there when he first came to the locality; Evan Evans, Gellideg, and Evan Jones—all three living there very many years ago. In more recent years there were John Webber and Richard Davies, men above the average talent in the musical world, whose names will go down to posterity as workers for the good of their fellow-men. Both have composed excellent hymn-tunes and anthems, which are very popular and often sung at the music festivals of the local churches. The hymn-tunes "Nantgau" and "Gellideg," and the anthem "Y Nefol Wlad," are the work of John Webber; while "Panteg," "Gethsemane" and "Rhagom, Filwyr Iesu" were composed by Richard Davies. Both of these local geniuses were self-trained. John Webber was a colliery under-manager at Gethin Pit, but he held a first class colliery manager's certificate. He died November, 8, 1926, at Pencoedcae, Brynteg, aged 74. Richard Davies was a blacksmith at Cyfarthfa and an expert at his trade. Pleasant and unassuming in demeanour, he gained the respect of all, and died at Nantygwenith Street on August 22, 1926, aged 71. There are others following in their footsteps to keep up the reputation of Gellideg.

We cannot leave Gellideg without referring to our most brilliant student-scholar, Mr. W. T. Owen, of 16, Gellideg, a student at Swansea University, and the son of Mr. John Owen, a working man, who is also a capable musician. In the last two years he has gained first class honours in French and German, with oral proficiency in both languages, and this at the age of 21. He has been awarded a University of Wales Scholarship valued at £200 for two years, and is now preparing for his M.A. degree. His feat is the more remarkable when it is realized that only one double-first has been taken at Swansea University during the last ten years, and reflects creditably on the instruction given in our Secondary Schools.

Gellideg Chapel was built in 1860 at the side of the Swansea Road. This religious cause of the Independents was commenced much in the same way as others of a similar nature by holding meetings at various private dwelling-houses in the district. The names of the most prominent persons who had met for religious worship before 1860 were : John Rogers, Thomas Watkins, Edward Hughes, Rees Price, Thomas Morris and David Jones. The majority of the worshippers in these house-to-house meetings were members of Bethesda Church, and in due course the number became so large that they felt a more convenient chapel was necessary. Mr. Rt. T. Crawshay was approached with the object of obtaining a plot of land on which they could erect a chapel ; and learning that most of the men were Cyfarthfa workmen who were dependent upon the works, he readily granted the necessary land and also the stones for building the edifice. The new Gellideg Chapel was completed and opened in 1860, during the ministry of the Rev. Rhys Gwesyn Jones at Bethesda. It was regarded as a branch of Bethesda, which church took over the responsibilities and debt of the new building. The Rev. R. G. Jones ministered to the church until he left for America in 1867. In May of the same year the Rev. James Evans was appointed to the care of the church, and continued to shepherd its flock up to the time of his death ; but since then there has been no regular minister at Gellideg. It relies entirely on " supplies " for conducting the Communion services.

Gellideg has done a great deal to foster music, especially in the direction of choral singing and the " cymanfa ganu," the two guiding spirits being the late Mr. John M. Webber and the late Mr. Richard Davies, both of whom were not only composers but conductors as well. Both were also strong pillars of the church at Gellideg, where they were for many years the two senior deacons. Mr. Richard Davies had acted as secretary for over 25 years and as precentor for over 30 years. There was only a space of three months between their deaths, and as their funeral processions wended their way towards the burial ground, the people sang the hymn-tunes they had composed with intense feeling. Truly a remarkable pair. Giants, in a way, in their own sphere. They had lived, worshipped and died together ; and I venture to say that it will be a long time before Gellideg will see their like in the sphere of music again. The burden of responsibility has for the time being devolved upon the younger generation, with Mr. David Lewis (who was a member of the late Board of Guardians for many years) as the senior. The father of David Lewis was also named David, and lived for a time at Cyfarthfa House and, later, at Tranch Bach.

On the other side of the Nantgau Brook is another old homestead, Nantgau Farm, to which William Richards moved in 1794 when he left Glyndyrus. The next tenants at Nantgau of whom I have any information were William Williams (Will yr Halier) and Catws his wife. They left the farm about 1874 and went to the Corner House Inn, Cefn Coed. Then Jenkin Jenkins, a contractor at the Coedcae Mine Pit and levels in the neighbourhood, came from Tai Canol Isaf, Heolgerrig, and occupied the farm. After his death, his widow took charge ; and then Lewis Jenkins, their third son, took it over until his death, which occurred on February 2, 1920. The farm then remained in the hands of the family until 1925, when William Harris bought the freehold of farm and lands, although a rearrangement of the property was made on that occasion.

Next we come to two old cottages, on the right of the road, built in the early days of last century. Thomas Williams (father of Alfred Williams) and his family lived here for many years. The present owner and occupier of these houses is Mr. Rees Morgan. On the left of the road, near the bridge, are some of the oldest houses in this district, and known many years ago as The Cottages. John Webber—father of Morgan Webber (sen.) and grandfather ot J. M. Webber, the musician—lived here, and in the meantime he built a public-house further up the hill. Morgan Webber used to say that when he was young, if he stood on the doorstep of this public-house, he was able to see the Six Bells Brewery. This must have been before the huge shale tips came into being. As Morgan was born in 1831, we can see that this extensive tipping took place within the last hundred years. It is said that old John Webber's wife was a near relative of William Richards, the leaseholder of Nantgau and other farms. The next to occupy The Cottage was John Morris, who converted the premises into a public-house, which was named The Travellers' Well. Both of these old public-houses have been closed as licensed premises for many years.

Before climbing the fairly steep hill above this ancient part of Gellideg, let us rest with our backs against the parapet of the bridge, under which flows the Nantgau Brook. A stranger, upon looking southwards, would be at once struck with amazement at the tremendous size of the mounds or tips which terrace the southern side of the Swansea Road from Nantygwenith Stables almost to the Finger Post, a distance of over two miles. Now, how can we account for this enormous amount of tipping ? Well,

I shall attempt to explain it geologically. It happens that the Swansea Road has been constructed on the outside of the northern outcrop of the coal seams and the iron-ore veins, which lie in an easterly and westerly direction. All the mine levels are comparatively near to this main road. The pits, on the other hand, are further away, southwards, because of the general downward inclination of the strata to a certain point, known as The Basin, in the neighbourhood of Abercynon. There are no levels on the northern side of Swansea Road, but there are two shale tips, the shale having been brought from the other side of the main road.

Near Gellideg Chapel there is a road branching off the Swansea Road and proceeding around the tip to Heolgerrig. It was made in 1909. If we follow this road we come to Cwm Mwyn, through which the main tramroad serving all the levels in the Clwydyfagwyr district ran. This tramroad commenced very near the Finger Post and ended at the Screen near Cyfarthfa Yard, and on the way it received the minor branches from the various levels. Proceeding up Cwm Mwyn from the point where the Cwmdu tramway branches off, we come to the site of an old level on the Rosser vein, and of another in which fire-clay was worked. On both sides of the Cwm huge shale tips tower, those on the left being the tips of Pwll Dafydd Beynon. The levels and tramroad have long fallen into disuse. Working our way upwards through the narrow gorge between the tips, we reach Y Lefal Ganol, which for many years was utilized as a horseway for Winchfawr Pit and in which the Gellideg coal seam was worked. Quite near this level is the old farm of Brynteg, which, previous to 1794, was occupied by John Williams and John Walters, and then came into the possesssion of William Richards. In 1842 Brynteg became vacant. Most of the land had been used for industrial purposes, such as tipping sites, levels and tramways. According to an old rate book, John Simon took possession after William Richards, the rateable value of the property being £10 10s. John Simon died at Brynteg, July 13, 1871, aged 68. His widow, Mary Simon, also died at Brynteg, July 17, 1889, aged 83. When she was young, Mary often assisted her father, Howell Giles, to haul boats along the Cyfarthfa Canal.

I have no record as to what became of William Richards, but it is known that he left three sons—Thomas, William and Jenkin. William was of a very poor state of health, and appeared to be suffering from some kind of wasting disease. After Dr. Edward Davies (Cyfarthfa) was consulted, he made a thorough examination of the patient, and came to the conclusion that there was something in the stomach, so William was ordered to abstain from all food for two or three days, after which the doctor would call again. When he came, he ordered a saucerful of milk, which he held to the mouth of William, who was directed to keep his mouth open. To the surprise of the persons present, a small lizard emerged from the patient's mouth, and dropped into the saucer! It was placed in a bottle and lived for some time. No doubt it had been swallowed when William consumed some of the spring water. After this strange happening he rapidly recovered his health. Jenkin Richards and his wife, Elizabeth, were members of Salem Church, Heolgerrig, and had a son, William, who became a minister of the Gospel, and, I believe, held a pastorate at Penywern. The other brother, Thomas, was known as "Thomas Brynteg," and married Esther, sister of Hywel Jacki Dafydd, the runner. They lived in one of the two houses known as Tai Brynteg. Esther, who predeceased her husband, died on May 20, 1900, and both attained the age of 80. Their daughter, Ann Francis, died in the same house on March 12, 1928, aged 82. All three brothers above mentioned were miners.

Opposite the old Brynteg Farm was an old mine level called Lefal Duke, while a short distance above was Lefal Ddima, working the Gellideg coal seam. Near Tai Brynteg was Lefal Twyn, in which the 7ft. seam was worked, and here Lewis Coed Meurig met with a fatal accident as far back as 1803. Next we come to a very old house, Tŷ William o'r Llwyn, named after William Richards. The name Richards was very common in this locality and it is rather difficult to differentiate between the families who bore it. The family I remember living in this particular house was that of Mr. William Wagstaff, a fitter by trade. That was about fifty years ago. The branch tramroad passing this house leads up to numerous levels, the chief of which were Lefal Lewis Pugh, Lefal Mynydd, Leflau John a Howell Simon, and Lefal Dafydd Lewis, Cwmdu.

Near Brynteg Farm, where the Gellideg seam crops to the surface, the main tramroad bears away in a sharp turn to the right. If we follow it we come to the site of an old bridge called Pont Tod, over which was taken the shale from Lefal Tod, a mine level nearby—Tod being the name of the contractor in charge of it. Further on we come to another old mine level—Lefal Pregethwr, on the left of the tramway. This level was driven very straight in a westerly direction for a considerable distance, nearly underneath Llwynygwcw. From inside it daylight could be seen from a distance of several hundred yards from the entrance. The old level was opened by John Williams, who lived at one of the Ffrwd farms. Besides being a miner, John was also a lay preacher—hence the name Lefal Pregethwr. Some of the miners employed at this level became fervid religious enthusiasts, and often practised preaching on the mine stacks—"cernydd mwyn"—outside.

Two of these eventually became ministers. One was the Rev. Richard Griffiths, Tabor, Cefn Coed. Richard was a member of Zoar Church, and began to preach as a layman before the formation of the church at Yr Hen Dŷ, Heolgerrig, in 1838. The other was the Rev. Lewis Evans, known to his fellow-workmen as Lewis Jack Evans. He was a member of the congregation worshipping at Ynysgau at first, but later threw in his lot with the Baptist denomination. After an absence of many years from Merthyr, he returned to spend the end of his days in retirement at Providence House, Tramroadside, Georgetown, where he died. I remember hearing him speak at the funeral of the late Mr. Evan Evans, Six Bells, in 1886. Many of the miners of those days went to work wearing top hats, and once inside the levels made a place to keep their hats, which they replaced with the ordinary working "duck" cap. Just above Lefal Pregethwr was Pont John Ivor, near the patch and level worked by John Ivor. Now we reach the house of Twmi Mali and Kitty Pugh, his wife, but more will be related of Twmi at a later stage. The present occupier is Mr. John Gower Richards, who is an assistant architect. Just above again is the site of another old mine level, and I have been told that two women and one man did all the transport work from the " face " to the tip, these being Ann Hopkins (of Winchfawr), Kitty Pugh, and Richard Rees (of Tranch Bach).

CHAPTER XIV.

PENLLWYNDERI—THE HARP INN—WILLIAM MORGAN — LEFAL TALIESIN—PARC PONT BREN—TWMI MALI, THE HARPIST—THE METHODIST CAUSE—JACKI PRICE—WILLIAM SMITH—WAUN CADU.

ASCENDING the hill from the Travellers' Well, we pass on our right what was formerly the old Mount Pleasant public-house, where first John Webber, and afterwards his son Morgan Webber, resided. On our left, some distance above, there is a row of houses, known as Tai Twmi, because they were erected, about 1850, by Twmi Jack Morgan, son of Jack Morgan, of Cwm Waun Newydd. It was here that Thomas Morgan, of the Finger Post, was born, but his family afterwards moved to the Dynevor Arms. Some of the family lived afterwards at Tai Twmi, and one of them—Thomas Griffiths, who is nearly 80—still lives there. Just here a public footpath, coming from the direction of Tai Mawr Road through what is known as The Coedcae, crosses the main road, and, passing the upper end of Tai Twmi, leads on to Brynteg and Winchfawr. Above, on the right, is Tŷ Rees Tai Mawr, thus named because its occupier at one time was Rees Edwards, who had previously lived at Tai Mawr Isaf.

Now we come to an old road coming up from Tai Mawr, which crosses the main road and leads up to Clwydyfagwyr and Winchfawr. It is a typical bit of country road between Tai Mawr and the main road. At the cross-roads there is a milestone, marking the distance from Nantygwenith as being one mile. On the right there is a large house called in the old days Penllwynderi ; in fact, the immediate neighbourhood bore this pretty name, which conjures up visions of copses of oak scrub, of which the vestiges are seen only in places at the present time. It was here that Edward Edwards (Ned Daffi) and his wife lived up to the time of their death. The land belonging to the house was originally part of Tai Mawr Farm and was called Tir Uchaf Tai Mawr ; it was given to Edward, together with a sum of money, to build a house thereon, by his parents David and Mary Edwards. David was a direct descendant of the Gurnos family, and Mary was a daughter of the Coedmeurig family named Reynolds (or Rheinallt). Edward Edwards had four children—Margaret, David, Mary and Lewis. Margaret is now nearly 82, and David is about 79. Both Mary and David live at Cefn Coed. Edward was a contractor on a fairly large scale, and kept a large number of horses for haulage purposes. At the back of Penllwynderi lived Thomas and Sarah Davies for many years. Thomas was an old miner known as Tomos Pendarren. On the left hand side, between the Clwydyfagwyr road and the main road, there were two old thatched cottages, in one of which lived William Toulds, while in the other lived Rees Roderick. William and Ann Toulds were noted characters in their day, but space does not permit my going into their history. Here is an anecdote concerning Rees Roderick. One day, on coming out of level Bwci with his horse and tram, a woman neighbour of his hailed him and told him that his wife had been confined. " Wel, shwd mae hi ? " asked Rees, " a fyddai'n well i fi ddod tua thre ? " " Na, na ; cerwch chi ymlaen. Mae hi'n lled dda," was the reply. And Rees continued on his journey. On coming out again with a second load, the same person approached him with the news that his wife had presented him with another child. " Wel, shwd mae hi ? " enquired Rees, " a fyddai'n well i fi ddod tua thre ? " His informant answered : " Na, na, Rees bach ; cerwch chi ymlaen. Mae hi yn alreit." Poor old Rees then entered the level again, and on bringing out his third " journey," who should be eagerly awaiting him again but the same kind neighbour with the following : " Wel, wel, Rees bach, be' chi'n feddwl ? Mae Mari yn y gwely eto ! " Whereupon Rees, seeing that things were getting beyond the limit, began to lose his temper and burst forth with : " Be' chi'n dweud ? Mae hi wedi cael *dau* o'r blaen ! " And with an air of determination went on : " Wel, dim shwrna arall, myn diawl ! " and made his way home.

Between the site of those two cottages and the Harp Inn are a number of houses built by Richard Jack Morgan and called Tai Newydd Penllwynderi. Here lived Edward Edwards (Cilhepste), Hywel Jacki Dafydd, and Tomos Dafis (Daff). Next we come to the Harp Inn, built about 1840 by Billy Jack Morgan, but later owned by William Jenkins of Ty'nycoedcae. The first person to occupy the Harp was Billy Jack Morgan. Edward Hughes was the next tenant, and it is interesting to note here the amount of information that I have been able to obtain from the notes recorded by Idris Ddu concerning certain sums paid by him at the house (the Harp Inn) of Edward Hughes in the months of August and October, 1847. Some of these payments were to his workmen. Being a contractor, Idris Ddu would pay his men at the Harp, Dyffryn, Grawen, Gwynne's Arms, Six (Six Bells), or the Miners' Arms ; sometimes he sent William his son to pay them. All the payments at these places took place in 1847, the earliest written record I have seen of the Harp Inn, but it was in existence before that date. This Edward Hughes took a great deal of interest in cock-fighting, and was also the trainer of Hywel Jacki Dafydd for all his races.

Jenkin Jenkins (later of Nantgau) next kept the Harp Inn, but only for a short period, and he then moved to Tai Canol Isaf, Heolgerrig. Then Rowland Thomas (Idris Ddu) moved from Bryngwyn to the Harp, Penllwynderi, March 5, 1856, but was only there a matter of ten months, for he died December 26, 1856, aged 67. Although he was called "Old Rowley," he was not so old after all as to justify this name. At the time of his funeral the frost was severe and there had been a heavy snowfall, with the result that the funeral cortege was unable to follow the road, so it had to traverse the fields on its way to the burial ground of Hen Dŷ Cwrdd, Cefn Coed. During the time Idris Ddu occupied the Harp, only one eisteddfod was held there. One of the subjects for competition was an essay on "The Union of the Four Nations of Great Britain," the winning effort being that of Mr. David Williams, Ynyscynon. Idris made the following remarks on the winning essay : "Ireland was fully conquered by King John in 1210 ; Wales was conquered by Edward I in 1283 ; Scotland was never absolutely conquered by the power of arms, but the two crowns were united in 1603. It was in 1707 that the union was completed. The union of Ireland and Britain was completed in 1801."

The next tenant of the Harp was William Morgan, who, when a young man, went to California, accompanied by his friend Jenkin Richards, and both worked at some quarries. Unfortunately, William was rendered totally blind as the result of a serious accident caused by an explosion of powder. His friends rallied to render the financial assistance needed to bring home the poor maimed fellow, and a reverend gentleman by the name of Phillips kindly volunteered to accompany him as far as New York, where he saw him safely put on board the ship that was to take him back to his native land. Now William, before going away, had been keeping company with Shenad, daughter of Idris Ddu ; and although the accident had disfigured her lover for life, that did not in any way mar the affection she bore him, but rather made it deeper and stronger, and William and Shenad were united in marriage. They went to live at the Harp Inn with the widow of Idris. William Morgan returned from California in 1857, soon after the death of Idris Ddu ; and when Ann Thomas, the widow, went to live with her son William at Winchfawr, she left the Harp to the newly-married couple. Both lived there for the remainder of their days. They kept a general provision business as well as the public-house, and it is remarkable that William was able to shave himself and was very accurate in changing all sorts of coins although he was blind. Their daughter Ann, and her husband William Elias Thomas, then took over the business ; but since their time the Harp has been kept by various other people.

Opposite the Harp there is one of the only two shale-tips on the northern side of the Swansea Road. A short distance above we come to a bridge over the Scwrfa Brook. If the brook is followed upwards for a little distance, we reach the site of an old mine level—Lefal Taliesin—in which were worked the lower mine veins, the Rosser and Garw groups. It is within 80 yards of the Bridge in the Cwm. We are still keeping on the border of the outcrop, and the shale brought out from this level was tipped on the other side of the main road, while the mine was despatched to the main tramway, southwards from the road. To get an exceedingly fine view of Pontycapel, I would recommend anyone to take up a stand on the tip above the brook, and I am sure he or she would be amply repaid by viewing the charming picture in the hollow below. The old mine-stacking place (or " llorfa ") has been fenced-in lately by Mr. Elias Thomas, and is now a nice field alongside which runs a public footpath.

We now enter into the midst of a number of houses alongside the mountain road. In one of these lived John Edwards and Bess his wife, who were the parents of the late William Edwards. The latter was somewhat of a scholar, and some years ago wrote a historical account of Clwydyfagwyr. He had spent most of his life in the Clwydyfagwyr district, but ended his days at Cefn, where he died on January 4, 1923. Following are the names of some of the past and present residents there : Mr. and Mrs. Thomas Richards (Thomas being the grandson of Twmi Mali), John Morgan (Cwmtwrch), John Davies (Daff), Thomas Jones and William Morgan. The latter was born next door to the Harp Inn, and for some time after the death of his brother, John the horse-dealer, William kept the farm of Coedmeurig. His father lost his life in the first Gethin explosion in 1862.

On the right hand side lived Mrs. Ann Thomas, widow of the late Mr. William Elias Thomas. She died quite recently, February 14, 1930, aged 70. Ann was a daughter of William Morgan and a grand-daughter of Idris Ddu. Rowland Morgan Jones, of Cefn, was also a son of William Morgan Jones of the Harp, and a grandson of Idris Ddu. Ann Thomas was born at the Harp Inn, and took possession of it after her father's death. Her son is Mr. Elias Thomas, our genial excise officer. A short distance above is Pontbren Park, where lived an old female character known as Catws Pontbren Park ; but the old house has been long since demolished. Opposite this place is the old residence of John and Gwenllian Harris. John Harris was at one time a great house-coal contractor, obtaining his coal from the mountain-side levels above. The house is called Plas Legan.

We are now on the main tramway. I want the reader to come with me back to the house of Twmi Mali, now occupied by Mr. J. G. Richards, a grandson of the old miner and harpist. In Twmi's house his old friends and acquaintances used to meet occasionally to spend a few hours with Twmi, and Kitty his wife. They diverted themselves by singing or stepping to the accompaniment of Twmi's marvellous harp, fashioned with his own hands and on which he was a skilful performer. One afternoon I paid a visit to the Cyfarthfa Castle Museum to see this quaint, rustic instrument. I was kindly directed by Mr. Llewelyn, the assistant curator, through the underground passages to the cellar, where the old relic was safely stored with the other paraphernalia of the Museum. The old instrument was in a very dilapidated condition, which fact did not warrant its being placed amongst the better-preserved examples of old harps in the Museum above for exhibition purposes. Now the remarkable thing about Twmi Mali's harp is that the old harpist, although totally untrained, fashioned it himself from wood that he had cut in the neighbouring Cwm Ffrwd. When gazing upon it we were not spiritualistic enough to fancy that we could hear the sweet strains issuing at the deft touches of the old miner as his fingers swept the strings, but it did give us a thrill of admiration, perhaps, tinged with a shade of regret that we were not fortunate enough to be members of those very happy gatherings in the house of Twmi Mali. Twmi and his harp were also in great demand at local weddings and dances. The merry company would congregate at the Harp Inn to celebrate the happy event, and the old harpist would provide the accompaniment. When he stopped playing the revellers would shout, "Gw on, Twmi." But Twmi would reply, "Mae y delyn wedi blino. Cerwch chi ymlaen : fe ddaw hi i diwn yn fuan." Both Thomas Richards and Kitty his wife were old natives of the district. Kitty was the sister of the three brothers, Lewis, Hugh and Hwmphra (Humphrey) Pugh, and I have been told that their parents lived at one time at Tai Mawr. Just above the cowsheds on the upper road, near Tai Mawr, there are the ruins of an old house, of which I could trace no account until Mrs. Margaret Simons, who lived at the farm for many years, told me. It seems that the parents of Kitty Pugh had lived at one time at this old house.

If we follow the tramroad we soon reach Clwydyfagwyr proper. In this district mining operations were carried on at a very early date. There are indications here of a system of scouring for iron-ore, which I shall deal with again. In connection with the industry that developed, it became necessary to build houses for the workmen, so the Company erected two rows of dwelling-houses. Further along, on our right, we reach Waun Bant, a substantial house built about forty years ago by John Lewis, Cwmdu, a contractor. It is now occupied by his son, John Morgan Lewis. Near here is the old mine-level—Lefal Bwci—worked very extensively for many years on the lower mine-courses, the shale being taken across to the northern side of the main road to be tipped. Years ago superstition was rampant. The "cannwyll gorff" and "bwci" (or "bwgan") were abroad every night according to some, and children were filled with awe at night if they saw any kind of light in an unusual place, or a dark form approaching them. Someone had very likely imagined that he saw something of the same sort here, hence the name Lefal Bwci. Isn't there a word "bogey" in English to correspond to the Welsh "bwci"?

Now we come to Carmel Chapel, Clwydyfagwyr, which is a Methodist church. The cause was commenced early in the last century (1823), the first meetings being held in the house of Thomas and Shan Thomas (Pontbren), Llwynygwcw. This old house had a thatched roof and was in a very central position for the worshippers. At that time there were very few houses in the locality. Most of the workmen were miners, many of whom came from Cefn Coed to work at the levels and patches. Of those who attended the early religious meetings at Llwynygwcw many were members of Field Street Chapel (Capel y Cae), Cefn Coed, which had been built in 1807 and was rebuilt in 1830. T. E. Clarke, in his "History of Merthyr," mentions in 1848: "There is a room belonging to Moriah Chapel, Cefn, at Clwydyfagwyr, about one mile from Coed-y-Cymmer, on the hill-side, which will hold about 150 persons. A school is held there every Sunday, and is supplied with teachers from Coed-y-Cymmer."

Those miners from Cefn met regularly, with others, at Llwynygwcw. Often Shan Thomas would prepare "llawn crochon o gawl, pen llwdn, a llysiau ddigon yn gymysg" for the Cefn folk during inclement weather, to save them the trouble of walking to and fro from Cefn. It was not unusual for them to attend their meetings in their working clothes, and thus, week in and week out, they carried on the work faithfully. Sunday School was held in the morning, and occasionally a minister would come over from Cefn in the afternoon. Thomas and Shan possessed a mare called Star, which they kindly placed at the disposal of the members, in order to bring the minister over and convey him back to Cefn after the service. The old mare continued to render noble service right up to the end, and deservedly merited the name "Seren yr Achos." Shan and Thomas Thomas were buried the same day.

The cause was carried on from house to house for 17 years. Although the week-night prayer meetings took place at Llwynygwcw, the Sunday School was held at various houses, such as those of Watkin Jones (Clwyd), Evan Williams (Gellideg), William Powell (Clwyd), Rees Powell (Mynydd), Evan Dafydd (Mynydd), William Harris (Coedmeurig), William Williams (Ffrwd), Margaret Davies (Mynydd), Elizabeth Thomas (Gellideg), Edward Evan (Clwyd), Catherine Pugh (Clwyd), John Jones (Tranch Bach), Philip Jones (Ffrwd), Rachel Mathias (Mynydd), John Hamer, Lewis Thomas (Penllwynderi), and others. At length it was felt that the time was opportune to build a chapel, and this was done. At the upper end of the present chapel Houses a building was erected in 1840, the ground rent being 10/- a year. It was 27 feet long and 15 feet wide, with benches serving for the seating accommodation of 150 people (according to Clarke). Against the upper end was built a stable to accommodate the minister's horse until the services were over. Pant-tywyll Chapel was then in course of erection, and a Mr. William Morris, of that place, offered to lend his horse for the convenience of ministers in their journeyings from one place of worship to another. The horse was named Jack Morris, and, as a result of continual practice, became thoroughly acquainted with the routes to the various chapels. The minister who borrowed the horse at Pant-tywyll was told he need have no fear about finding his way to the chapel at which he was to preach—Jack would see to that. All that was required of him was just to mount and throw the reins over his neck, then Jack would take him safely to his destination. The willing steed performed its work excellently for some years ; but alas ! on one occasion it made a terrible mistake. It happened in this way : Jack was often taken to Heolgerrig by the son of William Morris, and he would sometimes call at the Six Bells public-house. Now one Sunday a strange minister going from Pant-tywyll to Clwyd-yfagwyr received the usual instructions from William Morris and mounted the old horse. Jack ambled along, but his memory must have been at fault (or was it a joke on his part ?), for instead of arriving at the appointed place of worship, the minister found himself at the door of the Six Bells Inn !

This new chapel was illumined by the light of four halfpenny candles, two of which were in the pulpit and one on either side of the room. Daniel Jones was in charge of the lights, and occasionally he would go around snuffing them with his fingers. Soon after the new chapel was built, two of the most prominent members—Jackie Price and William Smith, who lived at Cefn—each built a house adjoining the chapel. As the chapel was rather small to hold the Sunday School comfortably, the elder women held their class in William Smith's house, while the elder men held theirs in the house of Jackie Price. Jackie was invariably the superintendent of the school, and, after dismissing the children, he would call at the private houses and order : "Casglwch y llyfrau." One Sunday a little girl came to school late, and, on being reprimanded by Jackie for her unpunctuality, pleaded in extenuation that she had seen a sheep that had fallen into a ditch on the Waun, and in the circumstances she did not know exactly what to do. Jackie immediately gave orders for the books to be collected, with the announcement: " Mae dafad wedi syrthio yn y ffos; dewch i gyd i geisio ei chael oddiyno."

At one time there was a strong temperance band at the Glwyd, under the conductorship of Edward Smith, and every Easter it would march in procession to Cefn, where temperance meetings were held. Jackie Price was always one of the flag-bearers. He was such a staunch temperance advocate that he would not allow even his pigs or cattle to have any of the grain sold at the Brewery mixed with their food.

The Rev. W. Evans, Tonyrefail, who used to preach occasionally at Clwydyfagwyr, would walk all the way from Tonyrefail and back again. One Sunday he was accosted by two men on the way, and one put to him the question: " What is the length of a Sabbath Day's journey?" The reverend man readily obliged his enquirer in this wise: " Why, certainly. It is from the house to the chapel and back!"

The second chapel, 36 feet by 21 feet—at present used as a public elementary school—was built in 1868. The old building was converted into dwelling-houses, with the old stable still at the upper end: the row is called Tai'r Capel. It may be interesting for the reader to know the names of the leading men who struggled on with the cause at the Glwyd through the lean as well as the prosperous years of its existence. They were: Jackie Price, William Smith, William Lewis (Cwmdu), John Edwards, David Evans (who was secretary of the church for 40 years), and Siams (James) Morgan. Siams was a very fluent speaker and was always appointed delegate to temperance meetings. He spent the closing years of his life as a lamp-locker in the colliery at Penygraig, Rhondda. Never having experienced an illness in his life, he used to say, some ten years before his death, how he would just like to have one week's illness before leaving this world. Upon hearing this, Morgan, his son, said to him one day: " Father, is that what you say after having had seventy years to prepare for the change?" But the wish of poor Siams was never realized, for he was one of the victims of the Penygraig Colliery explosion in 1880. His son, Siams Morgan Bach, was also a gifted public speaker and was always sent as a delegate to public and political meetings. During the 1868 Parliamentary Election, a public meeting was held at Ebenezer Chapel, Cefn Coed, and the building was so packed that Siams Bach had great difficulty in getting inside. Policemen were posted at the doors to prevent the youngsters entering the building, and as Siams was very small of stature he was taken to be one of the boys, and was promptly turned away. But Siams roared and argued that he had a wife and that he was a householder, whereupon he was admitted. No sooner was he inside than he was called to the platform and immediately asked to address the meeting. He very soon captured the crowded audience with his eloquent speech, interspersed with skilful descriptive illustrations, which soon made him the hero of the meeting. Shortly afterwards, Siams and his family emigrated to the U.S.A., settling down at Plymouth ; and this gifted son of Clwyd attained the age of 80 before he was called from his earthly labours to receive his reward.

Edward Smith, son of William Smith, was a musician who did a great deal to foster music at Clwydyfagwyr. He was one of a family, consisting of five sons and three daughters, and all took advantage of the music lessons given by Mr. J. Roberts (Ieuan Gwyllt), each one being able to play an instrument. One would play upon the flute, another on the harp, while another performed on the drum. It was Edward who founded and conducted the local band ; in fact, he directed most things musical in the district. This was in 1875 ; but shortly afterwards the family emigrated to the U.S.A. In 1913 Edward Smith paid a visit to the old country, and was most pleased to find that his early musical efforts at the Glwyd had not been in vain.

William Thomas (Shenad) took a leading part in all things connected with the church for many years.

William Shon Powell possessed wide Biblical knowledge, and was a very useful member of the Sunday School, in which he served as a teacher. He was also a faithful deacon of the church. Rees Lewis was a son of one of the founders of the cause. Thomas Thomas (Clwyd) was a deep thinker who had studied the books of Thomas Charles, James Hughes, and Barnes.

The following were the deacons during the third period of the history of the religious cause : that is, after the third chapel was built in 1902. This building, much larger than the previous one, contained a gallery and was furnished with electric light—a great improvement on the four halfpenny candles ! :—

John Lewis (Cwmdu), was the son of William Lewis, one of the founders, who, when unable to walk to chapel, came to the service occasionally on the back of his donkey. The son followed in the footsteps of his father, and he was treasurer of Carmel for 30 years, right up to the time of his death on January 12, 1925, at the age of 72.

James Thomas was another example of the son taking the place of the father and also of the grandfather. He was the son of William Thomas and a grandson of David Evans—one of the founders. James wrote a History of Carmel Church from its commencement, which was read at the centenary services held September 23, 1923.

William Davies was a quiet, unassuming officer of the church, a faithful and diligent worker for the good cause ; but just at the time when he was at the height of his usefulness, his cheerful life was brought to a close without a moment's warning on February 1, 1928, at the age of 51.

David Rees Jones was another grandson of Daniel Jones, one of the founders.

The present deacons are David Haines, Evan Richards, Wm. Davies (Daff), John Dl. Jones, Hopkin Hopkins, David Jones and Rees Williams.

The Elementary School at Clwydyfagwyr has been held in what was the old second chapel since its commencement in 1877. The first headmistress was Miss M. A. Rees, and there were 62 children on the register. The school has been very beneficial to the younger children of the district. Evening classes were also successfully carried on some years ago and were attended by many of the adults. On one occasion the head teacher was going around the students to see how they were progressing. He stopped by one who wore a heavy beard, and asked : " Shwd y'ch chwi yn dod ymlaen ? " The student answered, " O, lled dda, syr." " Gadewch i mi weld," said the master ; and after scrutinising the work, he added, " O wel, yr ydych yn gwneud yn dda iawn, o hen ddyn." The student must have taken it to heart to be classed as an old man, because the next evening he arrived minus the beard and was thus able to prove to the master that he was not so old after all as he was taken to be.

We are now on Waun Cadu. The name Waun is usually given to land lying between the upper and lower lands on the mountain slopes, such as Cwm-y-Waun Newydd, Waun Bant, Waun Cadu, Waun Brynteg, Waun Shon Dafydd Ifan, Waun Penyrheol, Waun Cwmyglo, Waun Cwmdu, Waun Felen, and Waun Darlwm (this is a corruption of either Daear Lwm or Derw Lwyn). It is not so easy to explain the word Cadu. If it signifies " conflict, fighting, or a struggle " (as is the meaning given by Spurrel), Waun Cadu would mean Waun y Frwydr or Waun y Brwydrau—quite a plausible meaning, as Carn y Frwydr is not far away. It is reasonable to think that both places originally had their names from the same cause. A possible explanation is that it was named after Cati, Catws, or Kitty (various forms of Catherine). A certain William Williams, with Catws his wife, who had lived at Nantgau, were tenants of this land at one time. This old Waun was once enclosed, and the fence can be seen in the old map of 1832. On the northern side the fence was nearly in line with the present road as far as the lower fence of Twyn Carmel House. It then ran south-east, then north-east in line with the rear fence of Llwynygwcw, which would thus be on the southern side of Waun Cadu. Pownd Cadu is situated in the flat stretch of the Waun near Carmel Chapel. The name Clwydyfagwyr has arisen from a gate entrance in this old fence or enclosure, called Magwyr ; hence the name Clwyd-y-Fagwyr.

CHAPTER XV.

LLWYN-Y-GWCW — WINGFIELD HOUSE — TWYN CARMEL HOUSE — CLWYDYFAGWYR PROPER—PANT BRYN MAN—LEFAL BWRLIN JACK MORGAN—THE SCWRFA BRIDGE—PONT WAUN BANT—COED MEURIG —ROWLAND THOMAS (IDRIS DDU), BRYNGWYN.

LLWYNYGWCW, which consists of a number of houses built together, is a very old place. Originally there was only a thatched house, with a stable, which is now in ruins. The first inhabitants at Llwynygwcw of whom we have any record were Thomas and Shan Thomas, Pontbren. Both were well advanced in years when the Methodist cause was started in 1823. There is no doubt that the surroundings were better wooded than they are at present, and that the cuckoo was a frequent visitor—hence the name Llwynygwcw. Nearby is Wingfield House, better known as Cuckoo Castle, built many years ago on the site of an older dwelling by the late Ebeneser Evans, who was a son of Mr. Isaac Evans, provision merchant at Castle Street, Merthyr. Ebenezer Evans carried on a jewellery business in the town for several years, then built the large house near Llwynygwcw, where his son and daughter afterwards resided. The latter, who died quite recently, was the wife of Mr. T. B. Greene, our esteemed journalist, who has been on the reporting staff of the *Merthyr Express* for over 30 years. Mr. Greene comes from a family of journalists.

Next we come to Twyn Carmel, the present house having been built on the site of an old dwelling known as Tŷ Shon Tai Cwpla built long ago by that remarkable old character Gwenni'r Meiswn, who had built many other houses besides. The house is now occupied by Mrs. E. Jones (widow of Richard Jones) and her sons. There is a great deal of land in this neighbourhood, the freehold of which was purchased by this family in 1926. The road to Winch-fawr passes quite near here.

Now we shall return to the site of the old main tramway, which passes between the old houses of Clwydyfagwyr and Carmel Chapel. A short distance above the first turning to the right there is a long and deep ditch opening upwards towards the mountain through Pant Bryn Mân. This is undoubtedly one of the ore scouring places of the old days when the iron-works were in their infancy. If we follow the ditch for a distance of 350 yards we come to what was once a large reservoir, but now the place is nearly filled-in with vegetation. In the embankment there were two outlets serving for the occasional release of water for the scouring process. At the sides of this ditch, called Y Gwter Fawr, veins of iron ore can still be seen. The sudden rush of a huge volume of water from the reservoir would dislodge the iron ore from its bed right along the sides of this ditch until the edge of the outcrop was reached. This brook running through the ditch was afterwards called Nant-y-Scwrfa, and enters Cwm Ffrwd near Pontycapel.

Returning to the main tramway and continuing along it, we pass numerous levels and patches—very few of the levels being on the right of the tramway, but all are connected with the tramroad. On the left we pass Cwar Lewis Cross Keys, a large quarry in which was worked the Gellideg Rock. Nearer the tramway the lower iron-ore veins were worked by open patch work. In the patch, worked by William Thomas (Wm. Rowley), the son of Idris Ddu, the Garw group, with the Garw coal seam, from 16 inches to 18 inches thick, were worked. Further on was an old level called Lefal Gwyr Tyncoedcae, which was near the Swansea Road and opposite the road leading down to Tyncoedcae Farm. The tip of this level comes to the edge of the main road to a point below the gate. A short distance above was Lefal Bwrlin (more correctly, Lefal Bullring). For about a quarter of a mile the Swansea Road just here is very flat and in the past scores of foot-races have taken place there. This district is called Pant-y-Bwrlin. The tip belonging to Lefal Bwrlin also came to the side of the main road. In this old level worked Jack Morgan, of Cwm Waun Newydd—first as a miner and afterwards as a contractor. The name of the level reminds us of the old custom of bull-baiting that existed many years ago in various localities. Somewhere in this Pant (hollow) there used to be a bull-ring, the site of which may have been covered by the tips. The bull-ring was a flat, circular space, with a strong post fixed in the centre, to which a rope was fastened. The other end of the rope was either fastened around the horns or to the nose-ring of the bull. The animal was driven around the ring at rope's length, worried by the dogs until it was goaded into madness. Many spectators came to see the cruel sport, and were highly delighted the more furious the bull got, cheering him when he gave one of the dogs a vigorous toss, and cheering the dog which clung the most tenaciously to the bull. Afterwards the bull was slaughtered. This cruel custom came to an end many years ago.

In the old levels miners did not pay as much heed to punctuality in coming to work as they were compelled to do later on. They would often come late in the morning and work to a late hour at night. One summer's evening, one of the Lefal Bwrlin miners, coming home rather late, was met by one of his neighbours, who asked : " Where have you been so late, William ? " " Late ? " was the reply, " why, the stars are not up yet ! " Oftentimes when the miners met together to have their meals, questions would arise and be discussed. One day the question of politics arose, and the first question asked was, What was meant by a Liberal ? After several attempts at a definition had been made, the others turned to Jack Morgan. " Beth y'ch chwi'n ddweud yw Liberal, Jack Morgan ? 'Ry'ch yn henach na ni ; ma' gyda chi dipyn o brofiad." After a little meditation, Jack answered : " Wel, boys, dyma fy marn i : Liberal yw dyn sydd yn rhoi dwy ddima am gincg " ! The next question that arose was, What was a Whig ? As no satisfactory answer was forthcoming, they again appealed to Jack Morgan. " Beth i chi'n ddweud yw Whig, Jack Morgan ? " " Wel," said Jack, " Whigs yw y rhai hynny sydd yn wigo " ! Then someone asked the meaning of the word Tory ; and after answering as best they could, they came to the conclusion that Jack was the only one present who could answer intricate questions of this kind. He was asked, " Beth y'ch chi'n dweud yw Tori ? " ; and he answered simply, " Wel, Tori yw dyn sydd yn torri rhywbeth " ! Many a happy half-hour was spent in this way by the miners of olden days. " Llun cyntaf yn y mis" (the first Monday in the month) was a specially notable day, for the miners spent it in fetching clay to hold their candles.

On the right hand side of the road, near the Scwrfa Bridge, there are two houses, in one of which lived David Davies (Dafydd Pegi), a noted racer in his day, who took part in numerous races. As we climb the hill, on the right we see another house, built by Thomas and Nancy Simon. Their daughter married Jeremiah Davies, and both lived there for many years. Simon Davies, their son, now occupies the premises. The next point we reach when following the main road is Pont Waun Bant, near which the shale from Lefal Bwci was conveyed across to the north of road. Just above there is a fairly level and straight stretch of road, about 130 yards in length, where many old-time runners have tried their paces. Near Pont Waun Bant a road branches off to the very ancient farm of Coed Meurig, a quarter of a mile away to the right. Various opinions have been expressed regarding the name Coed Meurig. In "Notes on the Old Parish Register," compiled by Major F. T. James, we find the name mentioned in 1716 (214 years ago). The people of Merthyr are indebted to Major James, who is a keen historian, for his very interesting work, which contains pages of indisputable and reliable facts. Mr. Charles Wilkins, in his work, also stated that the name occurs in the old parish register, but did not mention any date. He writes: "We must wander further back to find that the Meurig, who either sought refuge in the wood or gave the name to the place, was, in all probability, the father of Arthur, the British hero. Meurig, the Regulus of this County (Glamorganshire), was very popular with his people, and famed for his valour and wisdom. He was the hero after whom local positions of any striking character would be called."

Pant Rhiw Feurig, the hollow from which Nant Canaid springs, is one of these local positions, and in it are several small cairns. The old mountain road leading up the steep hill to Werfa Camp is known as Rhiw Feurig. Other examples are Ystrad Meurig and Ynys Meurig. Someone once said, "Enw mawr yw enw Meurig." The rateable value of Coed Meurig in 1769 was £6. In 1866, nearly a hundred years later, it was £40 15s. A certain David Edwards of Tai Mawr Farm is known to have married Mary, the daughter of Reynolds of Coed Meurig Farm. Now, in the parish register there is an entry to the effect that John Rheinallt (a Welsh form of Reynolds) buried a son, William, from Coed Meurig in 1795. This John Rheinallt is the Reynolds referred to, so the marriage must have been early in the last century. The next people I have traced as having lived there are David and Pegi Beynon. After the death of the former, his widow married Richard, son of Jack Morgan, Cwm Waun Newydd; and their son, Henry R. Morgan, a contractor, kept the farm after his parents for many years. Henry met with a fatal accident in his own level at Winch-fawr. There are living at present at Llwynygwcw children and grandchildren of Henry Morgan.

There is another very interesting reminiscence in connection with Coed Meurig which refers to Shon Llewelyn of Cefn, who was born in 1690, thus proving again that the farm is very old. Shon was an expert, among other accomplishments, in mowing hay or corn, and often mowed for the neighbouring farmers. When 72 years of age he mowed, unaided, in one day a hayfield of three acres. This field was at the rear of Coed Meurig, and the following lines were composed to commemorate the feat:

"Shon Llewelyn, â'r coes crwpyn,
Lladd tair erw yn y dydd;
Mae'n awr yn ddeuddeg mlwydd a thri'gain,
Os lladd bedwar, rhowch e'n rhydd."

On another occasion he was mowing a large meadow called Waun Coed Meurig, and it is said that he mowed a " swath," or " ystod," one mile long without once sharpening his scythe. The remarkable thing about this scythe was that it had been returned to the shopkeeper at Merthyr by a buyer as being worthless ; and when Shon went to buy a new scythe, the shopkeeper presented him with the returned one. After setting it and practising with it for some time, the scythe turned out to be one of the best he had handled. Shon named it " The Widow," because, as he said jokefully, " it had been left behind." It is said that Shon Llewelyn, at the age of 80, mowed a field in company with his son, grandson and great-grandson, in the order of their ages. Shon took the first swath, his son the second, his grandson the third, and his great-grandson the fourth—four generations of mowers.

Another who had associations with Coed Meurig was Lewis Coed Meurig, son of John and Ann Beynon, and born in one of the thatched dwellings at Penllwynderi. When Lewis was two years old, the family moved to Coed Meurig. At that time (about the middle of the 18th century) there were four houses in addition to the farm, and into one of these the family moved. Idris Ddu and T. E. Clarke mention that Lewis Coed Meurig tried lead-mining on Cilsanws Mountain, but without success. He was a very able man and a poet of some standing. At one of the competitive meetings held at the Patriot Inn he was awarded the prize for the best song on " Superstition." Out of 21 competitors' efforts, Lewis' song, " Signs before the Death of Flora," was adjudged the best. While working as a miner at Lefal Twyn Brynteg in 1803, Lewis met with a fatal accident. The following lines were composed to his memory :

" Lewis ddilys gerdd dda,—cynghorwr
A mwnwr mewn manna ;
Pregethwr a gwerthwr llyfra',
Coblar nêt—pwy ddwed na ? "

The following are names found in the old Parish Register :—

1763—Edward, son of David Williams, Coed Meurig, buried.

1769—Mary Gunter, wife of Lewis Coed Meurig, buried.

1777—Mary John Thomas, Coed Meurig, buried.

1787—William of Coed Meurig, buried.

1795—William, son of Rheinallt, Coed Meurig, buried.

1802—John, son of Lewis John, aged 19, of Coed Meurig, buried.

If we continue along the Swansea Road we soon come to an isolated house on the right hand side, called Bryngwyn, built about 1835 by Rowland Thomas (Idris Ddu). Rowland, the son of Edward Thomas, of Llanbradach, was born, according to his own written statement, at noon on the 25th of December, 1789, at Mhan Milwr in the Parish of Eglwys Elian (Eglwys Ilan), Glamorganshire. He died at the Harp Inn, Clwydyfagwyr, December 26, 1856, aged 67. Ann, his wife, was born in the village of Talyllyn, in the Parish of Llanfihangel, Breconshire, on March 27, 1796. It is very interesting to follow the movements of Rowley, a record of which he left in his MSS. Edward (Edward Rowley), his son, was born at Cwm-y-Capel, opposite Cefn-Coed-y-Cymer, and which would be just inside the Merthyr Parish boundary, on January 21, 1819. Another son, Thomas, was born at the new Grawen Houses, Cefn Coed, on June 15, 1821. He goes on to state that his son Aneurin was born in a house on the mountain-side (afterwards called Winchfawr) on March 11, 1824 ; Mary (February 1, 1826) and William (March 3, 1828) were other children born at the same house. His daughter Shenad, who afterwards married Wm. Morgan Jones, of the Harp Inn, was born at Lower Colliers' Row, Cyfarthfa, on May 2, 1831.

Rowley was a mathematician who took deep, practical interest in science. One of his mathematical experiments sought to discover how long it had taken Nature to wear away the great gorge at Cwm Ffrwd. His method of procedure was as follows. First he drew a plan of the Cwm, which showed the falls of Pwllyn Pren and Pwllyn Annie, and one day he visited the place to take measurements and place special marks near the falls—two nails being driven into a tree near each fall. All the data, such as heights and distances, were carefully entered into a note-book, which is still in the possession of his descendants. I do not think Rowley lived long enough to ascertain any definite results from his experiment, for time was an important factor to allow for the necessary wearing-away process. The date of the experiment was given as March 27, 1849, and the kind of tree into which the nails were driven was also faithfully recorded. Crude as this experiment appears to be, it reveals a brain of great mathematical ingenuity. Astronomy also claimed his attention. I remember many years ago seeing a sun-dial on the wall in front of Bryngwyn House, but which has now disappeared, there being no trace of the stone to be found. An iron pin was fixed in the centre of a circle inscribed in the stone, Roman numerals being used to denote the hours.

Having worked during the whole of his lifetime as a miner in various capacities, he was very conversant with the local geological formation. Not only was he a skilled practical miner, but also a scholarly geologist. The latter fact is clearly proved by the treatise he sent to the Cardiff National Eisteddfod of 1835, under the name of "Tubal Cain." It was a treatise on the mineral basin of Glamorganshire and the adjoining districts, and the printed leaflet had an explanatory appendix also by the same author. "Tubal Cain" dealt with all the coal seams and iron-ore veins in the district, the quantities yielded per cubic yard, their qualities, the names and thickness of the various coal seams and iron-ore veins as well as the intermediary rocks. The section dealing with the various rocks, seams and veins is highly instructive, and it is said that Rowland Thomas was one of the first to describe this locality, as regards its minerals, with such geological detail. He did not state whether his work won the prize at Cardiff, but Charles Wilkins said it was the best treatise sent in. In 1853 another treatise, in Welsh, on the same subject, was written, but this was much more elaborate.

To prove that the subject of my sketch was undoubtedly an expert in mining, who had gained a great deal of experience in the various grades of mining, at the time, we have only to read the following account written with the heading "House of Commons, February 19th, 1849":—

"On the motion of Mr. Hume on the subject of explosions in mines, I beg leave as a miner, and to some extent a little acquainted through my own experience on the subject, to give my opinion towards adopting a new plan of forming coal mines for the safety of our fellow-creatures, working and governing the pits, levels, drifts, etc." Then he proceeds to express his views that, "Firstly, all pits, levels, and drifts, should be made large enough to allow the easy passage of air and that all old workings should be shut up tightly. The pit should be made large enough to allow for a certain quantity of air for a given area. There should be an inlet and an outlet to every pit, level, and drift. A large pit is always safer to the sinkers." Continuing, he gives the cost of sinking, which shows that Rowley must have had some experience in that branch of mining operations. "Say twelve square yards at the surface. If that was cut one yard deep, 12 cubic yards would have been cut. If the cost per cubic yard was 15s., the first 12 cubic yards would cost £9; the second 12 c. yards would cost £9 plus one third—£12—etc." Secondly, he deals with the ventilation and how the air should be conducted through the workings. Thirdly, the power of ventilation is dealt with. "Natural ventilation," says he, "is not always reliable, and therefore a furnace should be placed near the upper outlet to assist the ventilation. Fourthly, the plan of sinking one large pit, only, ought to be prohibited; parting of a pit, for the purpose of ventilation, by plank partition, is often dangerous; a separate outlet for a pit is the safest."

These are only a few of the points which he advocated should be included in a Bill for the prevention of explosions in coal mines, etc. I take it to be evidence given by Rowland Thomas before a committee or commission at the House of Commons some eight days before the question of explosions in mines was to be dealt with by the House. And a more able or scholarly witness in this particular direction it would have been hard to find at that time.

At a Cymreigyddion meeting held at the Glove and Shears (Y Faneg a'r Gwelleif), Nos Calan, 1849, a debate took place between the miner and an iron-worker, in which Idris Ddu said:

> "Diffoddai tân Merthyr a'r gweithwyr i gyd,
> Heb gymorth y glowr a'r mwynwyr ynghyd:
> Y nhw sydd yn porthi, digoni'n dêg iawn,
> Pob tanwr o gwmpas y deyrnas o'i dawn."

Here we find Rowley as a bard. He was a frequent visitor to Fenni Eisteddfod. On August 1, 1834, he was a competitor for the best twelve englynion on the abolition of slavery in the colonies of Great Britain, which have appeared in the Welsh column of the local press. Among his writings there is an interesting account of the leases of Gellideg from 1742 onwards, as well as of the land that belonged to this old farm and to many other farms in the district. In 1835—the year of the first general election after Merthyr became a Parliamentary Borough—Rowley composed a song by way of an address to the electorate of Merthyr. Mr. J. J. Guest was returned unopposed as the first member for Merthyr, the other candidate—Mr. William Meyrick, solicitor—having withdrawn. At an eisteddfod held at the Swan Inn (Yr Alarch) in 1836, Idris Ddu gained the prize for the best six verses on the subject "Croesawiad y Gaeaf" ("Welcome to Winter"). He also composed an ode on the Hirwaun struggle between Iestyn and the Normans and Rhys ap Tewdwr, in which the dignity and honour of Wales were subjected to the ambitious schemes of Iestyn ap Gwrgant. Werfa Camp claimed his attention for another ode. One afternoon, when he was not in the best of health, he succeeded in climbing Aberdare Mountain. So overjoyed was he after reaching the summit, and so much did he enjoy the happy spell of health-giving leisure, that he immediately composed a song of praise to commemorate the event. All of his compositions are recorded in his own handwriting. At the Angel Inn, in 1838, he gained the laurels for the best six verses on the subject of the last new furnaces at Ynysfach, which had been completed early in 1838. In the same year, a meeting of the Cymreigyddion was held at the Rocking Stone at Pontypridd, and Idris Ddu presented an essay on "The Habits and Customs of the Welsh Nation from their Subjection to the Present Time." In this essay he mentions the various subjections suffered by the Welsh nation from 1184 B.C. to the time of Llewelyn the Last Prince, in 1282 A.D. Another ode (70 lines) was composed on "The Submission of the Egyptians in the Red Sea." According to Rowley, the Druids taught and encouraged love, good virtues, hatred of wickedness, and the belief in one God—The Most High. They called him the Creator of all things, the Unchangeable, the Almighty, and the Incorruptible Judge. The Druids would not allow an image of God to be made in any way whatsoever, neither were they allowed to think that God could be enclosed in any place or building, but maintained that it was in the meadows and woods that God could be worshipped most truly. Rowley composed two verses (16 lines in all) to the grave of his father—"Bedd Fy Nhad." They are very descriptive and full of a son's admiration. Next he composed twelve verses to the memory of the late Mr. David Jones, a Merthyr watchmaker, who had been president of the Cymreigyddion Society for over 27 years and who died about 1842, aged 80. Mr. Morgan Williams, of Penyrheolgerrig, was another who claimed the attention of Idris Ddu. Morgan had been compelled to leave the neighbourhood for North Wales on account of his Chartist activities. Idris, in a number of verses which he composed, implored Morgan to return to his native place, saying that there were plenty of his old friends there ready to welcome him back. During Rowley's illness, his friend the schoolmaster, Billy Dafydd Richard (Ceredig), came to see him, and addressed him in two verses of poetry which portrayed the sincere friendship that existed between them. In March, 1847, Rowley writes regarding his belief. From the answers which he wrote to ten religious questions, I gather that he was a staunch Unitarian. To question No. 8 he answers: "I don't believe that men who have risen under the narrow yoke of religious principles are qualified to govern any country." He had a wonderful knowledge and conception of the Bible, and wrote a great deal on various subjects therefrom, one of these being a treatise concerning the vision of the dried bones in the Book of Ezeciel. In a composition dated March 12, 1852, there is a curious account of the building of the Temple in Jerusalem. In the latter he worked out the cost under certain conditions. After finding the dimensions, quarrying the stone, transport of the stone for a distance of seven miles, the cost of the masonry, roof, lead and timber, he calculated the cost would be about 10/- a perch—or 4/- a perch more than the T.V.R. bridge at Quakers' Yard. In 1855 followed a treatise on the old chapel at Cwmyglo, and in the same year, at an eisteddfod held by the Ivorites, he presented an essay on "The Beginning, Progress and Name of Cyfarthfa Works," a very interesting and instructive effort. "Cadair Wag Fy Nhad" was the title of the poem of six verses which he composed to his father's empty chair. In 1841 Rowley wrote a detailed account of an operation carried out upon his son William on November 9 by Dr. Edward Davies, Cyfarthfa, assisted by Mr. John Evans, son of the late Rev. Samuel Evans, Soar, Pontmorlais. A stone weighing 15 drachms was extracted from the body of the boy during the operation, which was performed in less than five minutes. On the 21st—12 days later—the water-passage was restored to its normal condition again. William was then 13 years and 7 months old.

Rowley had a good knowledge of the compass and the variation of the magnetic point. He was one of the first to open patches on the mountain-side. In his writings there are records with reliable facts concerning these. There is also the following :—

"Appeal by Rowland Thomas to Mr. R. T. Crawshay, Mar. 19th, 1855.

"Sir, I wish to inform you that I have not received more to myself than £2 per month, or in other words 10s. per week, since I began on the Patches. That is known to Mr. Bedlington Kirkhouse, and David Skym, for I give them the account of every man's turns separately on a list every month, by setting that no man may have place for suspicion of overdraw. From July 13th, 1854, to March 3rd, 1855, we will have 33 weeks and 3 days at 10s. a week—£16 15s. Out of that I have to borrow £2 12s. to pay the men, so all that I have had since the beginning is £14 3s. to myself."

This gives some light on the wages earned in the early days in the Patches.

Rowland Thomas was truly a remarkable man: he was a mathematician, a skilled miner, an able bard, an essayist, a practical geologist, an astronomer, a historian, a philosopher, and a theologian. It is fortunate that he kept a faithful record of all his work, for it gives interesting side-lights on the local history of his time. His treatise on the coalfield of Glamorgan is most learned. He stands out as one of the most intellectual minds of the Merthyr of a hundred years ago.

After his removal to the Harp Inn, Edward, his eldest son, lived at Bryngwyn. He was the father of Wat. Rowley, the celebrated quoiter and sportsman, who died at Neath in November, 1926, aged 80. Edward's son, Thomas Edward Thomas, next lived at Bryngwyn until he was nearly 80 years of age, while at the present time it is occupied by Aneurin Thomas, his son.

CHAPTER XVI.

TYNYCOEDCAE FARM—RICHARD SHINKIN—LEWIS A GWENLLUAN, CWM WAUN NEWYDD—JACK MORGAN—PLAS Y FEDWEN—BRYN Y GWYDDEL—THE FINGER POST—COMPLETION OF THE TRAMP.

WHEN in Pant y Bwrlin we noticed a road on our right leading down to a farm. This farm is Tynycoedcae, and has been in the possession of the Jenkins family for over 130 years. The first of this family to occupy it was Richard Jenkins, whose ancestors lived at Vaynor, Merthyr and Aberdare centuries ago. Richard was born about 1764 and became a member of Hen Dŷ Cwrdd, Cefn Coed. He had four sons—Jacki, Lewis, Shinkin and William. Lewis and Gwenlluan his wife occupied the farm next. Jacki, the eldest son, had three sons and one daughter—Daniel, Jenkin, William and Ann. Daniel met with a fatal accident on an occasion when, accompanied by his son Richard, he went to a place called Brynmân, near the mountain-top, for coal. There the outcrop of the coal seams was not very deep, and the coal holes were known as Roman holes Richard, the son, was the only one near when the accident occurred.

Lewis Jenkins, who married Gwenlluan, was born there, and after the death of his father he lived at Tynycoedcae. He was a great friend of Idris Ddu, which is clearly shown in a song composed in honour of Lewis and his wife by the joint authors—Cawr Morlais (one verse) and Idris Ddu (two verses). This was written on March 4, 1853. Lewis and Gwenlluan had then been living happily together for 30 years, during which time Lewis and Rowley had been firm friends and companions. According to the wording of the song, the couple were very good-natured, and Lewis would often amuse the company with his melodious singing. Lewis Jenkins died April 19, 1866, aged 74, being predeceased by his brother Jenkin on January, 13, 1862, at the age of 63. After the death of Lewis, William, the son of Jacki Jenkins, occupied the farm. He was a contractor at the Winchfawr Mine Pit. After his death in December, 1894, Lewis, a nephew whom William had adopted, occupied the farm until his retirement in 1929. It is now in the occupation of Mr. Urias Beynon.

The old farm at Cwm Waun Newydd, the land of which has now been taken over by Tynycoedcae, and the buildings of which are in ruins, dates very far back. Many families lived there after it ceased being a farm. The first person of whom I have any record as having lived there was Jack Morgan, of Llanbrynmair—a miner as well as a farmer. He had four sons — John, Richard (who married Peggy, the widow of David Beynon, Coed Meurig), Billy (who built the Harp Inn), and Twmi (who built Tai Twmi, Swansea Road). Twmi Jack Morgan married Esther, the daughter of Jenkin Jenkins, of the Finger Post. Although he was uneducated, he was gentle, courteous, and of a very kind disposition. To his neighbours and associates he was always known as Jack Morgan, and each one of his sons bore the " Jack " after his name —e.g. John Jack Morgan. When the sons were all home they were robust and powerful—veritable sons of Anak. Other families came to Cwm Waun Newydd after Jack Morgan, some of them being quite noted. It is believed that Morgan Owen, the famous racer of Vaynor, lived there for a time. Now Morgan Owen had a sister, and during their stay she would often prove a match for her brother in a race across the fields. At the same time, Billy Bach Nicholas—afterwards called Billy Buttons—stayed there, and would often challenge Morgan Owen over a short distance of sixty yards.

When the Pugh family came to the district, Hwmphra Pugh found lodgings at Cwm Waun Newydd. This was about 1831, during the time of the Merthyr Riots. One day Humphrey decided to take a stroll to Merthyr, and on seeing him getting ready his landlady asked : " Ble i ti'n mynd, Hwmphra bach ? " " I'r dre am dro," said Hwmphra. " Wel, alli di ddim mynd. Ma' Billy bach wedi mynd a dy shiwt di ! " was the good lady's comforting rejoinder. It was always the rule at Cwm Waun Newydd that the first up in the morning put on the best suit. Again, the first one home from work would have the best pot of broth, or in fact the best of everything that was going. Thus there would be frequent fights for the best suit of clothes or to dispute the ownership of the best pot of broth. According to Mr. William Edmunds (the historian), it was a J. Jenkins who occupied the place in 1864.

There was an old house, called Plas y Fedwen, on the left hand side of the road, on the slope of Bryn y Gwyddel, which seems to have been on the southern side of the old fenced land of Cwm Waun Newydd.

Next we come to the Dynevor Arms, commonly called the Finger Post. There were a few dwellings below this inn, but they are not at present used as habitations. They were built, I should imagine, about the time of the construction of the Cwmynysmintan Waterworks, on land belonging to the Dynevor Arms. It was Jenkin Jenkins who built the first public-house in this place, its name being The Giant's Grave, and it was situated on the Aberdare side of the parish boundary. That took place about 1828. The present Dynevor Arms was built by the same person about 1831. Opposite this inn a road branches off from the Swansea Road through the Dyllas and Llwydcoed to Aberdare. Jenkin

Jenkins came here from Ton Beildra, Ystradfellte. His daughter, Esther, married Twmi Jack Morgan, of Cwm Waun Newydd, and both died at the Finger Post. They had five sons and one daughter, of whom only two survive—Thomas and Morgan. Thomas, who was born over 73 years ago at Tai Twmi, afterwards, with Catherine his wife, took possession of the Dynevor Arms, where he still resides. Catherine died December 2, 1929, aged 60. Great changes have taken place since the days of Jenkin Jenkins. When the Vale of Neath Railway Company opened their line from Neath and Swansea to Hirwaun and Aberdare in 1851, a brake service was instituted from a point between Hirwaun and Llwydcoed to Merthyr. The halt was called Merthyr Road, and the passengers were conveyed from there in brakes—four-wheeled carriages seating about a dozen persons—on to Merthyr. This continued to serve until the completion of the Abernant Tunnel in 1853. Now an excellent motor bus service has been instituted, buses passing the Dynevor Arms every twenty minutes, over a well constructed road. The water supply pipe-line from Tâf Fechan into the Aberdare Parish also passes over the mountain just here, the altitude being 1,180 feet above sea level. Now this brings my journeyings to a close. We have explored the Hamlet of Gellideg very thoroughly, yet I know the story is far from being complete; but I trust that, incomplete as it is, my work will be of interest, enjoyment, and of some historical value to the person into whose hands this little volume chances to fall.

OWNERS AND OCCUPANTS OF THE FOLLOWING FARMS IN 1930:—

Farms.	*Occupants.*	*Owners.*
Waun Wyllt	Morgan W. Davies	Lord Windsor
Penylan	,, ,,	,, ,,
Graig	,, ,,	Morgan family
Hendrefawr	Ebenezar Phillips	Wingfield & Mackintosh
Blaencanaid	Mary Williams	,, ,,
Wern	John Jones	,, ,,
Gelli-Ddu	Lewis & Jane Phillips	,, ,,
Old Factory	Dd. & Hannah Davies	,, ,,
Dynevor Arms (Finger Post)	Thomas Morgan	,, ,,
Plas y Gôg	Morgan J. Walters	,, ,,
Plas y Darren	Thomas Jas. Thomas	,, ,,
Corner House, Heolgerrig	Wm. Jas. Meyrick	,, ,,
Beiliglas, Heolgerrig	David Lloyd	,, ,,
Cwm-Du Cottage	Thomas Tong	,, ,,
Pleasant View (not a public-house now)	John Williams	Owner
Glyndyrus	William Thomas	,,
Rhydycar Isaf	Morgan Davies	,,
Rhydycar Uchaf	Mary Griffiths	,,
Llwyncelyn	Timothy Robertshaw	,,
Penycoedcae, Heolgerrig	William J. Morgan	,,
Penyrheol House	Miss Margaret Evans	,,
Penyrheolgerrig	Henry Thos. Davies	,,
Heolgerrig	Morgan Rees Davies	,,
Penycoedcae Brynteg	Phillip Lewis	,,
Nantgau	William Harris	,,
Tai Mawr (Central)	J. Blodeufryn Jones	Price Watkins
Tai Mawr (North-west)	William Miles	Price Watkins
Tai Mawr (North-east)	—— Johns of Ffrwd	Price Watkins
Coed Meurig	William Miles	Owner
Ty'nycoedcae	Urias Beynon	,,
Waun Bant	John Morgan Lewis	,,
Twyn Carmel	Emily Jones	,,
Yr Hen Dŷ (now Gerynant)	John Davies	,,
Nantygwenith (now a Stores)	Thomas & Evans	,,